Education for Citizensnip

Education for Citizenship

Edited by Denis Lawton, Jo Cairns and Roy Gardner

CONTINUUM
London and New York

Continuum

The Tower Building
11 York Road
London SE1 7NX

370 Lexington Avenue
New York
NY 10017–6503

First published 2000

British Library Cataloguing-in-Publication Data
A catalogue record for this book is available from the British Library.

ISBN 0-8264-7756-9

Typeset by YHT Ltd, London
Printed and bound in Great Britain by Cromwell Press, Trowbridge, Wilts

Contents

Contributors

Priscilla Alderson is a Reader in Childhood Studies, Social Science Research Unit, Institute of Education, University of London.

John Annette is the Assistant Dean and Director of Curriculum, Learning and Quality at the School of Social Science, Middlesex University, Enfield, Middlesex.

Tony Breslin is General Adviser, Vocational Education (14–19) in the London Borough of Enfield Advice and Development Service.

Jo Cairns is an Assistant Director of the Quality Assurance Agency and a Visiting Fellow at the Institute of Education, University of London.

Bernard Crick is Emeritus Professor of Politics, Birkbeck College, University of London and Chair of the Advisory Group (1997–8) on *Education for Citizenship and Democracy in Schools* (QCA, 1998).

Eva Gamarnikow is a Lecturer in Sociology and Human Rights, Policy Studies Academic Group at the Institute of Education, University of London.

Roy Gardner is a Senior Lecturer at the Institute of Education, University of London.

Anthony Green is a Lecturer in Sociology of Education, Policy Studies Academic Group at the Institute of Education, University of London.

Jagdish Gundara is the Director of the International Centre for Intercultural Studies, Institute of Education, University of London.

John Hammond is the Assistant Chief Executive of the National Council for Curriculum and Assessment (NCCA), Dublin.

Janet Harland is a Senior Lecturer in Education, Curriculum Studies Academic Group, Institute of Education, University of London.

Graham Haydon is a Senior Lecturer in Philosophy of Education, Institute of Education, University of London.

David Kerr is Senior Research Officer at the National Foundation for Educational Research (NFER), Slough, Bucks.

Denis Lawton is Professor of Education, Curriculum Studies Academic Group, Institute of Education, University of London.

Anne Looney is currently acting Assistant Chief Executive of the National Council for Curriculum and Assessment (NCCA), Dublin.

Henry Maitles is Head of Modern Studies in the Faculty of Education, University of Strathclyde.

Eirini Pasoula is a doctoral candidate at the Institute of Education, University of London.

Robert Phillips is Lecturer in Education, University of Wales, Swansea.

Alistair Ross is Professor of Education, University of North London.

Preface

A Message of Support from the Secretary of State for Education and Employment, David Blunkett

I greatly enjoyed speaking at the Institute of Education Conference on Citizenship Education in July 1999 and am honoured to provide the preface to this book, which arose from it.

Like the conference, the book is informative and enlightening. It also represents an interesting mixture of theory and practice. We want to build on the excellent good practice that exists in many of our schools and encourage others to develop their own approaches, be creative and identify opportunities across the curriculum and beyond to enhance the teaching of citizenship.

Citizenship education should give pupils the chance to exercise real responsibility and to make an impact on their school and community. Citizenship teaching, building on the curriculum, has the power to transform the lives of pupils in areas that many people have written off.

I welcome both the practical support and the critical inquiries contained in this book.

Part I

The Context

Chapter 1

Introduction to the New Curriculum

Bernard Crick

We aim at no less than a change in the political culture of this country both nationally and locally: for people to think of themselves as active citizens, willing, able and equipped to have an influence in public life and with the critical capacities to weigh evidence before speaking and acting; to build on and to extend radically to young people the best in existing traditions of community involvement and public service, and to make them individually confident in finding new forms of involvement and acting among themselves. (Report on *Education for Citizenship and the Teaching of Democracy in Schools*, QCA, 1998)

Citizenship gives pupils the knowledge, skills and understanding to play an effective role in society at local, national and international levels. It helps them to become informed, thoughtful and responsible citizens who are aware of their duties and rights. It promotes their spiritual, moral and cultural development, making them more self-confident and responsible both in and beyond the classroom. It encourages pupils to play a helpful part in the lives of their schools, neighbourhoods, communities and the wider world. It also teaches them about our economy and democratic institutions and values; encourages respect for different national, religious and ethnic identities; and develops pupils' ability to reflect on issues and take part in discussions. (From the prefatory page to the *Citizenship Order*, DfEE, 1999)

The one quotation is the language of stating a civic ideal to the public, and the other is the language of a 'mission statement' to teachers; but for once they are not so different. The electorate is concerned with schools and teachers; but teachers are citizens too, albeit with a very special and professional role which it has come now.

Last but not least of all countries in the European Union, the United States, Canada, Australia, New Zealand and most interestingly South Africa, 'citizenship' is now part of the National Curriculum in England. The curriculum, of course, like that for geography and history and English, demands knowledge of the United Kingdom as a whole, and stirrings are abroad in the other three centres of devolved power. A committee of the SCCC (Scottish Curriculum Consultative Council) is considering how citizenship can be strengthened and made more systematic in Scottish schools. Curriculum development work has been afoot in Northern Ireland even before the legislation for an Assembly, and is likely to be strengthened not thrown in doubt by the formation of a coalition government – because, of course, it is based on the idea of common citizenship, a broader concept than the existing EMU (Education for Mutual Understanding). The Qualifications, Curriculum and Assessment Authority for Wales (known by its Welsh language acronym, ACCAC), at the request of the government has developed a new guidance framework for PSE containing substantial elements of citizenship; this was approved by the National Assembly who will review after September 2002 whether or not it should remain non-statutory.

Last but not least because both the Report and the Order were able to draw on experience elsewhere for broad principles, as well as to build on Curriculum Guidance Paper 8, *Education for Citizenship* (NCC, 1990), even if the advisory group for the Report unanimously recommended that citizenship should be statutory, certainly for secondary schools, judging that in the context of the National Curriculum cross-curricular guidance was not enough to ensure an entitlement for all children. When it was decided by the Secretary of State, sensibly in my opinion, that it should not be statutory in primary schools, none the less the new 'PSHE and Citizenship' framework was constructed so that citizenship in Key Stage 2 leads directly into Key Stage 3 – that most difficult time of transition.

The idea of a curriculum defined by 'learning outcomes' was dominant in the Report. Some of its details were drawn from curricula in the Republic of Ireland and in Australia, albeit tuned to English conditions. Some voices were raised at the conference that gave rise to this book to say that 'learning outcomes are too rigid'. I think they are mistaken. For the only relevant and realistic comparison is with the still too heavy proscription (in my personal opinion) of some of the core subjects in the National Curriculum. To leave each school free to do as it chose would negate the idea of a common citizenship, the necessary cement of a highly pluralistic society. And considering political reality, if educators are to be as politically literate as pupils, to reject the theory of 'learning outcomes' is to imagine that when Labour was in opposition the party had discussed and then rejected Kenneth Baker's whole initiative for a National Curriculum. It did neither. Wild horses would not drag out of me what I felt at the time; but that is no longer relevant. The clock cannot be put back, except in seminars and earnest lectures to captive audiences. Besides, with hindsight that is ever golden, a middle way between national prescription and school autonomy might have been found. 'Learning outcomes' all round could have been the answer.

However, 'learning outcomes' may appear to have vanished from the

Citizenship Order and the Framework, indeed there is no explicit reference to the concept in QCA's guidance papers to either. It was decided by the QCA and the DfEE that the Citizenship Order had to be drafted in a form similar to the other revised Orders. So there are no formal columns of learning outcomes as in the Report. But consider the extraordinary brevity with which the Order is set out despite its considerable width, a width well caught in the mission statement quoted above. Take for example the programme of study set out under 'Knowledge and understanding' for Key Stage 3:

Pupils should be taught about:
(a) the legal and human rights and responsibilities underpinning society, basic aspects of the criminal justice system and how both relate to young people
(b) the diversity of national, regional, religious and ethnic identities in the United Kingdom and the need for respect and understanding
(c) central and local government, the public services they offer and how they are financed, and the opportunities to contribute
(d) the key characteristics of parliamentary and other forms of government
(e) the electoral system and the importance of voting
(f) the work of community-based, national and international groups
(g) the importance of resolving conflicts fairly
(h) the significance of the media in society
(i) the world as a global community, and the political, economic, environmental and social implications of this, and the role of the European Union, the Commonwealth and the United Nations.

That is all it says for a content so very wide, although academics need reminding that the level of content is more like general knowledge fitting to the age group of the junior forms in secondary schools, not pre or sub-disciplinary political science or sociology, nor in Key Stage 4 either (God forbid, that would kill it!). Brevity allows flexibility. That is one simple reason why compared to all other subjects it is so terse and brief.

David Blunkett himself has said on numerous occasions that this is deliberately a 'light touch' and a 'flexible' Order. I gloss this as 'strong bare bones', something sweated down to the muscle and deliverable at different strengths and with different emphases. Yes, but why? Not just because the Secretary of State has said so. He is well aware that he is not God. If anyone were to treat this as the word of God, it must only be because the word is good, just, right and fitting. I see two profound reasons for 'light touch' and 'flexible'. First, it would be wrong in principle – deep, deep principle, touching on the very nature of freedom and free government – for the state to prescribe the detail of a subject so sensitive as Citizenship (of course it is sensitive). Second, it is helpful to schools planning for a new subject to be able to build upon what many of them, in different ways and in different measure, have been doing already; and to adjust their delivery of the curriculum to what elements of or potential for citizenship learning they may find in other subjects – history, PSHE, geography,

RE, English, even some elements of maths and science, certainly information technology.

This seems to me wholly good. But some powerful, intense and utterly well-meaning lobbies feel that they have been left out or done down. I ignore those who would not wish citizenship to be there at all, say that vehement shadowy body the Campaign for Real Education, and others who appear to believe, often for better reasons (such as fear of overloading – which is surely a matter of school management not a structural absolute?) that the pre–1997 curriculum is part of nature, or if not ordained by King Edward the Confessor, at least frozen for aye and a day in the reigns of Ken Baker and Ken Clarke. No, I refer to the unhappiness of many in the human rights, the race relations and the world citizenship movements and lobbies. For quite obvious reasons they feel that the importance of their concerns are not sufficiently represented in the bare words of paragraphs (a), (b) and (i) above.

This was very carefully considered, both in the Report and in the DfEE working party that drafted the final order – replete with teacher representation, by the way. But two arguments counted against extension after, in the language of the Order itself, 'informed discussion'. To specify would subvert the general emancipatory idea of a 'light touch' Order and would also create all the political dangers and disputes of detailed specification. Also in the case of anti-racism, there is the uncertainty principle about method and the need to adjust teachers to different circumstances and different degrees of bigotry and prejudice. Certainly more is said in the Non-statutory Guidance documents that QCA has produced, but still not enough, I suspect, to satisfy some.

But here is where the 'flexibility' principle kicks in powerfully. The Qualifications and Curriculum Authority guidance paper for citizenship (QCA, 2000) says that so long as every element of the curriculum is covered, to the degree that pupils understand the meaning and usage of the institutions, terms and concepts laid down, there is room for considerable difference of stress; and anti-racism, human rights and global citizenship are not merely mentioned as the leading examples of this, but also as themes that can permeate many or most parts of the curriculum, not only in citizenship itself but throughout the school. And guidance is given to sources outside the government. It follows that those organizations, non-governmental organizations, voluntary bodies and charities, whatever, who can produce materials that are realistically attuned to the content of the curriculum, to the skills demanded, to specify ability, achievement and age levels, and to the time available to teach citizenship as a whole, will find their products in great demand. If their materials are either too generalized or inward-looking sometimes to please trustees not always equally aware of differing conditions in schools, they will fail. Here publishers will often be the essential intermediaries. Good causes are often thwarted by the inadequacy of their distribution system. There are in England about 18,300 primary schools and about 3500 secondary schools in the public sector. To reach them all, the normal publishing market can work well enough. So the principle of flexibility results not in detailed centralized guidance, but guidance to guidances; and these second level sources offer a variety of slants, approaches, materials, methodologies from which schools can choose if they wish, or mix and match.

This can never please, of course, those who might think that teaching human rights is actually a substitute for a comprehensive Citizenship curriculum, that human rights should not merely predominate but dominate. But social and political life is not only a matter of individual rights: any talk of 'group rights' should be sensitive to the authority that concept gives a group over the lives of its individual members – usually it is women who then suffer. The promotion of civic duties is also important – 'rights and duties indeed' – and sometimes we should persuade people that while they may have a right to act, they have a responsibility in such and such a case not to exercise that right. To give two very difficult examples. There are two sides to the argument, probably more, as to whether Salman Rushdie, with an undoubted right to publish, both in law and in any normal construction of human or natural rights, was acting responsibly in publishing The Satanic Verses if he had known the likely response of many believing Muslims. And don't get self-righteous! If we think that General Pinochet's vile complicity in and responsibility for great crimes against humanity are necessarily to be punished by a British or a Spanish court – no argument! For the new regime in Chile, liberals and socialists alike, had thought that a grim compromise was a necessary guarantee for ensuring peace, the stability of the republic, the ending of violence and the retreat of the army to barracks. Spain made such compromises, fortunately, I think. And Mandela made such compromises. The South African Truth Commission was a carefully, politically negotiated compromise compared to trials in courts of law, whether old or new law.

Two more less dramatic reasons why the Citizenship Order is light touch and flexible are to be found in its astonishing boldness in going beyond what I and my colleagues of the advisory committee thought possible to recommend: that participation in both school and the community is not simply a voluntary 'value plus', as we cautiously recommended, but is to be statutory. Imagine both the legal and the political difficulties if at this stage the government had tried to set down national rules, powers and procedures for school councils, and to determine what form participation in the community should take. The only guidance given at this stage is through examples of good practice already afoot. Perhaps later, as schools explore possibilities for themselves and as examples of good practice multiply on the national learning web and figure in the reports of the inspectorate, more precise guidance may follow.

While the Citizenship Order also uniquely puts a great weight on 'oracy', the 'informed discussion' of 'issues, problems and events', it makes no attempt to specify what these should be. Nothing is ruled in, but then nothing is ruled out. Schools and teachers are given freedom (and are advised to let the pupils have some choice too!), but then they also have no automatic protection if complaints are made at certain subjects being discussed at all. That is for governors, heads and parents to sort out locally, amid the perpetual temptation of the popular press to try to make a national issue of some bizarre local event. Such is life.

All the papers in this book discuss thoughtfully some of these issues. But the conference took place at the very end of the period of consultation on the draft proposals of the Secretary of State. But now they are law, so I have thought it worthwhile to talk only of the principles underlying the kind of Order that it is, not to indulge myself in the might-have-beens and the may-bes, although heaven knows we need independent, critical academic thought; and some ways of hoping that someone is listening outside the walls. Elsewhere I have written about the philosophy of citizenship education (*Essays on Citizenship*, Continuum, 2000).

To end by returning to the two quotations above this essay. One is addressed to the public, because the Citizenship Order is plainly part of a general stirring to try to make our society more democratic; it could be seen more specifically as an essential underpinning of the moves of constitutional reform by the present government which, even if not fully systematic, or not plainly so, are none the less impressive in number and scale. The other quotation is addressed to teachers and plainly citizenship is not meant to be just another subject but something that will permeate the ethos of the whole school and, hopefully, create lifelong habits of active citizenship, participation beyond simply voting, whether in the affairs of voluntary organizations or public bodies.

REFERENCES

Crick, B. (2000) *Essays on Citizenship*. London: Continuum.
DfEE (1999) *Citizenship Order*. London: DfEE
National Curriculum Council (1990) *Education for Citizenship: Curriculum Guidance*. Paper No. 8. York: NCC.
QCA (1998) *Education for Citizenship and the Teaching of Democracy in Schools* (Crick Report). London: QCA.
QCA (2000) *Guidance Paper for Citizenship*. London: QCA.

Chapter 2

Overview: Citizenship Education in Context

Denis Lawton

HISTORICAL BACKGROUND

It is tempting to date the current interest in citizenship education from the Report of the Speaker's Commission in 1988, but the story goes back much further. There were several earlier attempts to encourage schools to take preparation for citizenship more seriously, and it may be useful to begin by examining why such attempts were unsuccessful.

In the nineteenth century education for citizenship was often identified with a narrow version of moral training, and the extension of the franchise in 1867 provided some politicians with the notion that we should 'educate our masters'. No attempt was made to modify the curriculum directly at that time, but the kind of history that was taught clearly had some purposes beyond the subject itself:

> Throughout the nineteenth century, geography and history lessons had always had the intention of producing the *good citizen* rooted in anti-papist Protestantism. Imperial developments in the fifty years or so prior to the First World War, as well as the impact of social Darwinism, promoted patriotism, heroism and racism. (Phillips, 1998, p. 13)

By the beginning of the twentieth century there was an organization – the Moral Instruction League – one of whose aims was to influence the school curriculum. After the First World War, the League was reformed and renamed the Civics and Moral Education League. By the early 1930s, the League had virtually ceased to exist but the fear of Fascism and other totalitarian doctrines prompted a group of progressive educators to form, in 1934, the Association for Education in Citizenship that was supported by well-known figures such as Sir Ernest Simon and William Beveridge. They advocated *direct training* for citizenship rather than the indirect method of general education working through existing subjects. This *direct training* view was not, however, supported by the various official reports of the pre-war period. For example, the Spens Report (Board of Education, 1938) and the Norwood Report (Board of Education, 1943) seemed to suggest that economics and political science were beyond the capacity of pupils under 16 and that schools should concentrate on history and geography.

In 1945 the direct training point of view was revived by another short-lived organization – the Council for Curriculum Reform – which produced a remarkable report, *The Content of Education* (1945), advocating social studies as a compulsory subject in the core curriculum with politics and economics as important elements of that subject. The Report, however, had very little influence at the time. The curriculum was not a priority in post-war England where the immediate problems included a shortage of teachers and the building or rebuilding of many schools damaged during the war. In 1947, the Central Advisory Council for Education produced *School and Life* (Ministry of Education, 1947), which expressed concern about the danger of a moral vacuum and the need for schools to provide some kind of moral code for a modern secular society. But no curricular solution was suggested. Two years later the Ministry of Education in Pamphlet No. 16, *Citizens Growing Up* (1949), went a little further and suggested that more than an extra lesson a week on civics would be needed to produce good citizens. The pamphlet recommended the permeation approach: 'The study of man in society should permeate the matter of all organised studies.' One of the problems of this kind of citizenship education was that the new ideas tended to be taken up only by secondary modern schools.

In 1959 the Crowther Report (Ministry of Education, 1959) showed an awareness of a problem: 'The task of helping young workers, many of them of limited intelligence, to find their way successfully about the modern world', but did not produce a solution in curriculum terms. Similarly, the Newsom Report (Ministry of Education, 1963) warned schools of the dangers of an unstructured approach: 'Civics, current affairs, modern history, social studies, whether under those names or not, ought to feature in the programme. They need sensitive handling if they are not to go sadly awry.' But again, no detailed curriculum was suggested.

During the 1960s, several developments in social studies took place; one influence was the 'New Social Studies' approach advocated by many social scientists in the USA. In the UK the Association for Teaching the Social Sciences (ATSS) was founded in 1964 at the Institute of Education, University of London, explicitly to foster social science teaching in schools. The social sciences that were advocated included sociology, economics and political science. The Politics Association was also active at this time, but it tended to confine its work to more senior pupils, and especially to the teaching of A level Government and Political Studies. Some political scientists wanted much earlier teaching, however. For example, Bernard Crick (1969, pp. 3–4) wrote:

> As a Professor of Political Studies, I am interested in political education at the
> secondary level of education because it should be there both in its own right and in
> the public interest, not as a feeder to the university Moloch. At some stage all young
> people ... should gain some awareness of what politics is about. It is more
> important that all teenagers should learn to read newspapers critically for their
> political content than that they should have heard of Aristotle or know – may
> Heaven forgive us all – when the Speaker's Mace is or was over or under the table.

Crick later became active in a curriculum project financed by the Hansard
Society called the Programme for Political Literacy that produced a report
Political Education and Political Literacy (Hansard, 1978). Unfortunately, the
change of government in 1979 prevented any immediate action: most
Conservatives were then suspicious of political education – 'citizenship
education' might have been more acceptable.

The 1988 Education Reform Act included a National Curriculum. This might
have been an opportunity for citizenship education but the Baker National
Curriculum was based on a list of traditional subjects and was very crowded with
detail. The National Curriculum Council made provision for cross-curricular
themes, one of which was citizenship. But this reduced citizenship to a non-
statutory, optional part of the school curriculum: the statutory requirements of
the seriously overloaded National Curriculum pushed out non-statutory
suggestions such as citizenship.

There were several reasons for the failure of citizenship education in the past:

- Citizenship education was a classic case of 'high risk, low pay-off'.
  Citizenship education was a low status subject in schools but was dangerous:
  teachers can be accused of bias or even indoctrination.
- There was a shortage of good resources and of teachers who were
  competent to deal with difficult and complex issues.
- There was a lack of a clear definition of what political education or
  citizenship education was and what teachers could legitimately do.

Part of the problem of the definition of citizenship education was that there were
at least two views: the passive citizen view – training for conformity and
obedience; and educating the future citizen for active participation in a
democratic society.

The passive view would encourage the teaching of facts about government
and the (non-existent) British Constitution as well as the duties and
responsibilities of a good citizen. Advocates of the active citizen view would
want to concentrate on the understanding of political ideas and conflicts; and
developing democratic attitudes and values – including a willingness to be
critical of the status quo. The first approach runs the risk of boredom; the second

the risk of accusations of subversion.

The Report of the Advisory Group on Citizenship (QCA, 1998), chaired by Professor Bernard Crick, steered a very careful path between Scylla and Charybdis, and that care was also reflected in the Secretary of State's Proposals (DfEE, 1999) which became available for consultation in the general context of a revised National Curriculum (May–July 1999).

The Advisory Group chaired by Professor Bernard Crick, defined citizenship carefully and precisely, drawing on philosophical ideas dating back to ancient Athens, but essentially focusing on modern democracy. Three components or strands emerged to form a framework for school planning:

- Social and moral responsibility
- Community involvement
- Political literacy

Such general aims were probably uncontroversial, but to convert those three strands into a curriculum and a programme for action necessarily involved choosing curriculum design strategies that could have been controversial. The Working Group at first expressed their curriculum intentions in terms of *outcomes*, which may have been too close to a behavioural objectives model to be acceptable to those who favoured less prescriptive instructions to teachers and a more humanistic attitude to the teaching–learning process. (Janet Harland discusses this tricky question in Chapter 6 in this volume.) The outcomes approach was somewhat toned down in the Proposals which emphasized teacher autonomy to a far greater extent.

The learning outcomes recommended by the Citizenship Working Group were founded on four essential elements:

- Concepts
- Values and dispositions
- Skills and aptitudes
- Knowledge and understanding.

The four elements have now been welded into a learning programme for each key stage of the National Curriculum. It was recommended that at the two primary key stages the citizenship programme should be integrated with personal, social and health education (PSHE), and this will be Non-statutory Guidance; but for the secondary school key stages time will have to be found for teaching citizenship as a new foundation subject and this will be a statutory requirement. Perhaps most important of all, the ethos of many schools will need to change if young people are to be enabled to develop social and moral responsibility: this is simply not possible within highly authoritarian school structures. This problem was also discussed extensively during the conference.

Some schools may find teaching about democracy an uncomfortable experience which may require social changes within the school; as Priscilla Alderson suggests in Chapter 10 below, schools have, in the past, shown little interest in children's rights. Gamarnikow and Green (Chapter 9 below) also point out some theoretical as well as practical difficulties.

Citizenship education was an exciting issue in 1999 – not least because primary and secondary schools had to prepare for the incorporation of citizenship education into their curricula within a relatively short time. We hope that the publication of this book will illuminate their planning efforts in the first year of the new millennium.

REFERENCES

Board of Education (1938) Consultative Committee, *Report on Secondary Education* (Spens Report). London: HMSO.
Board of Education (1943) Secondary Schools Examination Council, *Report on Curriculum and Examinations in Secondary Schools* (Norwood Report). London: HMSO.
Council for Curriculum Reform (1945) *The Content of Education*. London: University of London Press.
Crick, B. (1969) *The Teaching of Politics*. London: Penguin.
DfEE (1999) *The Review of the National Curriculum in England: The Secretary of State's Proposals*. London: QCA.
Hansard Society (1978) *Political Education and Political Literacy*. London: Hansard Society.
Ministry of Education (1947) Central Advisory Council for Education Report, *School and Life*. London: HMSO.
Ministry of Education (1949) *Citizens Growing Up*. London: HMSO.
Ministry of Education (1959) *15 to 18*, Report of the Central Advisory Council for Education (England) (Crowther Report). London: HMSO.
Ministry of Education (1963) *Half Our Future* (Newsom Report). London: HMSO.
Phillips, R. (1998) *History Teaching, Nationhood and the State: A Study in Educational Politics*. London: Cassell.
QCA (1998) *Education for Citizenship and the Teaching of Democracy in Schools* (Crick Report). London: QCA.

Chapter 3

Social Diversity, Inclusiveness and Citizenship Education

Jagdish Gundara

INTRODUCTION

Discussions about the need for citizenship education in the United Kingdom have taken place at a time when powers were being devolved to Scotland, Wales and Northern Ireland. It has provided an opportunity to develop ideas about citizenship education as a major component in the National Curriculum especially if the imagination of young people can be captured because they are frequently reported to be disaffected with the political process.

This chapter will discuss the idea of developing a framework based on historical and contemporary aspects of diversity and their relevance to an inclusive curriculum, which integrates citizenship education. Issues of identity whether in singular or multiple forms are also relevant for citizenship education. Within complex democratic societies, where technological changes may be leading to high levels of unemployment, democracies and democratic institutions are subject to great stress. The need to deepen democracy entails a critical appraisal of issues of societal diversity and the development of collaborative community participation to set out a curriculum and appropriate pedagogies. Such strategies of collaboration open up discussions about the belongingness of diverse groups to a community and its institutions. In the final analysis, an issue has to be raised whether human nature is itself amenable to being educable.

CITIZENSHIP, CONTEMPORARY AND HISTORICAL DIVERSITY

Citizenship education should be an integral part of an entitlement to education. Entitlement to good education includes not only a grasp of languages but also competencies in literacy and numeracy. These skills are part and parcel of young people acquiring an understanding of political literacy and gaining an expertise and skills as active citizens.

It is not only what children are taught and what they learn but also their actual experiences at school which contribute to their understanding of their rights and their responsibilities as future citizens. So, a democratic school ethos is important and this needs to be experienced in the context of the wider community (ICIS, 1996). The role of youth work, further and other formal and non-formal lifelong learning are all-important. There is an African adage that 'it takes a whole village to educate a child.' There is obviously a lot to this adage but nowadays it is possible that the village itself will need re-educating. This is especially true because both young people and adults are not sufficiently educated to understand the historical and contemporary underpinnings of society and issues of citizenship and belonging within it.

The terms 'social diversity' and 'multiculturalism' raise issues about which there is no agreement. First, there is the common-sense notion that British society has become multicultural. The assumption is that it is the post Second World War immigrants, especially from the Commonwealth, who have caused diversity, leading to a loss of national identity. The comparative educationalist Nicholas Hans referred to factors such as languages, religion, social class and territory which formed the basis of nations. If one examines British society using this taxonomy then the society can be seen as being historically diverse. Lloyd and Jennifer Laing in the introduction to their book write:

> The term Anglo-Saxon has been used in the recent past for a variety of purposes – usually to denote a kind of fundamental 'Englishness'. Paradoxically, the origins of the term lie firmly embedded in late Roman Continental Europe, when a hotch potch of people crossed the English Channel. They intermingled with the Romano-British population, developing a new culture in what eventually became England. (Laing, L. and J., 1996, p.49)

In linguistic terms the use of Gallic and Celtic languages and different forms of regional English make the society historically multilingual. Likewise, in religious terms the pre-Christian religions, various denominations of Christianity and Judaism make Britain a multifaith society.

The historical distinctions between social classes and between rural and urban areas are indicators of differential access to public and social institutions, and education is, of course, critical to this context.

The polity has been constitutive of the Welsh, Scottish, English and Irish nations and, in addition, the presence of the non-territorially based and largely invisible Traveller/Gypsy communities. All of these form the historical basis of the multicultural part of the British nation. Hence, an understanding of the complex historical and contemporary aspects of societal diversity ought to provide educators and young people with a more textured and layered understanding of the polity.

Devolution within Britain presents an opportunity to develop a coherent historical and contemporary understanding of societal diversity within a framework which allows young people to view the complexity of the notions of belongingness of different groups.

CITIZENSHIP AND DIVERSITY

The challenge for citizenship education is the moulding of the one out of the many and to construct appropriate educational responses to difference and diversity within British society, especially in the light of the new and emerging constitutional and institutional arrangements.

The state, the education system and the anti-racist activists either purposively or by default have failed to develop frameworks based on historical and contemporary diversity using the disciplines of history and the social sciences. In devising programmes for citizenship education these issues need to be addressed.

Education policy initiatives of anti-racism or multiculturalism directed at 'immigrants' to the exclusion of the dominant groups are not useful. With devolution, this issue becomes even more complex and previous assumptions about dominant and subordinate groups require re-examination. Citizenship becomes an important issue within devolved nations because minorities within them may be created as second-class citizens.

The essentialist rhetoric of some anti-racist or multicultural policies has led to some communities becoming designated as 'other' groups and this has created binary oppositions (e.g. majority/minority, dominant/subordinate, belongers/non-belongers). This has negated the possibilities of creating an inclusive polity based on inclusive policies.

The most important current policy recommendation does not come from the field of education, but from the MacPherson Report on the Stephen Lawrence murder. The issue of 'institutional racism' is of major significance to issues of citizenship and of the rights of groups who are subject to institutionalized discrimination and exclusions. Institutional discrimination in both its direct and indirect forms needs to be tackled to provide a basis for equity in society. Since citizenship legally bestows equality, which is neither graded nor divisible, then racial justice and equity can only be actualized if institutional racism is absent. The issue becomes more critical as the rise of xenophobia, chauvinism and racism can have consequences for even the dominant nationalities such as the English.

Similarly, citizenship education ought to recognize the possibilities of the rise of reactive identities in England, which can take root in the aftermath of devolution. Amongst the minority communities there can be the development of a 'siege mentality' which is largely sustained by religion.

In historical terms, not only societies but also the nature and types of rights change. For instance, rights change over time, from the first generation of rights, which were largely civil in nature in the eighteenth century, to include political rights in the nineteenth century and the third generation of social rights in the twentieth century. Given the varying levels of inequalities, the state also tries, as Marshall states, to initiate a 'tendency towards equality' through citizenship (Marshall, 1977, p.49) by creating basic conditions leading towards social equality. This is a dynamic and an active concept, not a passive one.

However, political devolution within Britain introduces a new set of issues. They create a new political logic because, not only are there issues of inter-relationships between the devolved polities but also of the contemporary and historically diverse groups within them. The challenge is to build inclusive polities, which can accommodate notions of difference but also create conditions for belongingness of diverse groups. From an educational perspective this presents a 'creative moment' since notions of citizenship can be utilized to develop integrative mentalities based on concepts of differences and multiple identities. Diversities in their own right can be counter-productive if they conflict with citizenship and liberal democratic principles. Given that there are deep divisions, and uneven development, what can be done to develop new friendships, and constructive and creative imaginations? There is already a legacy of the exclusive and negative phenomena of racism, xenophobia, chauvinism and sexism. However, citizenship is a recent concept as part of the modern nation state because, in ancient and medieval societies (where monarchies, empires, chiefdoms existed), people were referred to as subjects and not citizens.

One of the ways history has been disarmed in democratic states is by settling disputes not by war but through the courts, tribunals and, of course, through elections. This access to institutions which provide citizenship rights is particularly important in relation to gender in a socially diverse society, where a group or community (not the state) wants to deny girls or women access to education or employment. The conferring of citizenship rights entails opposing such particularistic practices, which deny girls equality in education or in employment. However, the cultural practice of a Sikh wearing a turban or a Muslim girl wearing a headdress are legitimate because they do not impair acquisition of education or pose an impediment to gaining employment.

If citizens are excluded from or marginalized within the education system then should the state remain neutral or should it intervene? In other words, is the state fair or is it impartial? Rawls argues using the difference principle that the better-off should not do better than the 'worst off' (Rawls, 1971, p. 60). So, to accord equity, the state is 'fair' but not impartial. In a democratic state citizens are entitled to access to education and knowledge to equalize their life chances. If the state remains impartial it cannot create level playing fields in educational terms. It can only do so by intervening. We currently face an additional dilemma because old solidarities based on class have been destroyed, especially as the younger generation confront greater levels of polarization by being divided into those who are winners and losers. Such polarization, where the losers feel that they owe nothing to the winners, poses a new challenge to citizenship education. How can the schools build a set of resemblances or a stake amongst divided groups in society? Where groups who are losers contain black and white youth they may not share solidarities or a set of resemblances. Citizenship education, therefore, has the complex role of addressing the sense of exclusions and loss amongst both black and white youth. In this context genderized exclusions present an added level of complexity and need to be dealt with firmly but delicately.

The previous policies which privileged one or another group may prove to be counter-productive by exacerbating differences and reducing features of commonality amongst different groups. Hence, the state, through the school, the youth service or the career guidance service is not impartial but intervenes because both black and white groups are excluded. Schools and other institutions have the important task of turning the majority/minority issue into one of inclusiveness. The development of inclusiveness would entail reversing the polarities of majority or minority. This necessitates the development of complex common policies and strategies which include both white and black groups and establish a minimum level of resemblances. Furthermore, citizenship education ought to bridge the gaps between those who are considered a permanent minority, or majority, and nurture notions of the citizenship rights of both. Such policies and processes can instil the enduring notion of fraternity or new solidarities and develop 'communities of development and hope', as Judith Green (1998) describes it. Yet, this is easier said than done because Britain, like many other states, confronts complicated issues. Habermas writes:

> Today, as the nation-state finds itself challenged from within by the explosive potential of multiculturalism and from without by the pressure of globalisation, the question arises of whether there exists a functional equivalent for the fusion of the nation of citizens with the ethnic nation. (Habermas, 1998, p.117).

MULTIPLE IDENTITIES

So the real challenge is how the democratic processes in society and experiential democratic education can be a guarantor for social integration in highly differentiated contexts. Yet, there are already positive examples among many of the young British people. Das of the Asian Dub Foundation describes himself as a 'Hindi British Asian, English, Bengali European'. Pandit G who operates the decks describes himself as 'a half-Irish, Asian, Scot' (*The Times*, 2 July 1999). Andrew Marr stated that multiple Asian identities were a contributory factor in the better performances of children of Asian origin in education. He also wrote about the difference between Edinburgh and Belfast as follows. In Edinburgh:

> They began to juggle multiple identities – British, Scottish, European. The Scottish home rule movement, including the SNP, has been vigorously developing the rhetoric of liberalism and democracy. (*Observer*, 4 July 99)

Conversely in Belfast:

> The Ulster Unionist people meanwhile, huddled inside a simple, singular view of the world that deliberately avoided complexity or intermingling. As a result, today they have no open door to the outside world. Their identity is too strong, too single. In 1999, that is a tragic predicament for any people. Ask the Serbs. (*Observer*, 4 July 1999).

Hence Habermas, perhaps, ignores the graver dangers of the old historically entrenched ethnic identities of nationalities. These historical multicultural pasts may be more divisive than the ones arising from contemporary migrations.

Young people currently only demand their rights but do not necessarily accept that they have obligations. The public culture and domain therefore has to be inclusive of values derived from minorities and majorities and not just the dominant groups in society. Citizenship education, therefore, has to have an inclusive notion which symbolically and substantively captures the imagination and enchants the disenchanted young people. To engage the young people who are disaffected by the political process it is appropriate to use the constitutional and human rights principles, and other progressive and democratic struggles, as part of the curriculum.

Among young people the notion of being part of, and belonging to, complex localities is important. Hence, the notion of territorial belongingness, which is not exclusive but shared, is worth exploring within schools and youth clubs. There is a need to develop non-exclusivist neighbourhoods which are not no-go areas for others but are confederal communities. Such communities would be based on shared resemblances which are neither racist nor patriarchal. This necessitates the revamping of the old Greek concept of *paidea* or the German notion of *Bildung* to develop their interactive and intercultural aspects within complex schools and their communities. If this process is not undertaken through academic and formal political or citizenship education as well as through active citizenship engagement, the underclass or pauperized groups of whatever nationality or religion will activate their own separatist 'politics of recognition'. Such a dynamic could heighten notions of fragmentation and divisions with political consequences. Even if these groups are statistically small they cannot be written off as having no political consequence. Urban ghettos and rural blight have a way of permeating the body politic which prisons and internal security cannot contain, because of their corrosive potential (Habermas, 1998, p.123).

ACTIVE CITIZENSHIP AND UNEMPLOYMENT

Another major challenge is the growth of the economic, global and technological at the expense of the political, social and cultural. In socially diverse societies it becomes a critical issue because of the massive unemployment this will create amongst young people. Citizenship education which nurtures political knowledge, understanding and skills is crucial so that engagements in public life and the public domain are strengthened. Active citizenship which only relies on weak and impoverished civil society institutions is not sufficient because it does not currently possess leverage to interest young people. Dynamic young citizens who are involved in programmes of active citizenship are making a difference in schools and localities where they are involved in many parts of Europe. But such initiatives are sporadic and too few and far between, and young people's understanding of them is largely derived from the media.

The divisive aspects of the 'politics of recognition' is a powerful issue in the United States as well as in other parts of Europe. Groups which demand a recognition of their particularistic identities also demand separate schools and the 'curriculum of recognition' and such demands detract from the development of intercultural understandings and an inclusive curriculum.

Since there will be no jobs in the virtual and privatized technological factory and the governmental institutions are shrinking, how will social cohesiveness in the context of social diversity be strengthened? The need to bring the public domain and the public sector together with the civic and community sector is necessary because otherwise the only viable civil society of strength and glamour is the criminal fraternity which will increase levels of imprisonment and raise social and racial tensions.

Citizenship education requires a national as well as a wider focus. Hence, the notion of being 'Asian, Scottish, British and European' (and its English, Welsh or Irish equivalents) are all critical for citizenship education. This is especially important because Britain is a member of the European Union and a critical understanding and engagement by young people should enable them not to accept uncritically ideas of 'Fortress Europe'. Such a narrow interpretation of Europe is in social terms strengthened by a Eurocentric curriculum which has divisive consequences.

Most of the understanding of rights of young people in many European contexts come from the media and not the school. Young people are not taught to read these messages critically. This raises important considerations for teachers, curriculum planners, schools and other educators of what the education systems needs to do about citizenship education, either in tandem with or in response to the media.

DEEP CITIZENSHIP

Notions of how to develop deep democracy based on deep social participation and citizenship require urgent attention because the private market has no public obligations and the role of mixed economies becomes important. The role of social capital amongst citizens is now also recognized by the World Bank. This reflects at least the acceptance of possibilities of a multitude of voices at the universal level with social and civic virtues, which Paul Clark refers to as 'deep citizenship'. Deep democracy demands deep citizenship. The stimulation of civic values in public and private domains to activate civic virtues puts into place a new, non-traditional understanding of citizenship. Here deep democracy can be assisted by eliminating the previous private/public divide:

> The fundamental change in the way in which the particular and the universal are related to the public and the private is to admit the civic virtues to wide areas of life: most generally wherever one can act towards the universal, therein lie the civic virtues and therein lies deep citizenship. (Clark, 1996, p.118).

Part of the solution to resolving the contradictions, dilemmas and complexities lies in the recognition of multiple citizenships and a variety of political loyalties. In the contemporary British context, being an active member of a local street association, being Scottish or Welsh, British, European and global are all consistent with the notion of deep citizenship.

BELONGINGNESS

The other issue which should be raised is that of the 'belongingness' of all groups in British society. Dominant nationalities tend to see Britain as 'theirs', and 'others,' who are regarded as aliens who do not belong, are seen to encroach upon it. There are obviously specificities of different localities, communities, families and groups which provide a different colour, texture and hue to different parts of British society. There are also differences of local politics, economies and histories and these intersect and interact differently within the local, regional, national, European and global contexts.

The sharing of space by the dominant and subordinate, the colonizer and the colonized, the rich and poor, comes together in polities so as to make the functioning of modern democratic societies complex. This complexity includes the way in which material and social goods are produced and distributed, including the political, economic, literary, cultural and the media output. The 'other' is no longer out there, but here, and as Chambers states, there is an intersection of 'histories, memories and experiences' (Chambers, 1994, p.6). It is important to develop an agenda for public and social policy and create spaces where we can negotiate the complexity of our societies, both in rural areas and cities. Such an analysis should be inclusive of all groups who live in them. In establishing such a context, past and current exclusions need to be put to rights, making it possible to initiate a dialogue between all those living in Britain. The interaction and intersection of the histories of cultures and languages enables the construction of a more realistic understanding of the past, and better informs us of the present which may, in turn, have implications for constructing a less biased and a more meaningful future. For instance, the teaching of British history should include the contributions of Islam, Judaism, Blacks and the regional nationalities such as the English, Scottish and Welsh, their culture, civilization and history. This includes issues of antipathy, conflicts and co-operation.

Communities are not only situated within their localities but have other identities, both at national and supranational levels, which lends an enormous range of heterogeneity to the society and its life. The complexity of all this defies simplistic definition by either the dominant or subordinate cultures. Political systems, in most parts of the world, have not come to terms with the public policy implications of this reality.

Societies as such embody notions of 'belongingness' as well as of alienation. They have both features of a universalistic nature as well as particularisms and local differences. Yet, non-confederal localisms can become parochial, racist, insular, stagnant and authoritarian. There are thick and textured layers of political, social and economic contexts which intersect with history, culture and language. British society therefore provides possibilities and prospects of an infinite nature and, yet, can also be lonely and confining. The confederal nature of society requires that integrative thinking and structures should link individual groups and localities. The challenge for the political and educational system is to develop a shared and common value system in which inclusive rights and responsibilities will be developed as an outcome of the work of schools, social and political institutions.

Such a political initiative needs to establish broadly based social policies, measures, strategies, actions and institutional changes. These initiatives ought to be monitored to ensure that international standards are being met. Without the development of these strategies, combined with the analysis of the negative aspects of exclusion, there would be further proliferation of racial and ethnic conflict.

There is an urgent need for the formation of a network of institutions and structures to initiate further work: the collation of good public and social policy practices at the national level; the development of Internet and other informational networks; the dissemination of findings; and the establishment of educational and political strategies for different contexts.

CITIZENSHIP EDUCATION AND HUMAN NATURE

The role of citizenship and politics in society is predicated on the fact that citizenship education itself is necessary for all sections of society. Politically undereducated or ill-educated and inactive members of societies are dangerous because they can misrepresent the complexity of humanity and opt for simplistic solutions based on populist politics, often encouraging authoritarian and undemocratic solutions to complex societal issues.

The rationale for not engaging in citizenship education is the claim that ordinary people are not capable of understanding issues and are susceptible to propaganda. Elites sometimes suggest that, because human nature is largely negative, it is better not to inculcate interest in political or citizenship issues amongst the masses.

The assumptions being made in this chapter are twofold. First, that political awareness, knowledge and understanding is necessary for the masses to grasp both the inherent complexity of society and their rights and responsibilities within it. Second, the assumptions about the negativity of human nature also require scrutiny and comment. Thus, if human nature is considered to be negative, then selfishness, conflict and violence will be seen to be deeply embedded in human consciousness and educational and other socializing influences will have no role to play in changing patterns of behaviour and social relations. It is commonly argued that human nature is basically selfish and to expect human beings to be social is an uphill task.

The contention of this chapter is that there is as yet insufficient evidence to allow such definitive statements about human nature. In other words, human nature needs to be seen as neither good nor bad. The human capacity to be social or selfish is still an open issue and the potential for both exists among people. Human nature as such may neither be Hobbesian nor Rousseauian but has the potential, the proclivity and the capacity to be both.

Individuals may hold not only selfish but also social instincts and the interaction between nature and nurture can result in social contracts based on equality for both individuals and groups. This, however, is not a simple matter because minds are not tabulae rasae. They encode both personal and larger historical legacies which make the issue of equitable socialization very complex.

The role of citizenship education and involvement is to enable the establishment of a healthier balance between the selfish and the social by accepting the sanctity and autonomy of the learner. The development of such autonomous learners would enable them to negotiate some of the complexities of societies. Education systems with a citizenship education syllabus would enable the emergence of thinking citizens who would be less likely to seek solutions to conflicts through violence. The education of the young also ought to involve the unpacking of the underpinnings of 'evil' in society. However, this is also a broader task of public and social policy and requires an inter-agency approach, because in as much as truth and veracity are inherently human values so are lying and deception. Broader social and public policy measures are necessary to deny the roots of evil, lying and deception, and such policies include the curbing of the cruel treatment of children.

In educational terms, the common manifestation of children's ill-treatment and of violence against them leads to a lowering of their academic performance, higher levels of truancy and the drift into criminal and violent behaviours.

Intercultural public policies need to take cognizance of the diverse contributions and needs of girls and women. Girls and women from different communities and in different parts of the national context are represented in a range of positions in socio-economic terms. Their position has been impacted upon and they have been involved in changing the private and public domains with different capacities, especially in relation to their patriarchal and socio-economic positions. They have also contributed to resistance against racism and essentialized notions of their complex and multiple identities (Rattansi and Westwood, 1994, pp.15–31).

Such general social involvement and citizenship educational issues raise problems about the level of academic autonomy allowed by the state within its education system. If the state is insecure it will tend to control directly the education system for dominative or nationalistic purposes. Regional, national, European and other international organizations have a role to ensure that these tendencies are curbed and that states are held responsible for the international legal instruments they are signatory to.

Political and education systems also have a responsibility to determine the ways and directions in which technology will be developed and used. If it is allowed to be rationalized and instrumentalized to perpetuate violence, then technology reinforces the inherent evil forces in societies. The role of education and public policies to channel technological developments into peaceful and positive directions is essential to obviating conflict and violence.

In conclusion, devolution in Britain presents an opportune moment to integrate issues of citizenship education in the school curriculum. This can be accomplished by developing inclusive notions of British identities by building on the historical and contemporary diversities in British society within a common framework. Such developments ought to include the tackling of issues of institutional racism and xenophobia. Active citizenship needs to be strengthened by developing commitment to dealing with the challenge presented by unemployment arising from technological changes and the strengthening of institutions within the public domain and the civil society. This would ensure the legitimacy and belongingness of diverse groups to these isles.

REFERENCES

Chambers, I. (1994) *Migrancy, Culture, Identity*. London: Routledge.
Clark, P. B. (1996) *Deep Citizenship*. London and Chicago: Pluto Press.
Green, J. (1998) Educational multiculturalism, critical pluralism and deep democracy. In C. Willett (ed.) *Theorising Multiculturalism: A Guide to Current Debate*. Oxford and Malden, Mass,; Blackwell.
Habermas, J. (1998) *The Inclusion of the Other: Studies in Political Theory*. Cambridge, Mass: MIT Press.
International Centre for Intercultural Studies (ICIS) (1996) *Sagaland – Youth Culture, Racism and Education. A Report on Research carried out in Thamesmead and Roots of Racism – The Social Basis of Racist Action*. London: ICIS.
Laing, L. and Laing, J. (1996) *Early English Art and Architecture: Archaeology and Society*. Stroud, Gloucester: Sutton Publishing.
Marshall, T. H. (1977) *Class, Citizenship and Social Development*. Chicago: University of Chicago Press.
Rattansi, A. and Westwood, S. (1994) *Racism, Modernity Identity on the Western Front*. London: Polity Press.
Rawls, J. (1971) *A Theory of Justice*. Cambridge: The Belknap Press, pp. 60, 124, 132, 199.

Part II

Implementation: Some Issues and Challenges

Chapter 4

Moral, Social and Civic Education in Greece

Eirini Pasoula

INTRODUCTION

This chapter is concerned with the conceptualization and development of moral and social education in Athens. With regard to citizenship and education for it, I began to appreciate and deal with their relationship to moral and social education while trying to review some literature in the field of the latter. The chapter will present this relationship which I found while attempting, at the beginning, to reach some definition of *moral* education.

In this attempt, I initially encountered the following question:

> Can you tell me (Socrates) whether virtue is *acquired* by teaching or by practice; or if neither by teaching nor practice, then whether it comes to man by nature, or in what other way? (Plato, *Meno*, I, a, 1–4)

This question of Meno to Socrates about the nature of virtue and the ways of acquiring it can be seen in relation to Aristotle's suggestion that the acquisition of virtues requires practice in society:

> the best man is not the one who exercises his virtue towards himself but the one who exercises it towards another; because this is a difficult task. (Aristotle, *Nichomachean Ethics*, v, 1130a, 4–8)

Moral education is held to be as old as human society itself (Iheoma, 1995). Moral education is, to a significant extent, a social or political matter: societies have always been concerned with the moral and social development of the next generation. In schools, direct moral instruction and advice is given to the students while the structure and the relationships of the whole of school also transmit messages of this kind (Kleinig, 1982b; Pring, 1984). Further, society expects teachers to sensitize their students to *socio-political* issues such as the lack of respect for human rights, though it may often ask teachers to remain neutral and detached from politics (Kibble, 1998). The issue of making 'good' citizens is an old one, going back to Plato, while Dewey made democratic citizenship a major theme (White, 1996).

Before attempting to see what moral or social or civic education is, it is worth analysing the concepts of *education* and the *educated person* not only because moral, social and civic education are part of the wider concept of education but also because, as will be seen, moral, social and political issues dwell in these concepts. According to Peters (1965, 1966), *education* is not a concept that marks out specific processes or activities; rather it is associated with learning, for which an essential criterion is that something *valuable* should be passed on. Not all learning is educational – for example, learning how to pick pockets (Lawton and Gordon, 1996). Worthwhileness and improvement, as well as value judgements about what kind of learning that embodies them, are implicit in *education*. Accordingly, the concept of the *educated person* implies qualities and accomplishments, beyond cognitive improvement, that we value highly in people (Pring, 1994). It often happens, though, that a person is thought to be educated on the basis of his or her personal academic accomplishments, without reference as to how he or she relates to social improvement (Pring, 1994). The reason for this can be the exchange value of these accomplishments in the competitive market economy.

Along with the concepts of *education* and the *educated person*, it is relevant to attempt to examine what it is to be a *person*. I should also suggest that perhaps the best way to understand what the terms 'moral', 'social' and 'civic' mean is to see them in the light of what it is to be a person, where these attributes are observable. Dewey (1916, pp. 306–7) provided us with some valuable ideas:

> Each individual has of necessity a variety of callings, in each of which he should be intelligently effective . . . *No one is just* an artist and nothing else, and in so far as he approximates that condition, he is so much the less developed human being; he is a kind of monstrosity. He must, at some period of his life, be a member of a family; he must have friends and companions; he must either support himself or be supported by others, and thus he has a business career. He is a member of some organised political unit and so on. (emphasis added)

More than two thousand years ago, Aristotle stressed the social and political nature of Man, but more briefly:

> The man who is isolated, who is unable to share the benefits of political association, or has no need to share because he is already self-sufficient, is no part of a city, and must therefore be either a beast or a god. (*Politics*, I, 2, 1253a25) (italics added)

or

> no one would choose to have all good things by himself, for man is naturally constituted to live in company. (*Nichomachean Ethics*, ix, 1169b, 17f)

As these views suggest, to develop as a person requires meaningful involvement in a range of social relationships. To be a person is more than just to have an intellect; it is to have emotions and feelings, to relate to other persons in a distinctive way and to have responsibilities and obligations towards oneself and to the social context that so profoundly affects the quality of one's life (Pring, 1984, 1995). When we talk about an *educated person*, major issues about the quality of a politically organized society arise. Education thus appears to have, or at least ought to have, moral, social and political dimensions and aims. In this way, our question about what is moral, social and civic education has to be asked again.

Starting again with moral education, this has been taken to mean 'assisting young people in their moral development' (Ward, 1986, p. 72) or 'the conscious attempt' to do so (Lawton and Gordon, 1996, p. 147). These formulations seem to offer a quick way to define moral education, also tempting us to define social or civic education in a similar way. However, if what counts for *development* as a moral, social and political being is not examined, such approaches are superficial. The need for clarification is enhanced by the fact that no commonly accepted definitions exist (Wilson *et al.*, 1967; Beck *et al.*, 1971; Ward, 1986). A basic reason for this lack of consensus must be that the various terms involved are not easily and unambiguously defined; terms such as 'morality' and 'citizenship' can take different meanings, depending upon the context in which they are used (May, 1971; Carr, 1991). This diversity of meaning must be greater in modern pluralistic societies where there is no agreement on a consistent set of commonly accepted values and on what is morally or socially or politically right or wrong (Cox, 1986; Pring, 1984, 1994). Meanwhile, the confusion must increase because many relevant areas of study, whose delineation is unclear, have developed since the 1970s, such as personal education, peace education, human rights education, life education, political education, values education and sex education (Dufour, 1990; Stradling, 1986).

A good way to attempt to sort out the confusion is to attempt to approach the concepts of *morality* and *citizenship*. Starting with *morality*, it is worth noting that the word 'moral' derives from the Latin 'mores', which refers to the customs that any *society* demands that its members observe (Cox, 1983). The development of morality as inseparable from involvement in human relationships within the life of society – or the 'city' – was a widely held assumption in the ancient Athenian city state. To characterize a good man was to characterize the relationship in which such a man stood to others. The understanding of virtues provided him with standards by which he could question the quality of the life of his community and enquire whether this or that practice was just. At the same time, it was his membership of the community that was providing him with opportunities for the development of such an understanding (MacIntyre, 1981). In this context, Aristotle had suggested that 'the true student of politics is thought to have studied virtue above all things'

(*Nichomachean Ethics*, i, 1102a, 5). It is significant to note here that the base of the term 'politics' rests firmly in the Greek word '*polis*', namely 'a city, hence a state' (Partridge, 1958, p. 158). Thus, 'political relationships' were the relationships of free men (non-slaves) to each other, that is the relationships between members of a community who both ruled and were ruled (MacIntyre, 1981). It was in this context that a person was thought of as a 'political' being. Clearly, the term 'political' here is free from any current notion of party politics, partisan tactics and narrow personal interests. Instead, it directly concerns the *polis* as the context within which the person is to exist and develop as a human being. Poets and philosophers thought of the *polis* in this way, as illustrated in the *Philoctetes* of Sophocles, where Philoctetes was left on a desert island for ten years:

> You left me friendless, solitary, *without a city: a corpse among the living.* (MacIntyre, 1981, p. 127) (emphasis added)

It seems that Philoctetes felt exiled not only from the company of mankind, but also from the status of a human being; thus, friendship, company and city state appear to be fundamental to humanity. Similarly, Aristotle generally insisted that the person is indeed intelligible only as a political being, otherwise he is a barbarian (MacIntyre, 1981). Within this belief system, Pericles, in the Funeral Oration, despised the person who did not participate in the public life:

> You will find united in the same persons an interest at once in private and in public affairs ... For we alone regard the man who takes no part in public affairs *not as one who minds his own business, but as good for nothing* (Thucydides, *Peloponnesian War* II, xl, 2) (emphasis added)

The act of political participation – in the broader meaning of the term 'political' – was decidedly identified with moral goodness. This can make sense in that one cannot come to deal with the greater social good unless one is moral enough to care for it and, while doing so, to be able to move beyond one's personal interests. Both the quantity and the quality of engaging in the public good is dependent on one's moral maturity. More specifically, respect for others, a sense of responsibility and obligation towards them as well as protest when rights are infringed are political virtues firmly based on morality. As suggested by Pring (1995), participation was not just a right, it was an *obligation* to ensure delivery from tyrants, to protect one's self-interest, to promote the public well-being; but, above all, deliberation about what is *worthwhile* in the *political and moral* framework was a good in itself.

What seems to result from these thoughts is that one can only become truly moral by developing as a social and political being through participating in the life of the smaller groups and/or the larger society (analogous to the *polis*) one belongs to.

In practice, morality has not always been conceived of in its full 'sociological' or 'political' sense. Piaget and Kohlberg were criticized for thinking of moral maturation as marked by the development of moral reasoning through stages, underestimating the influence of cultural and subcultural factors. Criticism suggested that moral development does not take place in a vacuum but within a context of socio-political relationships as well as a body of relevant traditions, ideas and attitudes (Kleinig, 1982a; May, 1971; McPhail, 1982). Hirst (1965), attempting to establish morality as a distinct form of knowledge, offered mainly an intellectualistic view of it. Generally, intellectualistic and apolitical approaches to morality and moral education are said to have influenced academic attitudes to moral and social learning (McPhail, 1982). Perhaps one of the most telling critiques of the non- political, limited view of morality and moral education has been given by Dewey (1909, pp. 42–3).

> We have associated the term ethical with certain *special* acts which are labelled virtues and are *set off* from the mass of other acts, and are still more divorced from the habitual images and motives of the children performing them. Moral education is thus associated with teaching about these perticular virtues, or with instilling certain sentiments in regard to them. The moral has been perceived in *a too goody-goody way*. Ultimate moral motives and forces are nothing more or less than social intelligence (the power of observing and comprehending social situations) and social power (trained capacities of control) at work in the service of social interest and aims. (emphasis added)

In these lines, Dewey pinpoints the moral dimensions of everyday social practices, instead of associating morality with the 'lustre' of special, non-daily acts. He also recognizes the impact of moral motives and forces on human behaviour. Although these motives and forces may often be more 'personal' and subconscious than Dewey suggests (by defining them *solely* in social terms), it is true that they are developed and expressed in relation to one's society.

Moving from moral and social education to *civic* education, it is important to see how the above interrelation enriches or satisfies the concept of education for citizenship. It is valuable, though, to see first how *citizenship* may be defined. Citizenship has been a contested concept, the meaning of which changes according to context, especially depending on how democracy is understood. Democracy can be seen not merely as a political system but as a moral way of life characterized by fundamental human values such as self-determination and equality; such a view was taken by Dewey (1916, p. 87):

> a democracy is more than a form of government; it is primarily a mode of associated living, of conjoint communicated experience.

In this case, citizenship means participating positively in collective efforts to maintain or reshape society. If democracy is associated not with allegiance to a moral ideal but with a set of institutions and procedures, i.e. selecting between political elites for the exercise of power, citizenship is mainly associated with a set of arrangements, i.e. legal rights (Carr, 1991). None the less, citizenship has a basis in the Athenian *polis* (city state) (Carr, 1991). There, citizenship was marked by the idea that man was a *political* being, who could become truly human and develop himself only through participating in the life of his *polis* (Carr, 1991; MacIntyre, 1981). From the personal involvement of the citizen, the concept of citizenship evolved, after many changes across the ages, into subordination to the claims of the nation state, especially in terms of obeying the laws (Heater, 1992; QCA, 1998). In this context, a number of definitions have been given of citizenship (see, for example, Cogan, 1997; Marshall, 1950, quoted in QCA, 1998; McLaughlin, 1992).

These definitions relate citizenship to certain characteristics such as membership of a community, sense of identity, rights and entitlements, duties and obligations, participation in public life, as well as the values and virtues which are developed and required in this context. Regarding the characteristics of citizenship, McLaughlin (1992) suggested that there exists a *continuum* of interpretations of them, ranging from minimal to maximal. The *moral* aspect of citizenship is perceived as being fundamental to democracy (as a way of life) as well as to moral and social education. Klaassen (1996) made the significant point that citizenship concerns not only the relation between the state and its citizenry but also the relationships among the citizens themselves, especially their rights and duties while living together. I suggest that the moral dimension of democratic citizenship may be, in the final analysis, the *most* important of all, because a citizen may have the array of knowledge and skills required but, above all, he or she needs, as White (1996, p. 1) proposed, 'to be disposed' to use them *democratically*. In this respect, education for citizenship and moral education should be planned and developed in ways that address their mutual relationship.

> I have to note that I talk about democracy and democratic citizenship, because democracy is the only political system that generally seems to be more attractive and ever fully justifiable. (Wolff, 1996)

The interaction between moral, social and political aspects of development/education has been well stated by Hargreaves (1994, pp. 37–8):

> *Civic education* is about the *civic virtues and decent behaviour* that adults wish to see in young people. But it is also *more* than this . . . Active citizens are *as political as they are moral*; moral sensibility *derives in part* from political *understanding; politcal apathy* spawns *moral apathy*. (emphasis added)

It is not only political participation that rests on being moral enough to care for it and to exercise it in a morally good way. At the same time, moral sensibility develops through political participation, because deliberation on what is personally and socially good is involved. Therefore, each of them necessarily nurtures the other. This has serious implications for the conceptualization and development of education for citizenship. It seems that it cannot be limited to political literacy, as has repeatedly happened in the past (Whitburn, 1986; Wringe, 1992). Instead, it has to address related values, attitudes and skills.

Such a view of civic education offers a complete approach to moral and social education as well, since one cannot develop as a moral and social being without developing as a political being. Given this, any definition of moral and social education has to address this implicit mutual relationship. In these respects, moral, social and civic education could be perceived in the school context as 'the school activities, as part of the formal and informal curriculum, that relate to pupils' development as moral and social persons, which consists in the acquisition of relevant knowledge, values, skills and dispositions'. This definition is intelligible and acceptable on two conditions: first, that we understand the term 'moral' in its full sense and in relation to 'social' and second, that we clarify which are the relevant knowledge, values, skills and dispositions. Although lists of values and dispositions, attitudes and skills are commonly generated by studies on moral, social and civic education in an attempt to map its territory (see, for example, Iheoma, 1995; Pring, 1984; QCA, 1998; White, 1996), that is not the intention of my study. It is noteworthy that, while reviewing these studies, fundamental values of democratic citizenship such as co-operation, respect, equality and honesty were found to be the most prominent, showing again that the moral, social and political aspects of education are best conceived of in mutual relationship to one another.

It seems that we reached, through the ages, a conception of moral, social and civic education that is very akin to the Athenian assumption that growing and educating others to develop as moral beings is inseparable from growing and educating others to develop as social and political beings.

REFERENCES

Aristotle (transl. by E. Barker, 1995) *Politics*. Oxford: Oxford University Press.
Aristotle (transl. by J. A. K. Thomson, 1976) *The Ethics of Aristotle: The Nichomachean Ethics*. Harmondsworth: Penguin Classics.
Beck, C. M., Crittenden, B. S. and Sullivan, E. V. (eds) (1971) *Moral Education. Interdisciplinary Approaches*. Toronto: University of Toronto Press.
Carr, W. (1991) Education for citizenship. *British Journal of Educational Studies*, **39** (4): 373–85.
Cogan, J. J. (1997) *The Citizenship Education Policy Study Project. Final Report*. June 1997. Minneapolis: University of Minnesota.
Cox, E. (1983) *Problems and Possibilities for Religious Education*. London: Hodder and Stoughton.
Cox, E. (1986) The Belief System. In D. Lawton (ed.) *School-based Curriculum Planning*. Sevenoaks: Hodder and Stoughton.
Dewey, J. (1909) *Moral Principles in Education*. Boston: Houghton Mifflin.

Dewey, J. (1916) *Democracy and Education: An Introduction to the Philosophy of Education*. New York: Macmillan.

Dufour, B. (1990) The new social curriculum: the political, economic and social context for educational change. In B. Dufour (ed.) *The New Social Curriculum. A Guide to Cross-Curricular Issues*. Cambridge, Cambridge University Press, pp. 1–13.

Hargreaves, D. (1994) *The Mosaic of Learning: Schools and Teachers for the Next Century*. London: Demos.

Heater, D. (1992) *Citizenship: The Civic Ideal in World History, Politics and Education*. London: Longman.

Hirst, P. (1965) Liberal education and the nature of knowledge. In R. D. Archambault (ed.) *Philosophical Analysis and Education*. London: Routledge and Kegan Paul.

Iheoma, E. O. (1995) *Moral Education for Colleges and Universities*. Enugu, Nigeria: Fourth Dimension.

Kibble, D. G. (1998) Moral education: dilemmas for the teacher. *The Curriculum Journal*, **9** (1): 51–61.

Klaassen, C. (1996) Education and citizenship in a welfare state. *Curriculum*, **17** (2): 62–73.

Kleinig, J. (1982a) Moral education in a school setting. *Journal of Christian Education*, **74**: 37–47.

Kleinig, J. (1982b) *Philosophical Issues in Education*. London: Croom Helm.

Lawton, D. and Gordon, P. (1996) *Dictionary of Education*. Sevenoaks: Hodder and Stoughton.

MacIntyre, A. (1981) *After Virtue. A Study in Moral Theory*. London: Duckworth.

McLaughlin, T. H. (1992) Citizenship, diversity and education. *Journal of Moral Education*, **21** (3): 235–50.

McPhail, P. (1982) *Social and Moral Education*. Oxford: Blackwell.

Marshall, T. H. (1950) *Citizenship and Social Class*. Cambridge: Cambridge University Press, cited in QCA (1998) *Education for Citizenship and the Teaching of Democracy in Schools*. London: QCA.

May, P. R. (1971) *Moral Education in School*. London: Methuen Educational.

Partridge, E. (1958) *Origins: A Short Etymological Dictionary of Modern English*. London: Routledge and Kegan Paul.

Peters, R. S. (1965) Education as initiation. In R. D. Archambault (ed.) *Philosophical Analysis and Education*. London: Routledge and Kegan Paul.

Peters, R. S. (1966) *Ethics and Education*. London: Allen and Unwin.

Plato (1956) (transl. by R. W. Sharples, 1985) *Meno*. Warminster: Penguin Classics.

Pring, R. (1984) *Personal and Social Education in the Curriculum*. London: Hodder and Stoughton.

Pring, R. (1994) The context of education: monastery or market place? In J. Haldane (ed.) *Education, Values and the State. The Victor Cook Memorial Lectures 1993–1994*. St Andrews, Centre for Philosophy and Public Affairs, University of St Andrews, pp. 25–41.

Pring, R. (1995) *Closing the Gap: Liberal Education and Vocational Preparation*. London: Hodder and Stoughton.

QCA (1998) *Education for Citizenship and the Teaching of Democracy in Schools. Final Report of the Advisory Group on Citizenship*. London: QCA.

Stradling, R. (1986) Social education: some questions on assessment and evaluation. In C. Brown, C. Harber and J. Strivens (eds) *Social Education: Principles and Practices*. London: The Falmer Press, pp. 21–41.

Thucydides (transl. by C. F. Smith, 1917) *The Peloponnesian War. Books I and II*. London: Heinemann.

Ward, L. (1986) The morality system. In D. Lawton (ed.) *School-based Curriculum Planning*. Sevenoaks: Hodder and Stoughton, pp. 71–86.

Whitburn, R. (1986) The socio-political system. In D. Lawton (ed.) *School-based Curriculum Planning*. Sevenoaks: Hodder and Stoughton.

White, P. (1996) *Civic Virtues and Public Schooling: Educating Citizens for a Democratic Society*. New York: Teachers College Press.

Wilson, J., Williams, N. and Sugarman, B. (1967) *Introduction to Moral Education*. Harmondsworth: Penguin.

Wolff, J. (1996) *An Introduction to Political Philosophy*. Oxford: Oxford University Press.

Wringe, C. (1992) The ambiguities of education for citizenship. *Journal of Philosophy of Education*, **26** (1): 29–38.

Chapter 5

Personal Development and Citizenship Education: Setting the Agenda for Lifelong Learning

Jo Cairns

INTRODUCTION: CITIZENSHIP AND THE DRIVE TO LEARN

The crisis engendered by living in the postmodern age both for individuals and their communities as they share in common activities has been well documented. Writing in 1994 Hargreaves (1994, p. 58) argued:

> The decline of the Judaeo-Christian tradition as the prime purpose underpinning schooling and teaching in a context of greater religious, cultural and ethnic diversity raises penetrating questions about the moral purpose of education. One of the greatest educational crises of the post modern age is the collapse of the common school; a school tied to its community and having a clear sense of the social and moral values it should instil.

Reflecting on the more general lack of certainty and direction in the world now increasingly characterized by 'the inability of both public institutions and the collective behaviour of human beings to come to terms with it', Hobsbawm (1994, p. 15) writes:

> At the end of this century it has become possible to see what a world may be like in which the past, including the past in the present, has lost its role, in which the old maps and charts which guided human beings, singly and collectively, through life no longer represent the landscape through which we move, the sea we sail. In which we do not know where our journey is taking us, or even ought to take us.

Robert Reich in *The Work of Nations* argued that the consequences of these complex changes would be that:

> There will be no national products or technologies, no national corporations, no national industries . . . All that will remain rooted within national borders are the

people who comprise a nation. Each nation's primary assets will be its citizens' skills and insights. (1992, note 10:3)

A major response to this dramatic sense of cultural disjunction and absence of purposefulness at the end of the twentieth century has been the emergence of 'the Third Way'. Writing in 1998, Giddens (pp. 64–5) discussed the overall aim of Third Way politics as 'helping citizens pilot their way through the major revolutions of our time: globalisation, transformations in personal life and our relationship to nature. "Third Way politics" looks for a redefinition of rights and obligations'. It is clear that the New Labour government recognized the value of adopting the Third Way as its own and in the Green Paper, *The Learning Age* (DfEE, 1998), a clear echo of Reich's words is found: 'investment in human capital will be the foundation of success . . . the fostering of an inquiring mind and the love of learning are essential to our future success.' It went on to say, 'the government cannot force anyone to learn but we can help those who want to and we can change the culture to foster a love of learning.'

This chapter begins from the assumption that the government has chosen education as the vehicle to assist 'citizens [to] pilot their way through the major revolutions of our time'. More specifically it is focusing on the concept of the 'citizen' and 'citizenship education' to spearhead the drive to create a 'learning culture'. Thus by encouraging individuals to come to terms with their role as citizens, the culture will perceptibly change to accommodate the 'new relationship between the individual and community'. This is nothing short of creating a project to engage the imagination, co-operation, understanding and values of individuals and their communities.

CITIZENSHIP, LIFELONG LEARNING AND THE THIRD WAY

The project within formal and informal education follows on from the reworking of concepts of citizenship and citizenship education in the early 1990s. For example, the National Curriculum caused education for citizenship to become a cross- curriculum theme. The Speaker's Commission on Citizenship (1990, p. 3) reviewed the relationship between citizenship and adult education:

> If adequate support is to be made available to enable men and women to organise themselves, and influence decision-making locally and nationally, adult education and community development are of paramount importance.

In 1991 the Citizens' Charter (HMSO, 1991, p. 2) spoke of itself as 'a testament of our belief in people's right to be informed and choose for themselves'. Mayo (1997, p. 123) refers to Heater's comment that the Charter would bring about a focus upon individual rights, together with some reference to patriotism and voluntary work.

By centring the project on the citizen and citizenship education the government is thereby seeking engagement and purposefulness as characteristics of the educated person. As Hyland (1999, p. 188) argues from Gidden's text (1998, p. 70):

> The ultimate end of the (Third Way) programme is 'the social investment state' which 'defines equality as inclusion and inequality as exclusion'.

We might ask, however, to what extent the current lifelong learning programme, including the revised National Curriculum, actively takes forward the inclusion of individuals with its overarching Third Way framework? At present, the newly emerging educational framework remains more supportive of the development of pragmatic work-based skills, the needs for which are economics driven, and not specifically person-centred. The purpose of this chapter is to illustrate the difficulties which present approaches to lifelong learning create in relation to the 'big project'; namely that of changing the culture of our community in order to foster love of learning in the individual citizen. It is proposed here therefore that attention should shift to the engagement of the *individual* in the project by the support of educational initiatives which promote individual personal growth and values acquisition. Such a shift will facilitate a fostering of learning at times and with experiences which significantly shape individual identity. The chapter will also offer an illustration of the importance of engaging with specific curriculum areas to explore their place in the overall lifelong learning project for individuals through an analysis of religious education.

So far the government has reviewed its National Curriculum for compulsory education and set about revising policy and practice in 14–19 education and post compulsory and adult education.

In its introduction to the *Review of the National Curriculum* (DfEE, 1999), the government stated:

> We have set a challenging agenda to raise standards. We aim to raise the level of educational achievement of all young people, enabling them to fulfil their potential and to make a full contribution to their communities. We wish to help young people develop spiritually, morally, culturally, mentally and physically. And we want them to become healthy, lively and enquiring individuals capable of rational thought and discussion and positive participation in our ethnically diverse and technologically complex society.

This revised curriculum is to fulfil these aims by achieving four key functions: establishing entitlement, establishing standards, promoting continuity and coherence and promoting public understanding/participation (my words). A new focus of curriculum is to be established in which these functions can better be carried out, namely citizenship education. These changes to the National Curriculum are taking place within the wider educational context of a government committed to lifelong learning. Lifelong learning was itself described powerfully in the report of the Commission on Social Justice (1994, p. 120), where it is seen to 'raise people's capacity to add value to the economy, to take charge of their own lives, and to contribute to their families and their communities'. The Report continues (p. 141): 'Our aspiration is nothing less than the creation of a learning society.'

It is clear therefore that the context for personal learning and citizenship education is firmly rooted within the lifelong learning agenda. But what knowledge and which personal and community outcomes are therefore being sought and by whom as a result of lifelong learning? This question prompts a more fundamental question: to what do schools and any other institutions where learning takes place connect? As Gibbons *et al.* (1994) remind us, we must ask fundamental questions about the categories a society uses to make sense of itself and the physical world. Subjects or even broad fields like 'arts' and 'sciences' cannot be treated as if they exist independently of any social changes. Here we are helped by Young's (1998, p. 155) emphasis on the 'connectivity' of knowledge and learning. He speaks of his preferred model of a 'learning society' as 'connective'. Thus he argues the learning society will necessitate four sets of reconceptualizations – the form of specializations; the nature of qualifications; the relation between learning and production; and the concept of learning itself. He writes (p. 155):

> My hope is that these concepts will be of use in giving practical reality to three important ideas. The first is that a society of the future will embody an education-led economy rather than an economy-led education system. The second is that a curriculum of the future will need to be defined by the kind of learning we envisage young people preparing to be adults in the twenty-first century will need. The third idea is that instead of protecting young people from the dangers of work, work in a learning society could become, as Gramsci once hoped, an educational principle.

The potential for Young's ideas to be carried forward is clear. In *Success Against the Odds* (National Commission on Education, 1996) we see how pupils who are engaged, who are listened to, who have a sense of ownership and involvement in their school and their learning feel valued and in turn are able to value others. Yet we also know that one in twelve pupils leaves school with no qualifications. Further, according to the National Adult Learning Survey (Beinart and Smith, 1997), among those categorized as non-learners, nearly two-thirds were in the lower socio-economic groups, 16 per cent had obtained no qualifications by the time they left full-time education and half said that nothing would encourage them to do some learning. Interestingly, too, in *Learning to Grow Older and Bolder* (1999, pp. 11–12) Carlton and Soulsby argue that both younger and older generations share the same barriers to learning, such as:

- Lack of adequate and accessible advice and guidance on possible choices

- Lack of confidence about study skills and fear of failure
- A curriculum which does not relate to and build on their purposes and experience
- Location and distance, when transport is difficult and costly
- Personal and peer group attitudes about returning to learning, particularly when early experiences of school education had not been good

THE INDIVIDUAL AND THE LEARNING AGE

Our focus is therefore on the problems, concerns and learning needs and capacities of individuals within the current 'learning age' and their relationship with the national agenda of educational reforms. This is a focus articulated clearly by Sutherland in his address at the launch of Mayo's book, *Imagining Tomorrow* (1997). There he said:

> The relentless march of technology will require more radical responses than before, particularly if we are not only to equip our citizens for employment but also for personal fulfilment and participation in the processes of democratic action and social change. We need an effective balance between economic concerns and the empowerment of individual citizens.

If the national agenda is to succeed, then nothing less is called for than the wholesale participation of the population in the idea that 'we value learning for its own sake and for the equality of opportunity it brings' (DfEE, 1999, p. 7, Secretary of State). We might here usefully turn to the recent writing on the 'corporate religion' of business management to begin to grapple with the challenge of engaging the general population in 'learning for it's own sake'. The beliefs and values of individuals about the way they approach learning are being challenged by the new agenda. To what extent is this agenda item being taken forward? For example, Kunde (2000, pp. 2 and 10) writes:

> I use the word religion because it means binding together in a belief. I don't think it's possible to have any meaningful vision of the future without believing in something ... Only an organisation which wants the same things can work with the qualitative values which differentiate brands. It is not enough to employ people just for their skills – their attitudes and values must also match those of the company.

VALUES FOR THE LEARNING AGE

At the heart of the agenda is a quite remarkable concept of equity for, as Helena Kennedy writes in 1997, 'equity dictates that all should have the opportunity to succeed in personal, social and economic spheres' (p. 22). She goes on, 'Developing the capacity of everyone to contribute to and benefit from the economic, social, personal and cultural dimensions of their lives is central to achieving the whole range of goals we have set ourselves as a nation.' If the ability to learn is to become the most important skill, then we must examine how far current policies facilitate a shared perception across the population that this is indeed the case. Secondly, to what extent, we must ask, do initiatives to engage the widest population in learning in fact develop the capacity to learn. The remainder of this chapter will set about providing an evaluative framework by which to respond to these two questions.

The approach adopted will take as its starting point the core idea of Freire (1972, p. 28): 'Learning can only come about through praxis, reflection and action upon the world in order to change it.' Learning from this perspective becomes a vehicle for change and not for standing still. Such emphasis on learning will mean a significant cultural shift in our uncertain postmodern times. It calls for a holistic view of education which supports a multiplicity of partners in the process and complexity of change. Our concern is with a rationale which can underpin a culture which delivers learning for individuals, schools and communities which is transformative; that is, one which gives access to the ways and what of learning in a 'knowledge' society and thereby transforms attitudes, values and beliefs, including those about ourselves and our society. At its heart this new culture must be rooted in the experiences and expectations of the learners throughout their lives. Despite adopting readily the 'lifelong learning agenda', the government's present policies show little sign of attempting to take seriously the dilemmas which face the individual in the learning age. For example, Val Davis writing in *Inform* (1999) tells of an Italian Chief Education Officer's comment on the UK's Vocational and Educational Training, 'Where is the spiritual and moral dimension of our VET system?' It is left to the individual to attempt to join up their pre-school, compulsory school and adult learning experiences, achievements and failures. Currently it seems that the state's interest and funding plans for lifelong learning are wholly focused on a narrow understanding of the relationship between skills development and economic success.

The situation calls for the development of policies which cohere with the information already at our disposal about effective learning in individual and communal lives. We must engage with learners, their needs and contexts at times of specific importance for them both as human beings and as workers. For example,

- At times of identity formation, such as adolescence, parenthood, retirement
- At times of learning and training
- At times of major social change
- At times of work choices and changes
- At times of acting as a volunteer
- At times of returning to work

- At times of crisis, through perhaps sickness or bereavement

I would like to point to one critical time in a person's life, that of returning to work and making career choices, to highlight the importance of meeting individuals as they are at specific life changes. The experience of a team of tutors working with women returners in Oxford pointed up both the role of confidence development as a central 'content' of any course as well as the significance of reflective and personal definitions of 'love of learning' by individual course members. For a fuller description of a research project which took place around this theme, please refer to an article by Bachkirova (2000). The experience of the Oxford team supports the need for a firm base for taking forward the lifelong learning agenda for the individual as well as for the government. What is really at the root of the motivation to learn as well as at the heart of the processes of learning? The individual should feel confident that those who are setting the agenda for participation in a lifelong process are not simply involving them in a chase with the hope that on their return from the chase they will be required to enlighten them as to what were the processes involved in the chase and what was so highly prized by them to merit participation in a chase. This chapter will conclude with a call for:

1. A recognition within the lifelong learning agenda of the pivotal role of the individual in joining up the opportunities and the exclusions currently at work in both formal and informal learning settings;
2. A description of a framework for individual reflection and knowledge acquisition for participatory citizens at different life stages;
3. An educational model which defines opportunities for personal growth through learning at different life stages.

In calling for this realignment of the educational agenda of the new century in order to achieve access to it for all citizens, it is necessary to adopt both the call for connectivity by Young of the compulsory curriculum and a renewed understanding of adult education. Corbridge (1999) in the FEDA magazine, *Inform* (Issue No. 1) writes:

Adult education has gone through a painful change process over the past twenty years – from seeking to justify liberal adult education as an end in itself, through the instrumental argument that adult education exists only to provide an access route into vocational training, to a new balance. The new position recognises that the development of communities that value education for itself is an important part of the context in which economic and social regeneration can take place.

The Learning Age (DfEE, 1998) and *The Review of the National Curriculum* (DfEE, 1999) enable us to see a new order emerging in thinking about the place of education in the whole community. There are calls for coherence of provision and equality of access and opportunity. It is therefore worth exploring, in our ecologically sensitive times, how we might fit this new order ecologically into this developing new agenda. Odum (1959, pp. 250–2) quoted in Rappaport (1999, p. 512), speaks of an ecological dominant as 'an organism which is a major controlling influence on the community. As such, dominants are species that set the conditions encouraging or discouraging the presence of other species.' Our question is, 'What dominant species would we wish to see in our still liberal education framework?'

Hirst (1993, p. 198), for example, now favours an understanding of liberal education which is concerned to develop 'capacities for critical reflection across the range of basic practices necessary to any flourishing life within a given context'. Nussbaum (1998, pp. 293–4) argues that, like Seneca, we live in a culture divided between two conceptions of a liberal education. The first is the idea of an education that is liberalizing ('fitted for freedom'). This tradition looked for continuity and commitment of the tradition and discouraged critical reflection. The new idea sees education as 'fitted for freedom' only if it develops free citizens, those who call their minds their own. In this view of education as the cultivation of humanity, 'we ask schools, teachers, learning organisations to prepare everyone for citizenship, as well as to be economically and work active.' Nussbaum's vision of a liberal education involves drawing 'citizens to one another by complex mutual understanding and individual self-scrutiny, building a democratic culture that is truly deliberative and reflective' rather than 'the collision of unexamined preferences . . . And in this way we hope to justify our nation's claim to be a valuable member of a world community of nations that must increasingly learn how to understand, respect and communicate, if our common problems are to be constructively addressed' (p. 294).

A COMMON CULTURE FOR THE DEVELOPMENT OF CITIZENSHIP

Presumably here in the UK we share a consensus about a similar understanding of our own democratic community. In one so complex and fast-changing how might we best promote and engage with lifelong learning? The liberal understanding of education discussed above put alongside the Secretary of State's own vision of education demands informed participation in communal matters by everyone. In other words, each person or self must strive to become critically reflective of their community and their role in it. Hargreaves (1994, p. 71), however, reminds us that 'in the post-modern world the fragile self becomes a continuous reflexive project. It has to be constantly and consciously remade and reaffirmed.' It follows that in compulsory schooling and in adult education we must recognize and continuously strive to create a culture where the ecological dominant is 'a drive to learn', since, according to our botanical metaphor, it is the dominant organism which exerts a major controlling influence on the community. To best ensure a strong underpinning of those community structures, we must first seek out collaborative models of learning in community. Brown and Campione, for example, argue in Woods (1996, p. 125) 'that with repeated experience in "communities of learning" of explaining and arguing, justifying claims with evidence, students will eventually come to adopt these critical thinking strategies as part of their personal repertoire of ways of knowing.' Second, we must work with appropriate and helpful definitions of 'culture', in order to strengthen the new relationships and partnerships which will grow as a result of the drive to learn. White's (1949) definition is valuable here:

> Culture is the name of a distinct order, or class, of phenomena, namely those things and events that are dependent upon the exercise of a mental ability peculiar to the human species, that we have termed symbolling (that is the invention and use of symbols). It is an elaborate mechanism, an organisation of ways and means employed by a particular animal, man, in the struggle for existence and survival. (Cited in Rappaport, 1999, p. 464)

Similarly, Williams' (1976) perception of culture as a 'signifying system', whereby people in various groups and organizations have a system of signs to communicate with each other, is helpful. The sign system is not permanent but changes as members come into contact with others from within or outside the group. Thus the way human beings come to terms with situations is determined by their underlying sign system.

Symbols, myths and metaphors should now begin to emerge as a consequence of naming our present culture 'the learning age'. In this way, our experience of our current culture should begin to be included in an axis, 'participatory-liberal', with the majority of citizens joining in a wide variety of learning experiences, rather than 'high-low', in which the government dictates from above a seemingly good idea which it expects its citizens to share. Thus our culture might genuinely contain within its communities the seeds of survival for all. At present, the national agenda has been derived from the need for economic competitiveness in learners (Thorpe *et al.*, 1993) and, to some extent, social stability. Once again, the individuals who may be concerned, and some even traumatized, by the pressures of existing in such a rapidly changing 'knowledge culture' find little explicit guidance and support within the learning society as it is currently organized. Within our general culture, despite some high levels of human and economic satisfaction, a general unease persists. *The Times* (27 January 2000) refers to Halsey's *Social Trends* (2000), in which he argues that inequality remains the outstanding feature of income and wealth distribution. The struggle for existence and survival is not very far from either the individual or the state. A recent parable reminds us that, in times of change, learners will inherit the earth, while the learned find themselves beautifully equipped to deal with a world that no longer exists.

How then might we support individuals in 'joining up' the lifelong learning agenda for themselves? The imperative to survive is not the sole prerogative of the young. It is constant and links individuals as well as the individual and the state. The learning agenda must give access to ongoing individual development from birth to death. How might we encourage individuals to appraise their changing needs and map their achievements? As communities of learners and teachers, how might we map development according to what we already know of how adults learn?

The literature on adult learning (for example, Brookfield, 1986; Cross, 1981; Galbraith, 1990; Jarvis, 1987) describes and discusses many theories of adult learning. For example, Merriman and Caffarella (1991) provide a summary of four orientations to learning:

- behaviourist; the focus here is the reinforcement of stimuli in the learning situation which are intended to change behaviour
- cognitive; the focus here are the internal mental processes and how information is stored and retrieved in the change process
- humanistic; the focus here is learning guided by individual choice and responsibility, which in turn are affected by human nature and emotions
- social learning; here the focus is the interaction of the individual, the environment and behaviour of which learning is a function

With a renewed emphasis on the nature of citizenship and citizenship education, we might valuably explore those dimensions of humanistic and social learning which can support both individuals and communities in their learning agenda. By so doing we would of course highlight some traditional arguments in educational discussion between education and training and liberalism and subject centredness. For example, Knowles (1978) in developing his theory of andragogy included an ideal type of humanism for this purpose. We might also of course engage with the work of Carl Rogers here, particularly in his emphasis in humanistic education on the learner integrating new information in a very personal way. He writes (1969, p. 3) of 'the student who says "I am discovering – drawing in from outside and making – that which is drawn in a real part of me" '.

STRATEGIES FOR GOOD PRACTICE IN LEARNING AND TEACHING IN A LEARNING AGE

What pedagogies and pedagogic settings might take forward the lifelong learning agenda described here? Leach and Moon (1999) define a pedagogic setting as the practice that a teacher (or teachers), together with a particular group of learners, creates, enacts and experiences. They have used Lave's (1988) definition of a 'setting' and 'arena' to create the notion of a pedagogic setting. An arena she defines as a physically, economically, politically and socially organized space in time. Much of what is viewed traditionally as contexts for learning – the physical surroundings and materials used, the social, institutional and personal purposes at play, the people involved and the language used – 'are themselves an essential part of learning and thus of what is learned'. Working in this context, lifelong learning would not concern itself simply with skills and techniques but with the building and 'symbolling' of 'learning communities'. Further, we might reflect on the argument by Knowles (1996, pp. 96–8) that there are certain conditions of learning that are more conducive to growth and development than others, namely:

- the learners feel a need to learn
- the learning environment is characterized by physical comfort, mutual trust and respect, mutual helpfulness, freedom of expression and acceptance of differences
- the learners perceive the goals of a learning experience to be their goals
- the learners accept a share of the responsibility for planning and operating a learning experience and therefore have a feeling of commitment toward it
- the learners participate actively in the learning process
- the learning process is related to and makes use of the experience of the learners
- the learners have a sense of progress towards their goals

The content to be learned in these settings has been usefully defined by McDermott in Chaiklin and Lave (1993) as statements about the points of contact available to persons in various social settings. He argues that we can only learn what is around to be learned and only then by asking questions about what is to be learned, in what circumstances and for what purpose. The need for clear generalized approaches to the aims and content of lifelong learning for participatory citizens has been made. It is also of value to examine specific curriculum areas which might form the basis for a specialist curriculum coterminous with lifelong learning. It has, for example, been argued by Jackson (1997, p. 130) that to participate in religious education is 'a reflective activity personal to the student'. Jackson goes on to develop the importance of introspection in the learning of the educated individual.

For the philosopher Richard Rorty (1980), a person can be educated by studying his or her culture. Engaging in 'conversation', that is in hermeneutics, can lead to edification. This is a transformative concept. To be edified in this context is to be taken out of one's self. Through the challenge of 'unpacking' another world-view one can, in a sense, become a new person.

In this attempt to present the value of including a humanistic underpinning to the lifelong learning agenda, it is helpful to pinpoint the knowledge, attitudes and values with which the individual might engage in the particular specific curriculum area of religious education. Here the individual at all life stages is able to learn about and reflect upon some of the philosophies, values and challenges which underpin both the national/social and the individual learning agenda. The life experiences and conditions from which core human and social values are derived are present within the narrative frameworks of individual religious and humanistic traditions. For the individuals whom the 'big project' is seeking to encourage to become active and engaged citizens, the religious education curriculum offers the opportunity to learn about their own and other people's beliefs and values. Second, the learning in religious education is of a specific kind, namely a deliberative, sensitive involvement with others' perceptions and values as well as a structured reflection on one's own. The descriptions of current approaches to the subject below argues for the promotion of religious education as a means of supporting and encouraging the individual to participate in shared learning and shared values about living in our present pluralist and fractured cultures. At the same time, the descriptions point to a base being established among individuals to begin to work together on the common project of participating in 'changing the culture' with a coherent mode of 'symbolling' as inherent to the project.

Herein lies the strength of the argument to present religious education as a model for specific curriculum content and focus throughout lifelong learning. The goal of RE becomes transformation of the learner. The content becomes the 'stuff of living', namely our cultural environment and our symbolic interpretations of the content and business of living. Through our study we share others' ways of living and cultures, thereby becoming involved with other members and potential learners of our community. A diagrammatic representation of the personal learning outcomes which might result in lifelong learning is included in Figure 5.1. It is taken from Grimmett (1987, p. 256) who so finely summarizes the process of curriculum decision-making in religious education indicating the relationship of personal learning outcomes to the curriculum and the relationship of the curriculum to religious education's field of enquiry.

This understanding of religious education has stemmed from a thorough attempt to place the human being at the heart of the learning experience, while at the same time adopting a core set of human values as central both to the understanding of education and the person as the basis for curriculum development. This brief evaluation of the place of religious education as a specified curriculum area within lifelong learning can best be summarized by Jackson's (1997, pp. 133–4) own concluding statement on the aims of RE:

A fundamental aim is to develop an understanding of the grammar of religions and the interpretive skills necessary to gain that understanding . . . The achievement of this aim necessitates the development of critical skills which open up issues of representation and interpretation as well as questions of truth and meaning . . . There is too the inseparability of understanding and reflection in the interpretive

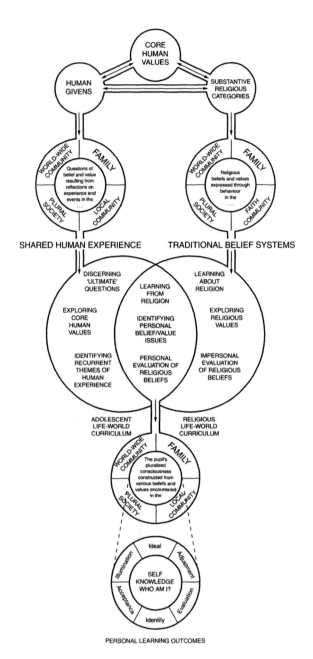

Figure 5.1: A summary of the process of curriculum decision–making in religious education, indicating the relationship of personal learning outcomes to the curriculum and the relationship of the curriculum to religious education's field of enquiry.

Source: M. Grimmett (1987) *Religious Education and Human Development*, p. 256

process, suggesting that 'edification' should be a further goal of the subject . . . [Finally] as others have pointed out, a religious education disconnected from learners' own questions and concerns will simply fail to engage them.

CONCLUSION: CITIZENSHIP AND THE NEED FOR INDIVIDUAL LEARNING

The illustration above from religious education asserts therefore the need for a greater 'embeddedness' of knowledge in experience and existence in adult education and in particular in lifelong citizenship education. (For a most useful discussion by Squires of 'Education for Adults', see M. Thorpe, R. Edwards and A. Hanson, 1993.) If we return finally to Leach and Moon (1999), we would commend their argument that pedagogy should be viewed from the perspective of the learner. The learning community then itself becomes a focus of study and analysis. They call for the following questions to be raised about pedagogic practice in relation to:

- educational goals
- learning purposes, including how these can be shared and created by learners
- the role of discourse (symbol, my word) in shaping, learning and creating identity
- the nature of knowledge that is the subject of learning
- learning activities, including the provision of collaborative tasks that enable reflection
- assessment activities that develop/demonstrate learners' understanding, including concept-mapping, journals and peer presentations

The basis for taking forward with coherence the national agenda for lifelong learning is already present. We might envisage a target date of say 2005 when individuals and the state can engage continuously and reflectively in their individual and collective educational development plans which would involve three levels, if we follow Lawton's (1996, p. 115) argument:

- vision
- mission
- practice

With praxis and practice in place, finally we would seek to ask:

1. How do we recognize learning in individuals and how do individuals, their communities and their workplace credit and acknowledge that learning?
2. How do we assist individuals in monitoring the quality of their learning?

3.   How will we know that we have ensured access to motivation, knowledge and learning to all age groups?

All of these questions can only be answered within the conditions set by this evaluative framework if moral, social and civic values are found together with economic values within national educational policies concerned with the aims of education and training. In conclusion, may I echo and support Carl Rogers' words in speaking of the role of 'the interpersonal relationship in the facilitation of learning':

> I have tried to indicate that if we are to have citizens who can live constructively in this kaleidoscopically changing world, we can only have them if we are willing for them to become self-starting, self-initiating learners. (from Thorpe *et al.*, 1993, p. 242)

REFERENCES

Bachkirova, T. (2000) How much would love of learning cost? Pragmatic versus humanitarian views of life long learning. *Journal of Further and Higher Education* (forthcoming).
Beinart, S. and Smith, P. (1997) *National Adult Learning Survey*. Sudbury, Suffolk: DfEE.
Brookfield, S. (1986) *Understanding and Facilitating Adult Learning*. Milton Keynes: Open University.
Brown, A. L. and Campione, C. (1996) Communities of learning and thinking. In P. Woods *Contemporary Issues in Teaching and Learning*. London: Routledge.
Carlton, S. and Soulsby, J. (1999) *Learning to Grow Older and Bolder*. Leicester: NIACE.
Chaiklin, S. and Lave, J. (1993)(eds) *Understanding Practice*. Cambridge: Cambridge University Press.
Commision on Social Justice (1994) *Social Justice: Strategies for National Renewal*. London: Vintage.
Corbridge, D. (1999) Scary times for local authority Adult Education. *Inform*, No. 1. London: FEDA.
Cross, K. P. (1981) *Adults as Learners*. San Francisco: Jossey Bass.
Davis, V. (1999) VET UK: how others see us. *Inform*, No. 2. London: FEDA.
DfEE (1998) *The Learning Age*. London: DfEE.
DfEE (1999) *The Review of the National Curriculum: The Secretary of State's Proposals*, London: DfEE.
Freire, P. (1972) *The Pedagogy of the Oppressed*. Harmondsworth: Penguin.
Galbraith, M. W. (1990) *Adult Learning Methods: A Guide for Effective Instruction*. Malabar, Florida: Kereiger.
Gibbons, M., Limoges, C., Moworthy, H., Swartzman, S., Scott, P. and Trow, M. (1994) *The New Production of Knowledge*. London: Sage.
Giddens, A. (1998) *The Third Way. The Renewal of Social Democracy*. London: Polity.
Grimmett, M. (1987) *Religious Education and Human Development*. Great Wakering: McCrimmons.
Halsey, A. H. (2000) *Social Trends*, cited in *The Times*, 27 January 2000.
Hargreaves, A. (1994) *Changing Times, Changing Teachers*. London: Cassell.

Heater, D. (1992) *Citizenship: The Civic Ideal in World History, Politics and Education.* London: Longman.

Hirst, P. H. (1993) Education, knowledge and practices. In R. Barrow and P. White *Beyond Liberal Education.* London: Routledge.

HMSO (1991) *The Citizens Charter: Raising the Standard* (CM1599). London: HMSO.

Hobsbawn, E. (1994) Age of extremes: the short twentieth century. In E. Baglin Jones and N. Jones (eds) *Education for Citizenship.* London: Kogan Page.

Hyland, T. (1999) *Vocational Studies, Lifelong Learning and Social Values.* Aldershot: Ashgate.

Jackson, R. (1997) *Religious Education: An Interpretive Approach.* London: Hodder and Stoughton.

Jarvis, P. (1987) (ed.) *Thinkers in Twentieth Century Adult Education.* London: Croom Helm.

Kennedy, H. (1997) *Learning Works.* Coventry: FEFC.

Knowles, M. (1978) Andragogy revisited, Part II. *Adult Education,* **30** (1): 52–3.

Knowles, M. (1996) Andragogy: an emerging technology in adult learning. In R. Edwards, A. Hanson and P. Raggett *Boundaries of Adult Learning.* London: Routledge.

Kunde, J. (2000) *Corporate Religion.* Harlow: Pearson Educational.

Lave, R. (1988) *Cognition in Practice.* Cambridge: Cambridge University Press.

Lawton, D. (1996) *Beyond the National Curriculum.* London: Hodder and Stoughton.

Leach, J. and Moon, B. (1999) *Learners and Pedagogy.* London: PCP/Open University.

McDermott, R. P. (1993) Acquisition of a child by a learning disability. In S. Chaiklin and J. Lave (eds) *Understanding Practice.* Cambridge: Cambridge University Press.

Mayo, V. (1997) *Imagining Tomorrow.* Leicester: NIACE.

Merriman, S. and Caffarella, R. (1991) *Learning in Adulthood: A Comprehensive Guide.* San Francisco: Jossey Bass.

National Commission on Education (1996) *Success Against the Odds: Effective Schools in Disadvantaged Areas.* London: NCE.

Nussbaum, M. (1998) *Cultivating Humanity.* Cambridge, MA: Harvard University Press.

Odum, E. (1959) *Fundamentals of Ecology.* Philadelphia: Saunders.

Rappaport, R. A. (1999) *Ritual and Religion in the Making of Humanity.* Cambridge: Cambridge University Press.

Reich, R. B. (1992) *The Work of Nations: Preparing Ourselves for Twenty-first Century Capitalism.* New York: Random House.

Rogers, C. (1969) *Freedom to Learn.* Columbus, Ohio: Merrill.

Rorty, R. (1980) *Philosophy and Mirrors of the Mind.* Oxford: Blackwell.

Speaker of the House of Commons (1990) *Encouraging Citizens*: Report of the Commission on Citizenship. London: HMSO.

Squires, G. (1993) Education for adults. In M. Thorpe, R. Edwards and A. Hanson *Culture and The Processes of Adult Learning.* London: Routledge.

Sutherland, J., Director of Education and Training, UNISON, speaking at the launch of V. Mayo (1997) *Imagining Tomorrow.* Leicester: NIACE.

Thorpe, M., Edwards, R. and Hanson, A. (1993) *Culture and the Processes of Adult Learning.* London: Routledge.

White, L. (1949) *The Science of Culture.* New York: Farrar Strauss.

Williams, R. (1976) *Keywords: A Vocabulary of Culture and Society.* London: Fontana.

Woods, P. (1996) *Contemporary Issues in Teaching and Learning.* London: Routledge.

Young, M. F. D. (1998) *The Curriculum of the Future.* London: Routledge.

Chapter 6

A Curriculum Model for Citizenship Education

Janet Harland

INTRODUCTION

I start from the assumption that a move to include education in citizenship within the provisions of the National Curriculum is both timely and welcome. Indeed I see it as one of the most positive and optimistic moves on the curriculum front for some time. The questions addressed in this chapter are therefore entirely focused on the how issues, and I leave to others any remaining concerns about why and whether, matters about which I have no anxiety.

For two decades I have taught curriculum studies to experienced teachers from both Britain and overseas. Not surprisingly, one of the aspects of the current initiative on citizenship education which has interested me has been the curriculum model proposed. When the Crick Report was first published, I was impressed by the breadth of the endeavour but also somewhat alarmed by the curriculum model espoused because of the ideological baggage which, I shall suggest, comes with that model. The Crick Report advocates a curriculum package expressed in terms of learning outcomes. In the event, when the Secretary of State's proposals for the review of the National Curriculum were published in May 1999, the terminology had shifted to that of a 'learning framework', which I for one welcomed. However it is, I think, still worth investigating the original proposal, as well as both the decision to abandon it and the possibility that learning outcomes may still be there *de facto* if not *de jure*.

My intention in this chapter is to begin by reviewing the place that learning outcomes occupied in the Crick Report, and then to explore more generally the emergence of this particular approach to curriculum planning. I shall review what I and others see as the advantages and the disadvantages of the approach. I shall then turn back to the Report to explore what I take to be the reasons why the committee originally adopted an outcomes-based model, and to suggest what I see as its inherent problems. Next comes an account of the revised proposals and some observations about both the possible reasons for and implications of this retrenchment. I conclude with some observations of my own about the nature of citizenship and what they signify for both curriculum planning and accreditation.

EDUCATION FOR CITIZENSHIP AND THE TEACHING OF DEMOCRACY IN SCHOOLS

The aims of citizenship education are described in the Crick Report as follows:

> to make secure and to increase the knowledge, skills and values relevant to the nature and practices of participative democracy; also to enhance the awareness of rights and duties, and the sense of responsibilities needed for the development of pupils into active citizens; and in so doing to establish the value to individuals, schools and society of involvement in the local and wider community. (DfEE/QCA, 1998, para 6.6)

The Report sets out the 'Key concepts', 'Values and dispositions', 'Skills and aptitudes', and, finally, 'Knowledge and understandings' which together represent 'the interrelationship of the essential elements'. It is stated that these need to be approached 'in a developmental and sequential way through the four key stages' (Figures 1 and 2, pp. 44 and 45). There follows a listing of the recommended learning outcomes for each key stage: for each the outcomes are divided between those concerned with Skills and Aptitudes, and those with Knowledge and Understanding. Key Concepts appear as and where they are judged appropriate to the developing maturity of pupils: Values and Dispositions are apparently subsumed within the more specific outcomes.

One feature to note about the outcomes as set out is that it would not be fair to describe them simply as behavioural objectives. Indeed they are replete with exactly the kind of language which is anathema to the out-and-out behaviourist: again and again we read terms such as *understand, know about, contribute, investigate* and *discuss*.

The Crick committee included the use of learning outcomes within its 'Essential recommendations'. The exact terms are worth a close reading:

> We unanimously recommend that

> 4.2 the statutory entitlement is established by setting out specific learning outcomes for each key stage, rather than detailed programmes of study. We advise substituting for the present input and output model of the existing National Curriculum subjects, an outcome model alone based on tightly defined learning outcomes. This offers flexibility to schools in relation to local conditions and opportunities, and allows the possibility of different approaches to citizenship education, involving different subject combinations and aspects of the curriculum based on existing good practice in each school;

4.3 the learning outcomes should be tightly enough defined so that standards and objectivity can be inspected by OFSTED – (DfEE/QCA, 1998, paras 42, 43)

THE CONCEPT OF LEARNING OUTCOMES

In reviewing the growing popularity of the outcomes model it is important to recognize that there is a considerable overlap between terms. Apart from the term used here, learning outcomes, we also find in common use (especially in the USA) the term outcomes-based education (OBE): and, more particularly in relation to vocational and professional education, this shades over into the notion of competence-based education (CBE).

In a very useful review of research concerning *The Competence and Outcomes Movement* Inge Bates quotes a definition from the early days of these developments which is still useful today:

> Competence-based education tends to be a form of education that derives a curriculum from an analysis of a prospective or actual role in modern society and that attempts to certify student progress on the basis of demonstrated performance in some or all aspects of that role. Theoretically, such demonstrations of competence are independent of time-served in formal educational settings (p. 9). (Grant *et al.*, 1979, quoted in Bates, 1998)

The origins of the movement are normally traced to the USA, and in particular to the Performance Based Teacher Education project of the 1960s. The continuing influence of Taylorism and of the behavioural objectives movement were both clearly apparent in this project, as well as the emergence of the notion of 'human resource development' as a technicized version of professional education and training.

In the UK it was the Youth Training Scheme (YTS) that first connected the notion of defined and measurable competences to the business of curriculum planning. This programme had been one of the more influential components of the New Training Initiative, launched by the Conservative government in 1981 in an attempt to address a perceived deficit in vocational skills and training across the British workforce as a whole. Gilbert Jessup, who worked with Margaret Levy on the core skills project within the YTS programme, took the model with him when he became Director of Research at the newly established National Council for Vocational Qualifications in 1986. Writing later about the curriculum framework for the YTS project, Jessup wrote

> The major impact of the 'new kind of standards' ... is that they make explicit the outcomes sought in education and training programmes. This contrasts with most previous forms of ... provision which has been defined in respect of learning 'inputs' in the form of syllabuses, courses, and training specifications ... This shift from an input-led system to an outcome-led system has fundamental implications

[which provide] the key to unlocking the education and training system. (Jessup, 1991, p. 11)

Not only has this model gone on to shape the provision of vocational and professional courses in the UK but we can also see its influence spreading. To quote a few examples at random: Western Australia has revised its whole school curriculum along these lines. Recent language programmes in Israel are employing this notion of learning outcomes to replace more detailed forms of specification which have previously been much preoccupied with course content and pedagogy. Hong Kong has been experimenting with the idea of a 'target-oriented curriculum'. And it appears that curriculum developers in Mozambique are actively considering reshaping the primary curriculum along these lines.

Looking at a list of examples as varied as this, we have to conclude that the notion of shaping educational practice through the specification of learning outcomes is likely to become increasingly popular, though as yet both what is gained and what is lost through this approach is unclear.

ADVANTAGES AND DISADVANTAGES

The advantages claimed for the outcomes model are numerous: it has been variously argued that it loosens the link between a specific mode of learning or length of course and a given outcome (or qualification); that it can do away with the tyranny of upper and lower age limits while also encouraging the accreditation of prior learning; that it means that individuals have more control over their own learning; that motivation is improved where there is clarity about targets; and that the concept of failure is replaced by that of 'not yet up to standard'. So overall we have a model where the destination is clearly, and usually very precisely, defined, but the journey is individual and may even be unique. Later we must consider the implications this may have for 'citizenship'.

Some advocates of outcomes-based education have stressed that the model lends itself to more equitable levels of achievement. For example, Boschee and Baron (1993) argue that 'the over-riding aim of OBE [their acronym] is to improve the opportunity for all children of whatever background'. They see outcomes as underpinned by a belief that 'all students can learn successfully'. Outcomes are 'future oriented, publicly defined, learner centred, focussed on life skills and contexts, and characterised by high expectations'. There is more than an echo here of Bloom's concept of mastery learning. The authors also put considerable emphasis on the need to create tight links between specified outcomes and assessment. Here there are clear overtones of what Madaus in the USA has called 'measure-driven instruction'.

However, others have seen problems with this model, and I am conscious that here I shall be condensing what is a complex argument. So I quote below the words of Hyland, who has for some time been an active critic of the competency movement and who gives here a particularly succinct critique:

> Instead of an holistic framework, competence-based education atomises and fragments learning into measurable chunks; rather than *valuing process and experience*, CBE is concerned only with performance outcomes and, most importantly, instead of encouraging *critical reflection on alternative perspectives*, CBE offers a mono-cultural view based on the satisfaction of narrow performance criteria and directed towards fixed and pre-determined ends. (Hyland, 1994, p. 54; my emphasis)

Here again there are implications for the teaching of citizenship. The journey of an individual or group of individuals towards the terminus may not be regulated in any precise form, but an outcomes-led model sets little or no value upon that journey except in so far as it delivers the traveller to a fixed destination. And there is certainly no space for alternative views of what the destination itself might be.

Bates himself insists that we see such curriculum planning strategies in a wider context:

> if we define the competence movement more broadly to include the increasing use of performance criteria to manage and measure organisational and individual performance, it is even more evident that we are dealing with a highly pervasive and seemingly relentless social trend. This suggests that we may need to view the arrival of competence-based pedagogy as epiphenomenal, as a surfacing in education of deeper changes in structures and processes of social control over work, education and training and as a means of synchronising these historically separate spheres. (Bates, 1998, p. 14)

If such a model were to be adopted in relation to citizenship education, then to the spheres of work, education and training identified by Bates, we might need to add that of civil society.

BACK TO THE REPORT

The question then remains: why did the original Report set out its recommendations in terms of 'an outcome model . . . based on tightly defined learning outcomes'? Of course there is the possibility that the committee was given a steer in that direction by the DfEE, or alternatively that they were unduly influenced by what Bates has called a 'seemingly relentless social trend'. But it seems that the motive was much more to do with avoiding undue prescription while nevertheless trying to ensure that the Report's priorities were actually achieved by schools. (This point has in fact been confirmed to me by more that one of those most closely concerned.)

As we have seen, the Report insists that teachers and schools must be free to find their own way towards the goals of citizenship education. It seems clear that the intention to emphasize outputs rather than inputs+outputs was intended to be teacher-emancipatory. Not only the examples of good and varied practice in schools with which the report is annotated, but also perhaps much current thinking about the depressing effect of unduly circumscribing professional autonomy, must have persuaded the committee that there needed to be space for local initiative and teacher creativity in determining the precise character of the citizenship curriculum in individual schools. A common-sense understanding of the term, learning outcomes, may have appeared to strike a balance between the need for some coherence in the goals to be met and, at the same time, for a productive degree of local independence. But this is to ignore the fact that there is – as so often – a gap between the common-sense use of the term and what the very same words have come to signify in the more specialized usage of curriculum development.

The problem with using the learning outcomes terminology to achieve the committee's purposes is that there is plenty of evidence that the competence or outcomes-based approach does not emancipate teachers. Despite the official discourse about the advantages of outcomes-based education in terms of learner emancipation, most such programmes appear to increase rather than decrease regulation and control over what is to be learned. Admittedly there is greater local discretion over the sequencing of the learning undertaken to achieve the specified outcomes. But it seems that the approach has tended to lead to more bureaucratic controls, more assessment, more self-policing by both teachers and students: in effect, more 'outcomes as syllabus'.

As examples of worrying impulses in this direction, we can look at two aspects of the Citizenship Report. First is the fate of Values and Dispositions. Even in the pages of the Report, we have seen how they vanished once an attempt was made to articulate learning outcomes for each key stage. How much further may they retreat in an environment dominated by talk of standards, league tables and OFSTED inspections, all dedicated to a conviction that qualitative judgements can be converted into quantitative measures? (Those with long memories will remember that in the 1970s the DES/HMI Assessment of Performance Unit was simply unable to complete a similar task in relation to Personal and Social Development.)

My second concern is the comment in the Crick Report about accreditation. Paragraph 6.4.2 points to the need to develop 'a range of appropriate qualifications ... including full, combined and short course GCSEs, GNVQ units, and Certificates of Achievement'. Such measures might well serve to reassure government that desirable outcomes are being achieved, but the danger is that measurable Knowledge and Understanding (and especially Knowledge) might come to overwhelm Skills and Attitudes in the process, while seriously threatening the crucial area of Values and Dispositions. The worrying assumption at work here would seem to be the notion, both here and – as we shall see – in the revised Proposals, that assessment is a kind of add-on to the business of curriculum design. Yet it is widely accepted that assessment procedures can and do dominate the teaching and learning process unless properly integrated with the overall aims and purposes of the curriculum. If the object of citizenship education is to move beyond the acquisition of facts and maybe the learning of skills, towards more demanding matters to do with process, critical reflection and experience, then a mode of assessment must be chosen which will support rather than undermine these purposes. Some forms of assessment can in themselves be educative (Gipps, 1994), but once the whole enterprise is associated with counting up the achievement of outcomes and the awarding of certificates, then the cart may well flatten the horse.

At its worst therefore the outcomes-led approach could well lead to a tightly regulated initiation into a government-endorsed conception of what it means to be a good citizen; where alternative perceptions are unlikely to meet with approval at the point of accreditation or inspection; and where the process and the experience of citizenship education is valued only in so far as it achieves pre-specified ends. I cannot think that this was the committee's intention: and this is why I have queried the use of this particular curriculum model.

THE SECRETARY OF STATE'S PROPOSALS: MAY 1999

The *Secretary of State's Proposals* of May 1999 (DfEE/QCA, 1999) for changes in the National Curriculum placed considerable emphasis on citizenship education and rightly recognize the very significant work of the Crick committee. This is not the place to describe the details of the proposals in this area but rather to comment on the fate of the recommendations concerning learning outcomes.

On the face of it, learning outcomes as such have disappeared. This may well be because arguments such as those sketched out in this chapter were in the minds of the politicians and officials who drafted the proposals, but it seems much more likely that they decided not to risk laying yet more overt prescriptions on to schools, especially in an area where it could be claimed that teachers have had no specific training and there are perhaps few acknowledged experts willing to take on responsibility for achieving defined outcomes. Perhaps simply adding another foundation subject to the mix was seen as challenging enough in terms of teacher response.

In place of outcomes, we have 'a basic framework within which schools can develop their own approaches'. However, the proposals are said to 'build directly from the recommendations [in the Report] ... and in particular from the framework of learning outcomes across the key stages' (p. 13). A little later it is said that 'The learning framework sets out what pupils may be expected to know, understand and be able to do but leaves the decisions about the detailed content and delivery . . . to schools' (p. 14). Why? because 'It cannot, by its nature, specify the many aspects of school life which contribute . . . such as the school ethos, out-of-school activity, community involvement, teaching styles and organisation . . .'. The proposals for the non-statutory framework for Key Stages 1 and 2 where citizenship is to be combined with PSHE are set out under the heading Skills, Knowledge and Understanding, accompanied by a note about the types of learning opportunities pupils might be offered. For Key Stages 3 and 4 where there is to be a statutory requirement to include citizenship as a new foundation subject, we are offered draft programmes of study plus attainment targets. Here a distinction is made between, first, Skills (which are about enquiry, communication, participation and action) and then, Knowledge and Understanding. The Attainment Targets duly refer to knowledge and understanding but they also use terms such as 'participate effectively' and 'demonstrate personal and corporate responsibility'. All mention of accreditation has been dropped.

The key question remains as to whether there is something here which is much more than a shift in words. As we have seen there is a clear endorsement of the learning outcomes as set out in the Crick Report. And the absence of any direct comment about accreditation should not be seen as an indication that it is not actively under consideration. Indeed this must be seen as the crucial issue because no one can deny the status problems of non-examined elements in the curriculum.

TOWARDS A RESOLUTION

A resolution of these tensions can perhaps only be achieved through a re-examination of the connections between curriculum aspirations, curriculum models and accreditation. To do this I shall, at this late stage, state what I see to be the two fundamental principles that underpin – or should underpin – the concept of citizenship within a democracy.

In the first place, it seems to me that democracy is open-ended. We cannot know the qualities that will be required of the citizen tomorrow – and we should not seek to constrain them. Within my own lifetime I can recognize very real shifts in how society understands what are the characteristics of a good citizen – and that within what, in international terms, is a particularly stable society. Democratic societies need to be in a state of permanent transformation. We need to foster attitude, motivation and a willingness to participate even more than specific knowledge about current political arrangements. The kind of functional analysis which is involved in defining outcomes tends to reduce the scope of teaching and learning to what can be specified now about an unknown and unpredictable future. So the essence of an education about democratic citizenship needs to be about precisely those things which Hyland (1994) argues are excluded from outcomes-based education: process, experience, critical reflection, alternative perspectives (see my earlier quotation). My argument is that the original Citizenship Report appears to advocate all those, but their preferred curriculum model militates against their achievement.

The second point is that citizenship as a concept implies a relationship between the individual and the community. What do we know about successful relationships? First, they are interactive and reciprocal. Second, they are based on a mutuality of both need and satisfaction. And third, they are voluntary and depend upon both an initial motivation and an adequate supply of persistence. This implies that not only must young people be helped to reach out to the community, but the community must reach out to young people. Inevitably a report about what schools should do must concentrate on their role. But an emphasis on outcomes reinforces a view that schools can do it alone. They cannot. A genuine advance in the cultivation of good citizenship will require a shift in national, not simply the school, culture. The community, or better still communities, must be encouraged to make positive moves towards young people: with honourable exceptions, too many of us currently prefer to ignore, criticize or even fear them, rather than seeking to invite them into the pleasures and responsibilities of participation in the adult world.

It is therefore to be hoped that the Secretary of State really understands the implications of the apparent retreat from an outcomes-based approach and has not simply dropped it for strategic reasons, only to reverse the process later by imposing an unimaginative system of accreditation and inspection. Keeping citizenship alive, open-ended and geared towards active partnership with the full spectrum of the community, both political and social, requires a bold approach to curriculum planning and also to accreditation. Within this we shall need a proper realization of the potential of a Record of Achievement. Through such means we may just succeed in creating a more active citizenry, young and old.

POSTSCRIPT

The final proposals for the revised National Curriculum (DfEE/QCA) were published in November 1999. The heading under which expectations for KS3 and 4 are set out is simply 'Knowledge, Skills and Understandings': Attitudes, Values and Dispositions have not made it to the final stage. The Statements of Attainment are drawn very broadly. Learning outcomes have not resurfaced, and no reference is made to the Crick Report approach. However, it is stated that further information about assessment will follow: as the Orders for Citizenship do not come into force until Autumn 2002, there is still time for further thought. This therefore remains a crucial issue and it is to be hoped that the DfEE will be prepared to listen to advice and to give advice to ministers which is based on sound thinking about the impact of testing on curriculum rather than on political expediency.

REFERENCES

Bates, I. (1998) *The Competence and Outcomes Movement: the Landscape of Research.* Leeds: University of Leeds School of Education.

Boschee, F. and Baron, M. A. (1993) *Outcomes-Based Education: Developing Programmes through Strategic Planning.* Lancaster, PA: Technomic.

DfEE/QCA (1998) *Education for Citizenship and the Teaching of Democracy in Schools* (Crick Report). London: QCA.

DfEE/QCA (May–July 1999) *The Review of the National Curriculum in England: The Secretary of State's Proposals.* London: QCA.

DfEE/QCA (1999) *The National Curriculum: Handbook for Secondary Teachers in England.* London: QCA.

Gipps, C. (1994) *Beyond Testing: Towards a Theory of Educational Assessment.* London: Falmer.

Grant, G., Elbow, P., Ewens, T., Gamson, Z., Kohli, W., Neumann, W., Olesen, V. and Riesman, D. (1979) *On Competence: A Critical Analysis of Competence-Based Reforms in Higher Education.* San Francisco: Jossey Bass.

Hyland, T. (1994) *Competence, Education and NVQs.* London: Cassell.

Jessup, G. (1991) *Outcomes: NVQs and the Emerging Model of Education and Training.* London: Falmer Press.

Chapter 7

The Emerging 14–19 Curriculum and Qualification Structure as a Context for the Development of Citizenship Education and the Role of the Social Sciences

Tony Breslin

EDUCATION, EDUCATION, EDUCATION: THEMES AND TENSIONS IN THE POLICY AGENDA

The current government's educational agenda has a number of themes. While this is not an exhaustive list, I will suggest that the following are of central importance: raising standards in quantitative terms; widening levels of educational participation especially among disaffected and disadvantaged groups so as to counter social exclusion; promoting lifelong learning howsoever defined; raising the profile of work-related and vocational learning and bridging the academic–vocational divide; enhancing numeracy, literacy and ICT proficiency at all levels within the context of a more flexible school and FE curriculum; encouraging democratic participation and developing life skills; developing rigorous assessment systems for measuring educational performance and the performance of educators.

What is immediately evident from such a list is that these objectives at least have the ability to contradict or undermine each other. As Stephen Ball remarks, policy-making is a messy process (Ball, 1994). Thus, focusing on achievement may serve to exclude further those students or schools or colleges that are not succeeding in the hard terms of examination grades, especially in a context of school competition and performance related pay. Likewise, using work-related schemes accessed through disapplication may encourage the excluded to participate but only at the cost of reinforcing the notion that work-related and vocational studies are of a lower status than conventional academic programmes. Finally, attempts to introduce curriculum flexibility while underlining the importance of Basic Skills and Key Skills, one of the overriding themes of the National Curriculum Review, may be at the cost of a broad, balanced, inclusive and genuinely comprehensive curriculum for all. In short, the objectives around raising standards threaten to impinge on those themes associated very broadly around the development of successful, participative citizens: social inclusion, increased participation, breadth and balance.

It is important to consider these tensions in appraising the current reforms proposed for the National Curriculum and the post–14 and post–16 qualifications structure and to bear in mind one policy commentator's observation that 'original intentions rarely mirror eventual outcomes' (Scott, 1996). This chapter concentrates on the changes proposed for Key Stage 4 of the National Curriculum and for the 16–19 qualifications structure. These changes, notably the rise of Education for Citizenship and the emergence of a commonly unitized and broadened post–16 agenda have profound implications for teachers and curriculum planners, especially those concerned with PSHE and the Social Sciences. This chapter does not attempt a detailed critique of these changes. Rather, it presents them, offers some evaluative observations and attempts to draw the separate National Curriculum and post-16 changes together into something approaching a coherent 14–19 context.

KEY STAGE 4: FLEXIBILITY, KEY SKILLS AND CITIZENSHIP

At Key Stage 4, the curriculum is about to change significantly. Most of the changes are set to impact on classroom delivery from September 2000. The key themes are citizenship, Key Skills and flexibility. The flexibility has largely been achieved by reducing the content burden within Programmes of Study and providing specific opt-outs rather than through the removal of certain subjects. Part of the rationale for this is to retain a conventional notion of 'breadth' and part is to head off the risk of the kind of subject turf war that characterized the formation of the original National Curriculum. The main features of the revised National Curriculum, the associated qualifications structure and the related guidance structure are:

- the retention of the existing subject menu, including religious education, but the introduction of a range of detail changes in specific areas which are detailed in the recently published booklets for each National Curriculum subject;
- the addition of a statutory citizenship strand designated as a foundation subject;
- the designation of PSHE within a non-statutory delivery framework at Key Stages 3 and 4;
- a move towards greater flexibility, as outlined above, through a focus on slimmer, less prescriptive Programmes of Study and access to a greater range of qualifications including NVQs and Entry Levels;

- increased access to 'disapplication' and a broadening of the use of disapplication, as an exceptional measure, beyond the 'disaffected', so as to reach students with particular needs or talents;
- a facility for schools to suspend the Programmes of Study for technology, modern foreign languages and science for groups of students so as to 'permit courses leading to a wider range of qualifications specified for each subject area', a process described as 'modification' as distinct from 'disapplication';
- an increased focus on work-related learning and the development of a stronger vocational element;
- a 'light touch' (content-based) rewriting of the GCSE specifications in all subjects for first examination in 2003;
- the alignment of Programmes of Study in English at Key Stages 3 and 4 with Key Skill units in Communication;
- the alignment of Programmes of Study in mathematics and ICT at Key Stage 4 with Key Skill units in Application of Number and ICT;
- the launch of 'new model' Part One GNVQs, and their availability at Key Stage 4 and in the post-16 phase;
- the launch of the Connexions programme, a post-13 mentoring framework that is set across the 14–19 continuum for those identified as at risk of becoming disaffected;
- the restructuring of careers service provision around the needs of those at risk of disaffection and the subsequent recasting of Youth Service and Careers Service provision within a common framework.

In terms of the main changes around flexibility, Key Skills and citizenship itself, the following points are worth emphasizing:

Flexibility

From a curriculum planning perspective schools now have two routes to increased flexibility. The first of these is disapplication. Since September 1998 schools have been allowed to 'disapply' individual students at Key Stage 4 from two subjects drawn from modern foreign languages, science and technology in favour of alternative work-related learning provision sometimes delivered through an FE context. This type of disapplication, which will remain available, has been focused on the disaffected and raises issues about entitlement. However, a range of additional disapplications now exist. These include:

- disapplication to allow exchange of a National Curriculum subject for a further subject in a particular curriculum area;
- disapplication to allow the study of fewer National Curriculum subjects;

- disapplication through a statement of Special Educational Need;
- disapplication through temporary exceptions.

Each of the above relates to the disapplication of individual named students. A further option, which is available through application to the Secretary of State, involves disapplication for development work or experiments in the curriculum and allows the broader disapplication of subjects and assessment procedures, a facility that has hitherto only been available to those at schools in Education Action Zones.

The second route to greater flexibility is through what has been termed 'Curriculum Modification'. This involves the retention of the full National Curriculum subject menu but the substitution of non-National Curriculum Programmes of Study based around different (and specified) qualifications such as Entry Level courses and NVQs. As distinct from most forms of 'disapplication', 'modification' involves changing the curriculum for identified groups of students and may offer a means of providing differentiated Programmes of Study within a common and comprehensive entitlement.

Key skills

The realignment of the Programmes of Study in mathematics, English and ICT in relation to the 'first three' (or 'harder') Key Skills (Application of Number, Communication and ICT) is likely to lead to a similar refocusing of the GCSE specifications in these areas. Success through the Key Skills qualification in any one Key Skill will require the passing of a test and the submission of a portfolio at a given level (1, 2 or 3). The likelihood is that GCSE success will remove the need for a student to sit the related Key Skills test. Thus, the challenge in these three subjects will be to design Key Stage 4 schemes of work that generate portfolios in each of the Key Skills.

Citizenship

The key issue about citizenship is its new status as a 'real' subject with a designated timetable location set alongside other delivery contexts. This raises questions about delivery and about teacher training and teacher expertise. For this reason, citizenship does not have to take its place in the National Curriculum until September 2002. A comprehensive citizenship programme is likely to have a timetabled component and a cross-curricular aspect as well as finding expression through the operation of the school as a community and the operation of the school within the wider community. Thus, while some elements of a school's citizenship provision are likely to be delivered through whole school initiatives such as the creation of School Councils, the formation of more democratic organizational structures, cross-curricular exercises and the development of revised assembly programmes, a part is almost certain to be based around explicit 'citizenship' lessons, howsoever titled, timetabled in the traditional way, encompassing or timetabled alongside PSHE lesson provision, the latter being augmented by strengthened pastoral, guidance and mentoring structures. While the DfEE and the QCA are at pains to stress that they do not prescribe the time allocations for individual subjects, schools are likely to be encouraged to weight the discrete timetabled component within citizenship programmes at around 5 per cent of curriculum time at Key Stages 3 and 4.

In this context, it is worth saying a little more about the relationship of PSHE to citizenship. PSHE and citizenship are combined at Key Stages 1 and 2. However, at Key Stages 3 and 4, they are separated. Within this context, much of the social education or 'social studies' content within PSHE is likely to be recast within a citizenship education framework. Thus, PSHE is likely to be more concerned with personal development and the pastoral structure while citizenship is likely to concentrate on social, political and economic literacy and participation. Schools will still have a statutory responsibility to address the plethora of issues covered in PSHE but will not be required, at Key Stages 3 and 4, to deliver PSHE as a 'subject'. In part, this is because many of the key elements in PSHE (such as health, sex and relationship education and drug and alcohol awareness programmes) are likely to be delivered, substantially, within a pastoral guidance, tutoring and counselling context rather than a conventional subject teaching one.

Summary

Taken together these changes constitute an interesting mix. The promotion of citizenship education for all through the creation of a new foundation subject is clearly a statement about the duty of schools to contribute to the creation of active adult citizens and constitutes a reflection on a range of areas of concern: a lack of participation in political life, the apparent breakdown of a range of social structures (notably the family), concerns around the essential civility of the young arising from a series of high profile murder cases (Jamie Bulger, Philip Lawrence and Stephen Lawrence) and, as a context for much of this, the reality of social exclusion.

If citizenship education and PSHE, though, seek to build participation and social inclusion, the danger that other changes might pull in another direction is real. For example, the continued focus on disapplication and the design of a curriculum that, from the outset, a proportion will not be able to access risks the persistence of such exclusion. In terms of the trade-off that 'flexibility' implies for the 'comprehensive' or 'entitlement' curriculum, these notions of disapplication and modification (whatever the detail) raise questions that impact on education for citizenship and the broader project of social inclusion.

Moreover, the disjuncture within the Key Skills framework between the 'first three' or 'hard' and the 'wider' or 'soft' skills (each of which constitutes, one might argue, a core skill for the practice of successful citizenship) and the focus on the 'hard' (i.e. easier to assess) Key Skills points, at the very least, to a missed opportunity and, more worryingly to an overtly assessment-led model. This is a concern that the proposals for the post-16 phase do little to dispel.

POST-16 DEVELOPMENTS: FROM *QUALIFYING FOR SUCCESS* TO *LEARNING TO SUCCEED*

In the post-16 domain, the qualifications structure, rather than the curriculum as such, is the focus of reform, the proposed changes having emerged from the post-Dearing *Qualifying for Success* research and consultation exercise instigated by QCA shortly after the 1997 General Election (QCA, 1998b). Again, most of the changes are set to impact on classroom delivery from September 2000. Here, unitization and the 'common sizing' of GNVQ and GCE qualifications, the emergence of a new Advanced Subsidiary qualification and the promotion of a broader offer in the first year of post-16 study are the key changes. In this context, the political trick is to introduce these developments while retaining a notion of 'excellence', in terms of the so called 'gold standard' in the second year. Against this background, the main developments are:

- the common sizing and 'unitizing' of GNVQ, AS and Advanced level courses, the extension of the GCE A–E grading scheme to GNVQ Advanced programmes, and the 'rebranding' of GNVQ Advanced programmes as Vocational A levels;
- the launch of 'new model' post-16 GNVQs (and vocational A levels) to complement the new model pre-16 GNVQs noted above;
- the creation of a Single Award Vocational A level as a 6-unit qualification, probably labelled the '6 Unit Advanced GNVQ', a move which may raise question marks about the continuing viability or purpose of the existing '12 Unit' or 'Full Award' Vocational A level;
- the introduction of two new 3-unit qualifications: the Advanced Subsidiary level and the Part Award Vocational A level;
- the restructuring of Advanced level as a 6-unit qualification that incorporates the new AS level, pitched at the ability level of the notional 17-year-old, and 3 additional 'A2' units, pitched, as the current A level is, at the ability level of the notional 18-year-old;
- the creation of modular and linear pathways within all AS and A level courses based on January and June examinations for more popular courses

and June examinations for those that are less popular;
- a combination of internal (5 per cent) and external (15 per cent) synoptic assessment (based on the combined AS and A2 Specifications) delivered through the examination of the A2 units;
- a restriction on the number of times that a candidate can be re-examined in an AS or A level module (one resit per module unless the whole qualification is retaken);
- the raising of the 'internal assessment' (formerly 'coursework') ceiling within A level courses to between 25 per cent and 30 per cent according to subject;
- a push towards offering at least 4 courses in the Lower Sixth, while retaining 3 in the Upper, as the standard sixth form curriculum;
- greater breadth, in terms of subjects, vocational areas and the broader academic–vocational divide, especially in the Lower Sixth;
- a possible shift in the GCE A level selection point from 16 to 17 (i.e. post-AS level);
- the development of a set of free-standing 'World Class Qualifications' to sit above standard GCE A level, provisionally labelled as Advanced Extension (AE) papers and restricted to a list of traditional academic subjects;
- the 'decoupling' of Key Skills from GNVQ and Vocational A level and their assessment through the new separate 'profiled' Key Skills qualification detailed above;
- the 'signposting' of Key Skills within GNVQ, vocational A level and GCE A level course specifications to support portfolio development;
- the launch of a new 'profiled' Key Skills qualification, noted earlier, based initially around the first three Key Skills, assessed initially at Levels 1, 2 and 3 and examined partly through a portfolio constructed on the basis of the courses that a student is following and partly through external tests.

Thus, the assessment theme persists and is strengthened by the creation of targets and the strengthening of testing regimes. Further, while the promise of a broader and increasingly unitized programme in the first year of post-16 study creates the space and the opportunity to create citizenship units and develop 'broader citizens', the focus on excellence thereafter is likely to include socially rather fewer than it excludes. Citizenship and standards (notably 'gold' standards) do not always sit easily together.

TOWARDS A 14–19 CONTINUUM: OPPORTUNITIES AND THREATS

As the planning and consultation processes draw to a close, the changes outlined here become more, rather than less, concrete. Key decisions around the accreditation of distinct GCE AS and A level units, the assessment of the wider

Key Skills (Working With Others, Problem Solving, Improving Own Learning) and the place of the core Key Skills in pre-16 GNVQ and GCSE programmes still need to be taken. None the less, the general trend appears to be towards the formation of a 14–19 curriculum and a qualification structure that is unitized and progressive through four levels from Entry through to Advanced. In this, the changes proposed represent a series of small but significant changes rather than a smaller number of giant leaps. They are more interesting in terms of the foundations that they lay for further change than in the initial changes that they will produce from September 2000.

Here, the review of the GCSE qualification, that the awarding bodies and QCA are about to conclude does not go far enough. A more extensive structural review of GCSE (rather than the current review of specification content) is vital to the evolution of the 14–19 framework. A restructuring of GCSE so that it follows the above changes and becomes a unit-based course examined at Foundation and Intermediate levels (derived from the recently expanded tiering framework) offers the possibility of a coherent 14–19 track across both the academic and the vocational domains. Presently, with GNVQ Part One, there is the potential for a coherent 14–19 offer within the vocational domain while the drawing of Key Skills development forward to the beginning of Key Stage 4 from September 2000 develops this 14–19 stream. No such coherence, though, currently exists in the academic sphere, the sphere that for most students will remain the dominant component in their curriculum. With the proposals as they stand, a clear break will remain at 16 in terms of progress through this suite of GCSE and GCE courses. However, a new GCSE model that has progressive levels that are 'nested' within each other (as the new GNVQ model does), rather than the current tiered levels, offers the prospect of coherence across the curriculum and qualification structure and hints at the potential for a shift away from the notion of separate vocational and academic spheres itself. Indeed, the unitization of GCSE in the style of GNVQ and GCE programmes would allow the dropping of the current range of course titles (GCSE, GNVQ, GCE) and their subject-based organization in favour of a structure that offers four levels of course (Entry, Foundation, Intermediate, Advanced), a description of achievement by level rather than by qualification type, a mix of academic and vocational units drawn from a range of academic disciplines (including the full range of social science subjects) and vocational competency areas and a shift away from the mass examination of young people at fixed points towards a credit accumulation framework which is entered at 14 and reaches on through lifelong learning.

If GCSE does not evolve in this way, the danger is of a reinforcement of the academic – vocational divide whereby those who are struggling with the mainstream academic curriculum opt out of GCSE and into so-called 'work-related' programmes, delivered through FE colleges, at 14, while the more able (or more successful) continue with 'academic' studies. Such a scenario casts FE colleges as post-14 secondary moderns for those who cannot access the higher status academic Programmes of Study and has profound implications for the social inclusion and citizenship agendas.

And the future development of FE is a critical component in this curricular and qualificatory landscape. At a practical and immediate level, these changes need to be considered in the context of the emergence of a level funding regime (and common funding source) across school sixth forms and further education colleges, as detailed in the recent *Learning to Succeed* White Paper, within the context of the promotion of models of lifelong learning (DfEE, 1999). Herein lies a central contradiction that underpins much of the above. The curricular and qualificatory trends appear to be towards 14–19 integration. However, institutional and funding structures appear to be reinforcing a pre-16/post-16 divide. Even if the proposed level funding regime across school and college regimes fails to reduce the unit funding of students in school sixth forms to FE levels, and this remains a contested point, the tide is still flowing strongly against smaller sixth forms such as those typically found in schools in rural areas and in struggling schools in the inner city. Thus, the recent formation of Lifelong Learning Partnerships and the promised emergence of Learning and Skills Councils to co-ordinate and commonly fund post-16 provision on an area and subregional basis coupled with the proposal for an essentially common inspection regime across the sector represent attempts to bring coherence to post-compulsory schooling and lifelong learning provision. However, in so doing, these changes risk accentuating the creation of an institutional framework that seems to run counter to the curricular reforms that these institutions, schools and colleges are asked to carry through.

BUILDING A CRITICAL CITIZENSHIP: THE ROLE OF THE SOCIAL SCIENCES

These concerns about a mismatch between the apparent evolution of the curriculum, the qualifications structure and the institutional infrastructure and about the way in which the development of successful citizenship education appears to jar with certain of the reforms should not, though, mask the very positive messages, especially for social science teachers, in the proposed changes. The emergence of statutory and, in part, explicitly taught Citizenship Programmes at Key Stage 3 and Key Stage 4 and the continued promotion of post-16 citizenship as a curricular entitlement (Thornton, 1999) provide tremendous scope for colleagues with a social science expertise in terms of delivery, co-ordination and in-house training. Moreover, GCSE Social Science and Sociology and GCE AS and A level Sociology, Social Science and Social Policy provide excellent foundations for the development of Programmes of Study in what one might call 'Critical Citizenship' as, of course, do specifications in politics and, to some degree, economics. Indeed, when allied to the likely growth of the Advanced Supplementary level within a broader Year 12 programme and the downsizing of GNVQ into 3 and 6 unit sets, the opportunity to promote a full range of social science subjects as a means of developing a critical citizenship for the citizens of the new millennium is considerable. It is an opportunity that social science teachers cannot afford to miss.

Through initiating, with the support of the Citizenship Foundation, the *Citizenship 2000* group, a gathering of practitioners and organizations concerned with all aspects of the social education curriculum, late in 1997, the Association for the Teaching of the Social Sciences (ATSS) has made a considerable contribution to recent thinking in the development of Education for Citizenship in both the pre-16 and post-16 sectors and is acknowledged as such in Professor Bernard Crick's Report (QCA, 1998a). It is now time for ATSS and its associates, including the Politics Association, to carry that work forward. The initial QCA document that contained the Secretary of State's *Proposals for the Review of the National Curriculum* devoted almost half of its content to PSHE and Education for Citizenship (QCA, 1999) and subsequent publications have followed this lead. Indeed, the initial document points out that:

Personal, social and health education and citizenship give pupils the skills, knowledge and understanding to lead confident, healthy, independent lives and to become informed, active and responsible Citizens. (QCA, 1999, p. 17)

Moreover, within this framework it is the task of citizenship, as a statutory foundation subject at Key Stage 3 and 4, to enable pupils to be: 'informed, critical and responsible and aware of their duties and rights' (QCA, 1999, p. 17).

PSHE and Education for Citizenship can, of course, secure these objectives but they will not do so simply by being on the curriculum. A compulsory citizenship programme that is poorly designed and delivered by those without social science expertise will serve to undermine rather than enhance the cause of social education as a whole and will fail to satisfy its curricular intentions as, so often, PSHE programmes have in the past (Shelton, and Rowe, 1998), a point underlined in Bernard Crick's report (QCA, 1998a). Only when underpinned with a genuine social scientific rigour can such programmes expect to succeed in what is clearly a laudable educational cause. The implication is clear: given the foundation subject status of citizenship, schools now require the expertise of social scientists to deliver what will become an inspected aspect of the National Curriculum (Barnard, 1998). This status coupled with the prominence of the citizenship focus in a whole range of recent QCA publications, in the social inclusion and widening participation debates and in the public enquiry into the killing of Stephen Lawrence give an official legitimacy to the curricular claims of social scientists that simply has not existed in the recent past.

CONCLUSION: THE REBIRTH OF THE SOCIAL SCIENCES IN THE SCHOOL
AND COLLEGE CURRICULUM

In the 1990s, as a social-science-free and sociologically ill-informed National
Curriculum swung into action, as Margaret Thatcher declared that there was no
longer any such thing as society and as Maureen Lipman, in a famed advertising
campaign for the just privatized yellow-vanned BT, claimed of sociology itself
'well ... it's an ology', a government document with quite such a focus would
have been unthinkable. Of course, this focus might emphasize conformity,
responsibility and a range of other 'quiet life' ideals; a model of citizenship
around 'good behaviour'. There is, though, much about activity, participation,
informed choice making, political understanding and social structure. Such stuff
is not for the making of 'quiet citizens'; as the quotation above reveals, the term
'critical' has even found its way into the official documentation and the
Secretary of State's pronouncements. In a recent speech at a conference staged
by the Demos think-tank, David Blunkett called for compulsory citizenship
classes in the post-16 phase and introduced a radical outlook that one might not
always associate with New Labour:

> It doesn't matter what we call it. It's about ensuring people are aware of the power
> structures in society around them, and are able to have some influence over it. If we
> are to succeed, we have to empower people by giving them consciousness of what's
> happening around them. (Blunkett, 1999, cited in Thornton, 1999, p. 6)

Of course, writing from a sociological perspective, the temptation is to say 'let's
call it Sociology', and I must confess to having done so elsewhere (Breslin, 1999)
but such a call risks opening up precisely the kind of subject battle that the
broader reforms seek to avoid, one that would see sociologists, historians,
religious education specialists, political scientists, economists and others
competing with each other to supply their own solution to the citizenship
challenge. The statistics suggest that collaboration might be more successful: in
terms of post-16 Advanced level courses, over 50,000 candidates are currently
entered for the social science specifications offered in Sociology, Politics and
Economics, all of which can make reasonable claims to building the kind of
awareness and offering the sort of empowerment that the Secretary of State
advocates and all of which can make an important contribution to a post-16
framework for citizenship education (McNeill, 1999). Indeed, given the
popularity of the social sciences at Advanced level, it might be argued that it will
be easier to establish the structural, staffing and resourcing foundations of a
Critical Citizenship programme in the post-16 domain, a matter, perhaps, for the
recently formed DfEE Advisory Committee concerned with the development of
Citizenship Education programmes for the 16–19 age range. For now, though,
with or without such foundations, the pre-16 domain remains the priority.

Let me, then, soften the plea and suggest only that these new citizenship programmes, at all levels, be informed by an inclusive social scientific perspective that embraces sociological, political and economic standpoints and sits alongside the proper contribution of other areas beyond the social science arena: history, business studies and religious education for instance. As David Blunkett's statement indicates, Education for Citizenship is at least partly about the development of sceptical and critical understanding and about empowerment and this can certainly be achieved through the development and exercising of the sociological imagination (Mills, 1959) and the wider social scientific one. Heads, principals, curriculum managers, teacher trainers and the writers of the next generation of examination specifications, whether these are citizenship specific or simply more 'citizenship friendly', need to be aware of this. Moreover, to reiterate a point made earlier, a broadly social scientific outlook, both pre- and post-16, has one further thing to offer citizenship programmes: a rigour that, too often, conventional PSHE schemes have lacked. In this rigour, citizenship programmes are likely to find the sort of credibility that has been absent from many PSHE schemes in the past (HMI, 1991). Whatever, the advantages of cross-curricular, experiential and ethos based models, as the experience of cross-curricular themes reminds us (Whitty *et al.*, 1994), this is a credibility that Education for Citizenship requires if it is to survive and prosper in what remains an essentially traditional subject-based framework.

REFERENCES

Ball, S. (1994) Some reflections on policy theory: a brief response to Hatcher and Troyna. *Education Policy*, **9** (2): 171–82.

Barnard, N. (1998) Missing sociologists: threaten reform. *The Times Educational Supplement*, 20 February 1998.

Blunkett, D. (1999) cited in K. Thornton (1999) Citizenship may become compulsory post-16. *The Times Educational Supplement*, 28 May 1999.

Breslin, T. (1999) A 14–19 framework for the new millennium? A summary and appraisal of the curriculum and qualification structure proposals at the fore of New Labour's plans for 14–19 education. *Social Science Teacher*, **28** (3): 11–14.

DfEE (1999) *Learning to Succeed*. London: The Stationery Office.

HMI (1991) *Social Science Within PSE Courses – Courses in Personal and Social Education in Twenty Secondary Schools*: A Report by HMI. London: HMI.

McNeill, P. (1999) Unpublished collation of GCE Advanced level results, 1996–99. Patrick McNeill Education and Publishing Consultant, Hertfordshire.

Mills, C. W. (1959) *The Sociological Imagination*. New York: Oxford University Press.

QCA (1998a) *Education for Citizenship and the Teaching of Democracy in Schools* (Crick Report). London: QCA.

QCA (1998b) *Qualifying for Success: The Review of 16–19 Qualifications*. London: QCA.

QCA (1999) *The Secretary of State's Proposals for the Review of the National Curriculum*. London: QCA.

Scott, D. (1996) Education policy: the secondary phase. *Journal of Education Policy*, **11** (1): 133–140.

Shelton, I. and Rowe, D. (1998) *Citizenship Programmes in Schools and Colleges*. London: Citizenship 2000.

Thornton, K. (1999) Citizenship may become compulsory post–16. *The Times Educational Supplement*, 28 May 1999.

Whitty, G., Rowe, G. and Aggleton, P. (1994) *Subjects and Themes in the Secondary School Curriculum in Research Papers in Education*. Pre-publication draft copy. London: Institute of Education, University of London.

Chapter 8

Education for Citizenship, Civic Participation and Experiential and Service Learning in the Community

John Annette

INTRODUCTION

In the 1999 Secretary of State's Proposals (DfEE/QCA, 1999) for the National Curriculum, David Blunkett asked the Qualifications and Curriculum Authority (QCA) to consult on proposals for the teaching of citizenship and democracy in schools through a non-statutory entitlement for PSHE and citizenship education at Key Stages 1 and 2 and as a statutory entitlement for Key Stages 3 and 4. This statutory framework for citizenship education and service learning in the community, outlined in the Secretary of State's proposals, is different from the recommendations of the final Crick Report which stated that

> We also discussed whether service learning or community involvement initiated by schools should be part of a new statutory Order for citizenship education ... However, we have concluded not to ask for their inclusion in a statutory Order at this time, mainly for fear of overburdening schools and teachers. But this question should be kept under review by the Commission on Citizenship Education. (QCA, 1998, pp. 25–26)

This decision was reached despite the evidence of the consultation process, in Appendix C of the Crick Report, which indicated that there was strong support for learning in the community and that this was seen as an important way of linking the proposed three strands of citizenship education which are values, community participation and political literacy. Indeed, many examples were provided to support the inclusion of community based leaning or service learning in the Order for citizenship education. More recently, Professor Bernard Crick has indicated that he now more fully recognizes the importance of community participation in civil society as an important element of an education for citizenship and supports the Secretary of State's decision to include service learning as a statutory entitlement for students at Key Stages 3 and 4.

In this chapter I would like to argue for the importance of service learning (community-based learning or active learning in the community) as an essential component of citizenship education because it encourages civic participation as well as the development of civic virtues and political knowledge. I will briefly examine the concept of citizenship and argue that a civic participation model of citizenship, based on the ideas of civic republicanism, is a preferable 'third way' model of citizenship in comparison to the liberal-individualist and communitarian models because it both requires civic participation and virtue and is based on a defence of negative liberty (Annette, 1999). I will then provide some background to the development of service learning as a basis for citizenship education and democracy. The capability/competency, knowledge and understanding framework of learning outcomes, which is proposed by the Secretary of State's proposals and also the Crick Report, will be best achieved, I will argue, by linking the learning of political knowledge and the ability to engage in critical thinking about values with experiential learning in the community. In particular, I would like to consider the importance of reflective practice in experiential learning. In conclusion, I will consider the problem of assessing such experientially based learning outcomes and argue for the need for increased evaluation and research into the learning outcomes of citizenship education and service learning.

What is active citizenship? Professor David Marquand in a reassessment of social democratic politics has written that,

> the civic republican tradition has more to say to a complex modern society in the late twentieth century than the liberal individualist one; that the protagonists of 'active citizenship' are right in laying stress on duty, action, and mutual loyalty. (Marquand, 1997, p. 50)

Critics of the social democratic conception of citizenship as outlined by T. H. Marshall in his famous essay, *Citizenship and Social Class* (1950), argue that, while he recognized the importance of the notion of social rights, he did not sufficiently emphasize the importance of civil rights and especially political rights. Recently, Michael Sandel (1996), Benjamin Barber and other communitarian writers have identified with the political language of civic republicanism with its emphasis on civic virtues and civic participation. In a number of recent articles and in his inaugural lecture as Regius Professor of Modern History at Cambridge University, Quentin Skinner has outlined a republican conception of freedom which is critical of the negative conception of liberty and its history as outlined by the late Isaiah Berlin. What is important in the civic republican conception of freedom, according to Skinner, is that the idea of negative liberty or the absence of restraint is identified with the idea of political liberty and citizen virtue. The main threat to freedom for republican theorists from James Harrington to Adam Smith is the 'corruption' of civic virtue which can lead to a decline in citizen participation. According to Skinner, modern contractualist liberals are indifferent to the conditions which are necessary for the maintenance of liberty (Skinner, 1998; and Dagger, 1997). What is important to note is that for the civic republican, the defence of liberty is best achieved through the development of civic virtue and civic participation. Rights require both responsibilities and civic participation.

One of the major challenges facing civic republicanism is that it traditionally identified citizenship with being a male property holder. The creation of a shared political identity underlying citizenship should also allow for multiple group identities based on gender, race, ethnicity, social exclusion, etc. It may be that the civic republican politics of contestability, as recently argued for by Philip Pettit (1997), may provide a more pluralist basis for citizenship in contemporary Britain than traditional republican politics. Equally recent theorists of liberal democracy like Eamonn Callan also argue that an education for citizenship must hold a constitutive ideal of liberal democracy while allowing for religious and cultural pluralism (Callan, 1997). A more differentiated but universal concept of citizenship (Lister, 1997), which encourages civic virtue and participation while maintaining individual liberty and allows for cultural difference, will create a way of understanding citizenship that is appropriate for an education for citizenship and democracy.

David Marquand (1997), in his argument for civic republicanism, states that voluntary service is not an important feature of active citizenship. Here I believe he places too much emphasis on formal political participation and the state and does not recognize fully enough the importance of the associations, institutions and practices of civil society. In the USA an increasing number of political scientists, for example Robert Putnam, are noting the decline of 'social capital' with a decrease in voluntary activity and a growing concern about the vitality of civil society (Putnam, 1995, 1996; Skocpol and Fiorina, 1999; Wuthnow, 1998). The evidence in the UK is complex and a recent study indicates that 'social capital' is still strong but may indicate a decline in public 'trust' (Hall, 1999). A 'strong democrat' like Benjamin Barber argues for the importance of civil society in maintaining a participatory civil society and calls for the maintenance of public spaces for civic participation. In a comparative survey of attitudes towards citizenship in both the UK and the USA, Professor Ivor Crewe and his colleagues state that,

There is now ample evidence that electoral turn-out, attention to political and public issues in the media, involvement in election campaigns and demonstrations are all strongly and consistently related to motivations that are reinforced through participation in informal groups and voluntary associations. (Crewe *et al.*, 1997, p. 7)

According to Barber,

> We live today in Tocqueville's vast new world of contractual associations – both political and economic – in which people interact as private persons linked only by contract and mutual self-interest, a world of diverse groups struggling for separate identities through which they might count for something politically in the national community. (Barber, 1992, p. 128)

For Barber, the fundamental problem facing civil society is the challenge of providing citizens with:

> the literacy required to live in a civil society, the competence to participate in democratic communities, the ability to think critically and act deliberately in a pluralist world, the empathy that permits us to hear and thus accommodate others, all involve skills that must be acquired. (Barber, 1992, p. 128)

As we will see later, Benjamin Barber and other political analysts see education for citizenship and service learning as a key factor in maintaining civic virtue and civic participation. Equally, Robert Wuthnow sees civic participation in civil society as an important way in which people increasingly develop both civic virtues and public spiritual and moral values and engage in what the liberal Jewish theorist Michael Lerner has termed the 'politics of meaning' (Wuthnow, 1998; Lerner, 1997)

What about young people and the ideal of active citizenship? Several studies indicate a relatively high level of voluntary activity among young people. The study done for the Commission on the Future of the Voluntary Sector (CFVS), alongside studies done by the Trust for the Study of Adolescents, the National Centre for Volunteering and recent research done by Roker *et al.*, for the National Youth Agency (Gaskin, *et al.*, 1996; Gaskin, 1998; Roker *et al.*, 1997, 1999a, 1999b) provide evidence of support for volunteering among young people. Indeed the CFVS study indicates that young people see the voluntary sector as a more meaningful arena for political action than the more formal political process. The Demos Real Deal project also found serious cynicism among young people about politicians and formal politics (cf. Bentley and Oakley, 1999; also Wilkinson and Mulgan, 1995; and Wilkinson, 1996). It is debatable whether or not this reflects a generational change (Parry *et al.*, 1992) or a life-cycle explanation (Jowell and Park, 1998). The evidence appears to show that young people, while having an antipathy to politicians and formal politics, do see civic participation as a meaningful political activity. It will be interesting to see whether the evaluation of the government's new scheme, the Millennium Volunteers, will provide evidence of changed civic or political attitudes. It is not clear how the UK government, which believes in joined-up political thinking, will link this scheme with its proposals for citizenship education. According to David Blunkett, the Millennium Volunteer Scheme will help to create a sense of citizenship which will counteract the 'alienation, disaffection and individualism' that young people experience. While recent research by Ivor Crewe *et al.* (1997) and Dean and Melrose (1999) provide a framework for examining attitudes in the UK towards citizenship, much more research is needed to understand more fully the complex political attitudes of young people.

What about active citizenship and citizenship education? While education for citizenship briefly appeared in 1990 as a cross-curricular theme, the evidence for its development in schools since then is uneven. David Kerr, in his NFER Report on the findings of the first phase of an international study of citizenship (Kerr, 1999a), demonstrates that while there are a large number of examples of best practice in PSE and citizenship education in schools, its development faces some deep-seated obstacles. He also argues persuasively that there is a need for much greater research into the practices and learning outcomes in these areas. There are a number of research initiatives involving the National Foundation for Educational Research (NFER) which include the two-phase international comparative study of citizenship education, which is linked to the International Association for the Evaluation of Educational Achievement (IEA) and funded by the Department for Education and Employment (DfEE). There is also a review of citizenship education in sixteen countries sponsored by the QCA (Kerr, 1999b). Recent Demos 'newthink' studies by David Hargreaves and Tom Bentley recognize the importance of citizenship education in schools and demonstrate the need for an open and contestable approach to moral reasoning (Bentley, 1998; Hargreaves, 1994). It should be noted that the civic republican conception of citizenship, as argued by Skinner and Pettit, requires citizens to be able to engage in 'dialogic reasoning' in the public sphere as well as to identify with citizen virtues. Ivor Crewe and colleagues' research indicates that nearly 80 per cent of pupils aged 15–16 said that they engage in little or no public discussion either at school or after school. Don Rowe and colleagues at the Citizenship Foundation have been involved in a number of interesting projects in critical thinking concerning values and citizenship. The NFER research needs to be supplemented by much more research into the learning outcomes of various initiatives among students in schools in PSHE and citizenship education.

What is the purpose of civic education? Melanie Phillips, the Jeremiah of contemporary social democracy, recently criticized proposals for citizenship education in her editorial entitled, 'The indoctrination of Citizen Smith, Jr.' (*The Sunday Times*, 17 March, 1999, p. 17). She paints a picture of Bernard Crick as the dark figure behind David Blunkett who is attempting to indoctrinate young British citizens. This is surprising in that in the recent Crick Report and the earlier Hansard study of political education, Bernard Crick, along with Alex Porter and also Derek Heater, saw education for citizenship not as a form of political indoctrination but instead as involving critical thinking and political literacy. She goes on to write that,

> Even more strikingly, it wants teachers to promote a particular form of democracy called active citizenship ... This is not so much political literacy as political activism. (Phillips, 1999, p. 17)

In this chapter I have been arguing that civic participation, which includes more formal political participation, is an essential duty for a citizen in a democracy and that an education for citizenship must provide the means to encourage young people to engage in participatory politics. The studies referred to above offer a number of ways in which citizenship is taught, from greater political discussions to community service learning, which will lead to greater political efficacy among students. Elizabeth Frazer (1999a), in her recently edited volume of the *Oxford Review of Education* (1999, Vol. 25, Nos.1 and 2) on citizenship education and in a paper presented to the PSA on citizenship education (May 1999), has identified the problematic relationship between education for citizenship and the study of politics. In the PSA essay she identifies 'six kinds of antipathy to politics' which lead to a hostility to political education. She is critical of those proponents of citizenship education who are more concerned with instilling values and knowledge about British political traditions than in encouraging students to become active citizens (Frazer, 1999b). I will argue that an education for citizenship which increases civic participation among young people, especially through service learning in the community, also importantly develops civic virtue and political literacy and can indeed lead to spiritual and moral values. According to David Kerr,

> Citizenship education is as much about the communities in which schools are situated and the nature of society, as about the school curriculum. All too often in the past this fact has not been sufficiently acknowledged. (Kerr, 1999a, p. 26)

What about active citizenship, citizenship education and service learning? There is a growing movement of educators, students, community leaders and politicians who are proponents of service learning as a key element in establishing a meaningful form of citizenship education. 'Service learning' is an educational method which provides a structured learning experience in civic participation which can lead to the development of the key skills necessary for being an active citizen. It also facilitates the acquisition of political knowledge and the ability to engage in reflective understanding which leads to personal development and civic virtue. In the UK, the Community Service Volunteers (CSV), especially through its Education for Citizenship programme under its Director John Potter, have been working in partnerships with schools, universities and local schools and communities in effectively establishing service learning programmes. A recent study for the CSV by Peter Mitchell, *Education for Citizenship: The Contribution of Active Learning in the Community* (Mitchell, 1999) provides an argument for what Mitchell terms 'active learning in the community' (or service learning or community-based learning). He sees the learning outcome of citizenship education as not only being an increased knowledge and understanding of civic rights and responsibilities but also employability and the ability to engage in lifelong learning. This raises another question of joined-up policy-making about how the provisions for the New Deal and Lifelong Learning will be linked to the initiatives in citizenship education. In addressing the linkage between citizenship education and lifelong learning, Mitchell stresses the importance of effective learning and notes that active learning in the community involves active learning, collaborative learning, responsibility in learning and learning about learning, which are the main elements of a strategy for effective learning (Mitchell, 1999, p. 20). In a previous essay I have argued for the importance of service learning within higher education (Annette, 2000) and have argued for its linkage with post-Dearing key skills in higher education and education for citizenship. What is impressive about the work of the CSV's Education for Citizenship and its partners is that there are now a large number of examples of successful service learning programmes both within schools and also higher education institutions. According to John Potter,

> Learning through community service, therefore, when carefully structured, promotes all three strands of citizenship education (values, community participation and political literacy). The approach is central, not peripheral, to the education agenda. Learning through community service does, however, require careful implementation by teachers who are clear about its purpose and proficient in its execution. It has to be linked with the whole and taught curriculum and be embedded within the explicit mission and purpose of the school. (Potter, 1999, p. 17)

There are a number of schools in which CSV education for citizenship programmes, run in partnership with the Institute of Service Learning (Philadelphia, USA), provide students with the opportunity to engage in service learning in local communities. In addition, a number of university service learning programmes associated with the CSV have formed the Council for Citizenship and Learning in the Community (CCLC), which promotes the development of service learning opportunities for students in higher and further education (Annette and Buckingham-Hatfield, 1999; Annette, 2000).

In the USA, service learning, both in schools K–12 and in higher education, has been growing in importance since the 1970s (cf. Zlotkowski, 1999). The National Society for Experiential Education (NSEE) is a national organization which promotes service learning in both schools and in higher education (community colleges and universities) and the American Association for Higher Education (AAHE) facilitates innovations in teaching and learning in higher education, including service learning. The University of Michigan's Center for Community Service and Learning publishes the *Michigan Journal of Community Service Learning*, a leading journal in this area and the National Service-Learning Clearinghouse at the University of Minnesota, under the directorship of Dr Robert Shumer, provides invaluable access to research and databases. The Corporation for National Service, which was founded as a result of President Clinton's Federal National and Community Service Trust Act of 1993, provides federal funding to support service learning in schools and higher education. More recently, the AAHE, under the editorship of Edward Zlotkowski, has been publishing a number of volumes of theoretical analysis and case study presentations by leading academics in the USA who advocate service learning. This includes a volume edited by Joseph Erickson and Jeffrey B. Anderson, entitled *Learning with the Community: Concepts and Models for Service Learning in Teacher Education* (Erickson and Anderson, 1997) which provides a useful framework for introducing service learning into teacher training. In a large number of teacher training programmes in colleges and universities in the USA there are innovative examples of the pedagogy of service learning in schools. Recent data from the National Service-Learning Clearinghouse based at the University of Minnesota shows that the total number of students in secondary schools doing service and service learning in the USA is over 12.5 million and that the growth in the number of students engaged in high school service learning between 1984 and 1997 was 363 per cent (cf. www.nicsl.coled.umn.edu/who/status). In addition, there are more than 6.7 million students in universities and colleges engaged in service learning. Rahima Wade, a leading advocate of community service-learning in the school curriculum, writes,

> Service learning is a comprehensive teaching strategy with great potential for bringing about positive outcomes for students, schools and communities. (Wade, 1997, p. 34)

Underlying the provision of service learning both in schools K–12 and in higher education are the theories of development and learning of experiential learning and the reflective practitioner. According to Barbara Jacoby (Jacoby, 1996), a major influence on the theoretical framework for service learning has been provided by the experiential learning theory of David Kolb's *Experiential Learning* (1984). David Kolb's experiential learning theory is based on the ideas of John Dewey, Kurt Lewin and Jean Piaget and it provides a pedagogy for structuring service learning activities and assessment. Central to Kolb's learning cycle is the activity of reflection which follows from concrete experience and precedes abstract conceptualization. It is important to note that the concrete experience for service learning is a structured learning experience which provides the opportunity for reflection. This model was adapted by Dennison and Kirk as *Do, Review, Learn and Apply: A Simple Guide to Experiential Learning* where experiential learning is characterized as an important example of active or effective learning (Dennison and Kirk, 1990). There is a great deal of diversity in theory and practice among proponents of experiential learning (e.g.

Boud *et al.*, 1985; Warner-Weil and McGill, 1989; and Moon, 1999) relating to the use of reflection in learning and the complex question of analysing the exact nature of the relationship between reflection and learning. The challenge for students is to learn how to reflect upon experience and not simply to describe experiences. The structured learning experiences within which students undertake reflection will involve interaction with other people. It will be useful to note that the student's level of emotional intelligence will influence the levels of learning outcomes that the student will be able to achieve. The 'light touch approach' to the introduction of the new 'subject' of citizenship will hopefully encourage teachers to think how the learning of political knowledge, perhaps through history, geography, literacy, religious education, etc., can be linked to active learning which encourages critical thinking about values and also experiential learning through service learning in schools and local communities.

In order to consider what will be the best ways to approach the teaching and learning of citizenship in schools much more research will be needed. There is a growing amount of research in the USA, Australia, etc. which examines the teaching and evaluation of citizenship education. Carole Hahn in her book *Becoming Political* (Hahn, 1998) uses both qualitative research based on focus groups and more quantitative data based on surveys in schools in England, Denmark, Germany, The Netherlands and the United States. She examines comparatively both civic education and adolescent political attitudes. She writes that,

> The purpose of this comparative study of citizenship education in five Western democracies was to identify similarities and differences in adolescent political attitudes and secondary school curriculum and instruction. It is hoped that through such a study civic educators might gain insights into how school policies and practices can effectively prepare youth for their roles as participating citizens in pluralistic democracies in an increasingly interdependent global society. (Hahn, 1998, p. 235)

Her study supports the view that, despite the effects of citizenship education, most young people have a low level of 'trust' in formal politics and political leaders. In the USA there have been a number of more detailed empirical studies which attempt to evaluate the learning outcomes of education for citizenship. Norman Nie, Jane Junn and Kenneth Stehlik-Barry designed and conducted the 1990 Citizen Participation Survey in which the authors attempt to assess the effect of levels of educational attainment upon political influence through networking and what they term 'cognitive proficiency' (Nie *et al.*, 1996, pp. 39–44). More recently, Nicholas Emler and Elizabeth Frazer have analysed the published research concerning the relative influence of education on political engagement (Emler and Frazer, 1999) and confirm the correlation between levels of education and political participation in the UK as analysed by Parry, Moyser and Day, (1992). A more specific study of civic education has been recently done by Richard Niemi and Jane Junn (1998) who base their assessment of civic education on the 1988 National Assessment of Educational Progress (NAEP) Civics Assessment. The authors examine the influences of differences according to race, gender, type of school, family backgrounds, etc., and test a theoretical model to explain the cognitive process by which students learn about politics. The authors note that

> In light of these factors, it is unsurprising that our interpretation offers such a striking contrast to the conventional wisdom on the utility of the civics curriculum in promoting knowledge about American government and politics. While Langston and Jennings suggested that their results did not support the 'thinking of those who look to the civic curriculum in American high school as even a minor source of political socialization', we argue that our analysis demonstrates that the civics curriculum has an impact of a size and resilience that makes it a significant part of political learning. (Niemi and Junn, 1998, p. 145)

While there is an existing literature which examines the practices of citizenship education both in the UK and comparatively abroad, there is still only a small amount of research which analyses the assessment methods and learning outcomes of citizenship education and especially service learning. In the UK there have been some initial research projects into student tutoring in schools which have evaluated learning outcomes in the development of cognitive development and the acquisition of transferable or key skills. (Goodlad, 1995, 1998; Topping and Hill, 1995) There has, however, only been limited research into the learning outcomes of service learning resulting from recent pilot projects organized by the CSV (Potter, 1999). In higher education the HEFCE FDTL CoBaLT, or Community-Based Learning and Teaching, has begun to assess community-based learning and its impact upon local communities. In the UK the Council for Citizenship Service Learning (CCSL), the CoBaLT FDTL project and the CSV (Community Service Volunteers) Education for Citizenship programme are planning in partnership a research project into service learning and its outcomes both in schools and in higher education.

This is in striking contrast to the USA where there have been major research projects on evaluating the learning outcomes for service learning both in schools K–12 and also in colleges and universities. The National Society for Experiential Education (NSEE) and the American Association for Higher Education (AAHE) both support and disseminate research in service learning and the National Service-Learning Clearinghouse at the University of Minnesota provides a critical guide to research findings related to service learning both in K–12 schools and higher education (cf. Giles *et al.*, 1991). What is also impressive is the increasing number of PhDs in the area of evaluating the learning outcomes of service learning (e.g. Furco, 1997) which are listed on the National Service-Learning Clearinghouse (cf. www.nicsl.coled.umn.edu/res/bibs/imps.htm).

There have been a number of studies in the USA which have attempted to analyse the correlation between service learning and a variety of learning outcomes. More recently, Janet Eyler and Dwight Giles of Vanderbilt University (USA) have been involved in an extensive research project involving over fifteen hundred students at twenty colleges and universities. This involves examining the variety of learning outcomes from service learning and also considering how differences in the types of service learning programmes influence learning outcomes (Giles and Eyler, 1994; Eyler and Giles, 1999). This important research will be useful not only for reviewing educational practice but it will also provide a model for further research which attempts to look at the relationship between experiential learning, cognitive development and learning outcomes. A. W. Astin and colleagues at the UCLA Higher Education Research Institute have also been engaged in research into the range of effects of service learning on undergraduate students (Astin and Sax, 1998; Astin, 1999). In 1991 Dan Conrad and Diane Hedin reported on an Experiential Education Evaluation Project which was based on research in 1978 which was administered to 4000 secondary school students in 33 programmes (Conrad and Hedin, 1991). The main findings indicated that experiential education programmes had a positive impact on students' psychological, social and intellectual development and that the opportunity for students to act autonomously increased the positive impact. In May 1998, Rand Education (a non-profit research institution) published its findings on *Coupling Service and Learning in Higher Education: The Final Report of the Evaluation of the Learn and Serve America, Higher Education Program*, which was sponsored by the Corporation for National and Community Service. The research findings measured impacts of service learning both for students and for communities and included in its conclusion an analysis of the value for money of the Learn and Serve America Higher Education programmes. The Rand survey involved 725 service learning students and 597 comparison non-service learning students with a total of 1300 students participating in 28 institutions. According to the report,

> Results reveal that students in service-learning courses compared to those in similar courses without a service component report larger gains in civic participation (especially intended future involvement in community service) and life-skills (interpersonal skills and understanding of diversity) . . . A conservative conclusion is that participation in service-learning does not appear to slow or hinder student learning and development and carries some modest benefits, particularly in the area of civic and life-skills. A less conservative conclusion is that service-learning may carry stronger positive effects on certain students when specific elements are in place, especially strong links between course content and service experience. (Rand Education,1998, pp. xvi–xix)

An extremely interesting piece of research in evaluating learning outcomes in service learning in secondary school students has been done by Richard Niemi,

Mary Hepburn and Chris Chapman (Niemi *et al.*, 1999) and is based on the 1996 National Household Education Survey which was a telephone survey of 21,000 parents and 8000 of their sixth to twelfth grade students. The particular report by Niemi *et al.* is based on interviews with 4212 nine to twelfth grade students and their parents. This report notes that, although increasing, there is still only limited empirical data concerning the learning outcomes of service learning (Conrad and Hedin, 1991; Verba *et al.*, 1995; Wade and Saxe, 1996; Youniss and Yates, 1997; Melchior, 1997; Astin and Sax, 1998; Eyler and Giles, 1999). In their report, they provide a comparative analysis of their findings with existing empirical studies. They note that there is an important difference between 'community service' and 'service learning', with the latter being linked to the school curriculum and being a structured learning experience. They note that there are few studies which link service learning outcomes with academic improvement (cf. Shumer, 1994). They also raise the question about whether service learning has any long-term effect upon political participation. Verba *et al.* (1995) have found linkages between civic skills gained and adult political participation. Several other secondary school studies demonstrate evidence of civic participation (Niemi *et al.*, 1999, p. 5). Their findings confirm those of Shumer which is that the design of the service learning programme and especially the length and intensity of the experience increases considerably the positive learning outcomes of the students (Niemi *et al.*, 1999, pp. 5–6; Shumer, 1996). In evaluating the extent of participation in community service they note that levels of participation are very high and are holding steady, with recent studies indicating 60 per cent and 67 per cent levels of participation (Hodgkinson and Weitzman, 1996; Wirthlin Group, 1995). They also stress, however, that levels of participation do not necessarily indicate sustained participation. They examine the influence of such variables as gender, ethnicity, parental education, type of school, family background and school policies towards participation. They describe their overall findings as 'a mixed-bag' of results. Niemi *et al.* conclude that sustained service learning produced the greater effects and that service learning

> appears to stimulate greater political knowledge, more political discussions and with parents, enhanced participation skills and higher political efficacy but not more tolerance of diversity. (Niemi *et al.*, 1999, p. i)

This summary does not do justice to the level of sophistication of the research methodology and the analysis of research outcomes which provides an impressive model for similar research in the UK. As indicated earlier (Kerr, 1999a), there is a significant need for research into the evaluation of assessment and learning outcomes in all types of citizenship education in order to inform the policy-making decisions of the QCA and the 'educational judgements' of OFSTED.

In conclusion, I would like to argue that the proposals for citizenship education in the UK should integrate service learning in the community with critical thinking about values and the learning of political knowledge. The introduction of citizenship education as a type of effective learning should involve experiential learning in the community and the ability of the student to engage in reflective practice. In order to substantiate the claims of service learning in schools at Key Stages 3 and 4, more extensive research should be undertaken. The teaching of citizenship as a 'subject' should therefore include the approaches of 'values in education', 'political literacy' and 'experiential learning in the community'. The evidence of high youth civic participation and at the same time increasing political disaffection and alienation should help to indicate that an education for citizenship should be about introducing active learning which can lead to greater civic and political participation. As the civic republican conception of citizenship recognizes, both civic participation and civic virtue are necessary for the protection of our liberties as citizens.

REFERENCES

Annette, J. (1999) Is citizenship British? Civic republicanism and the political languages of citizenship. Unpublished paper presented to the conference on Citizenship, University of Leeds.
Annette, J. (2000) Citizenship and higher education. In J. Cairns, R. Gardner and D. Lawton *Education for Values: Morals, Ethics and Citizenship in Contemporary Teaching*. London: Kogan Page.
Annette, J. and Buckingham-Hatfield, S. (1999) *Student Community Partnerships in Higher Education*. London: CSV Publications.
Astin, A. W. (1999) Promoting leadership, service and democracy: what higher education can do. In R. Bringle, R. Games and Revd E. Malloy, *Colleges and Universities as Citizens*. Boston: Allyn and Bacon.
Astin, A. W. and Sax, L. J. (1998) How undergraduates are affected by service participation. *Journal of College Student Development*, **39** (3), 251–63.
Barber, B. (1992) *An Aristocracy of Everyone*. New York: Oxford University Press.
Barber, B. (1998a) *A Passion for Democracy*. Princeton: Princeton University Press.
Barber, B. (1998b) *A Place for Us: How to Make Society Civil and Democracy Strong*. New York: Hill and Wang.
Bentley, T. (1998) *Learning Beyond the Classroom*. London: Routledge/Demos.
Bentley, T. and Oakley, K. (1999) *The Real Deal: What Young People Think about Government, Politics and Social Exclusion*. London: Demos.
Boud, D., Keogh, R. and Walker, D. (eds) (1985) *Reflection: Turning Experience into Learning*. London: Kogan Page.
Callan, E. (1997) *Creating Citizens: Political Education and Liberal Democracy*. Oxford: Oxford University Press.
Conrad, D. and Hedin, D. (1991) School-based community service: what we know from research and theory. *Phi Delta Kappan*, **72**, 745–57.
Crewe, I., Searing, D. and Conover, P. (1997) *Citizenship and Civic Education*. London: Citizenship Foundation.
Dagger, R. (1997) *Civic Virtues: Rights, Citizenship and Republican Liberalism*. Oxford:

Oxford University Press.

Dean, H. and Melrose, M. (1999) *Poverty, Riches and Social Citizenship*. London: Macmillan.

Dennison, B. and Kirk, R. (1990) *Do, Review, Learn, Apply: A Simple Guide to Experimental Learning*. Oxford: Blackwell.

Emler, N. and Frazer, E. (1999) Politics: the education effect. (Secretary of State's proposal). *Oxford Review of Education*, **25** (1 and 2), 251–73.

Erickson, J. and Anderson, J. (eds) (1997) *Learning with the Community: Concepts and Models for Service Learning in Teacher Education*. Washington, DC:AAHE.

Eyler, J. and Giles, D. (1999) *Where's the Learning in Service-Learning*. San Francisco: Jossey Bass Publishers.

Frazer, E. (1999a) Introduction – The idea of political education. *Oxford Review of Education*, **25** (1 and 2), 5–22.

Frazer, E. (1999b), *Citizenship Education – The Advisory Group on Education and the Prospects For Curriculum Reform in England*. PSA Conference Paper, University of Nottingham, May.

Furco, A. (1997) *School Sponsored Service Programmes and the Educational Development of High School Students*. PhD dissertation. University of California, Berkeley.

Gaskin, K. (1998) *What Young People Want from Volunteering?* London: National Centre for Volunteering.

Gaskin, K., Vlaeminke, M. and Fenton, N. (1996) *Young People's Attitudes to the Voluntary Sector*. Loughborough: Commission on the Future of the Voluntary Sector.

Giles, D. E. and Eyler, J. (1994) The impact of a college community service learning laboratory on students' personal, social and cognitive outcomes. *Journal of Adolescence*, **17**: 327–39.

Giles, D. E., Porter-Honnet, E. and Migliore, S. (1991) *Research Agenda for Combining Service and Learning in the 1990s*. Raleigh, NC: National Society for Experiential Education.

Goodlad, S. (ed.) (1995) *Students as Tutors and Mentors*. London: Kogan Page.

Goodlad, S. (ed.) (1998) *Mentoring and Tutoring by Students*. London: Kogan Page.

Hahn, C. (1998) *Becoming Political: Comparative Perspectives on Citizenship Education*. Albany: SUNY.

Hall, P. (1999) Social capital. *British Journal of Political Science*, **29**: 417–61.

Hargreaves, D. (1994) *The Mosaic of Learning*. London: Demos.

Hodgkinson, V. and Weitzman, M. (1996) *Giving and Volunteering in the US*. Washington, DC: Independent Sector.

Jacoby, B. (1996) *Service Learning in Higher Education*. San Francisco: Jossey Bass.

Jones, G. and Wallace, C. (1992) *Youth, Family and Citizenship*. Buckingham: Open University Press.

Jowell, R. and Park, A. (1998) *Young People, Politics and Citizenship*. London: Citizenship Foundation.

Kerr, D. (1999a) *Re-Examining Citizenship Education: The Case of England*. London: NFER.

Kerr, D. (1999b) *Citizenship Education in International Comparison*. London: QCA.

Kolb, D. (1984) *Experiential Learning*. Englewood, NJ: Prentice Hall.

Lerner, M. (1997) *The Politics of Meaning*. Reading, Mass: Addison and Wesley.

Lister, R. (1997) *Citizenship: Feminist Perspectives*. London: Macmillan.

Marquand, D. (1997) *The New Reckoning*. Cambridge: Polity.

Marshall, T. H. (1950) *Citizenship and Social Class*. Cambridge: Cambridge University Press.

Melchior, A. (1997) *National Evaluation of Learn and Serve America School and Community Based Programs: Interim Report.* Boston, Mass.: Brandeis University, Center for Human Resources.

Mitchell, P. (1999) *Education for Citizenship: The Contribution of Active Learning in the Community.* London: CSV Publications.

Moon, J. (1999) *Reflection in Learning and Professional Development.* London: Kogan Page.

Nie, N., Junn, J. and Stehlik-Barry, K. (1996) *Education and Democratic Citizenship in America.* Chicago: University of Chicago Press.

Niemi, R., Hepburn, M. and Chapman, C. (1999) Community service by high school students: a cure for civic ills? Unpublished paper.

Niemi, R. and Junn, J. (1998) *Civic Education.* New Haven: Yale University Press.

Oldfield, A. (1990) *Citizenship and Community.* London: Routledge.

Parry, G., Moyser, G. and Day, N. (1992) *Political Participation and Democracy in Britain.* Cambridge: Cambridge University Press.

Pettit, P. (1997) *Republicanism: A Theory of Freedom and Government,* Oxford: Oxford University Press.

Phillips, M. (1999) The indoctrination of Citizen Smith, Jr. *The Sunday Times,* 17 March.

Potter, J. (1999) *Education for Life, Work and Citizenship.* London: CSV Publications.

Putnam, R. (1995) Bowling alone. *Journal of Democracy,* **6** (1): 65–78.

Putnam, R. (1996) The strange disappearance of civic America. *The American Prospect,* **24** (Winter): 34–48.

QCA (1998) *Education for Citizenship and the Teaching of Democracy in Schools, Final Report.* London: DfEE and QCA.

Rand Education (1998) *Coupling Service and Learning in Higher Education.* Washington, DC: Corporation for National Service.

Roker, D., Player, K. and Coleman, J. (1997) Exploring adolescent altruism: British young people's involvement in voluntary work and campaigning. In M. Yates and J. Youniss (eds) *Roots of Civic Identity: International Perspectives on Community Service and Activism in Youth.* Cambridge: Cambridge University Press.

Roker, D., Player K. and Coleman, J. (1999a) Young people's voluntary and campaigning activities as sources of political education. *Oxford Review of Education,* **25** (1/2): 185–98.

Roker, D., Player, K. and Coleman, J. (1999b) *Challenging the Image: Young People as Volunteers and Campaigners.* Leicester: National Youth Agency.

Sandel, M. (1996) *Democracy's Discontent.* Boston: Harvard University Press.

Secretary of State's Proposals (1999) *The Review of the National Curriculum in England.* London: DfEE and QCA.

Shumer, R. (1994) Community based learning: humanizing education. *Journal of Adolescence,* **17**, August, 357–68.

Shumer, R. (1996) What we know about service learning. *Education and Urban Society,* **28**, 36–47.

Skinner, Q. (1998) *Liberty Before Liberalism.* Cambridge: Cambridge University Press.

Skocpol, T. and Fiorina, M. (eds) (1999) *Civic Engagement in American Democracy.* Washington, DC: Brookings Institution Press.

Topping, K. J. and Hill, S. (1995) Summary of evaluation research. In J. Potter (ed.) *Learning Together: Student Tutoring Research and Evaluation.* London: CSV Publications.

Verba, S., Schlozman, K. and Brady, H. (1995) *Voice and Equality: Civic Voluntarism in American Politics.* Cambridge, Mass: Harvard University Press.

Wade, R. (1997) *Community Service Learning.* Albany: SUNY.

Wade, R. and Saxe, D. W. (1996) Community service learning in the United States, theory and research, *Social Education*, **24**: 71–87.

Warner-Weil, S. and McGill, I. (1989) *Making Sense of Experiential Learning.* Buckingham: SRHE/Open University Press (reprinted 1996).

Wilkinson, H. (1996) But will they vote? The political attitudes of young people. *Children and Society*, **10**: 230–44.

Wilkinson, H. and Mulgan, G. (1995) *Freedom's Children.* London: Demos.

Wirthlin Group (1995) *The Prudential Spirit of Community Youth Survey.* Camden, NJ: Prudential Life Assurance of America.

Wuthnow, R. (1998) *Loose Connections.* Cambridge, Mass: Harvard University Press.

Youniss, J. and Yates, M. (1997) *Community Service and Social Responsibility in Youth.* Chicago: University of Chicago.

Zlotkowski, E. (1999) Pedagogy and engagement. In R. Bringle, R. Games and Revd E. Malloy (eds) *Colleges and Universities as Citizens.* Boston: Allyn and Bacon.

Chapter 9

Citizenship, Education and Social Capital

Eva Gamarnikow and Anthony Green

INTRODUCTION

On 19 November 1997 the Secretary of State for Education, David Blunkett, set up the Advisory Group on Citizenship, chaired by Professor of Politics, Bernard Crick, with the following terms of reference:

> To provide advice on effective education for citizenship in schools – to include the nature and practices of participation in democracy; the duties, responsibilities and rights of individuals as citizens; and the value to individuals and society of community activity. (quoted in QCA, 1998, p. 4)

In policy terms this development is widely viewed as both innovatory, and a belated development of a key foundation of the National Curriculum, which from its inception in 1988 was always intended to promote students' spiritual, moral, social and cultural development. The novel features of citizenship education (CE) are its elevation to a subject within the National Curriculum and its connections with anticipated ambitious political outcomes, namely, democratic renewal in the UK. The Speaker of the House, Betty Boothroyd, outlined these expectations in her Foreword to the Crick Report:

> Citizenship as a subject appeared to be diminishing in importance and impact in schools . . . This . . . has been a blot on the landscape of public life for too long, with unfortunate consequences for the future of our democratic processes . . . Citizenship Education will enhance understanding of and participation in our democratic, legal and other civic processes. (Ibid., 1998, p. 3)

CE is thus different from the other National Curriculum subjects which are located within an overall standards, assessment and qualifications framework intended to raise educational outcomes, 'to overcome economic and social disadvantage' (Secretary of State for Education, 1997, p. 3) and to invest in human capital to increase employability.

> We are talking about investing in human capital in the age of knowledge. To compete in the global economy . . . we will have to unlock the potential of every young person. (Secretary of State for Education, 1997, p. 3)

While CE may contribute to these aims, the chief objective behind this new curriculum subject is to enhance the civic and political development of children and young people in a social and political context where fears about young people's alienation from Britain's democratic institutions and processes are increasingly evident (Wilkinson and Mulgan, 1995; Roberts and Sachdev, 1996; Social and Community Planning Research, 1997; Bentley, 1998). CE is therefore a key element of the wider policy concerns of New Labour to combat social fragmentation and exclusion which was amplified by eighteen years of Conservative government.

It is these wider policy concerns which form the starting point of our analysis. New Labour won the 1997 General Election at a time of extensive and growing social, economic, political and cultural polarization. By the end of the Conservative era the UK had the highest levels of poverty in Europe (Atkinson, 1998), with one quarter of all children living in persistent poverty (HM Treasury, 1999), in several thousand 'worst estates' characterized by high rates of unemployment, teenage pregnancy and crime (Social Exclusion Unit, 1998b). Long-term poverty and hardening social exclusion have resulted in growing health inequalities 'from womb to tomb' (Acheson, 1998), as well as increasing educational polarization (OFSTED, 1998; Mortimore and Whitty, 1999) and disaffection from school (Social Exclusion Unit, 1998a). New Labour inherited not just a fragmented society, but a profoundly unequal one, where the gaps between the haves and have-nots were increasing on most, if not all, dimensions of life chances. The wide-ranging social policies of the present government are committed to eradicating this growing polarization. Regenerating social capital is a key policy instrument in these endeavours.

Our concern in this chapter is to explore critically how CE fits into these wider policy concerns and to pose critical questions about the likely effectiveness of social capital as a strategy for creating a more equal and equitable society, in the context of continuities in structural inequalities. Our argument is that the central policy direction, under the banner of the Third Way, prioritizes social and cultural change as a key strategy, over equity-enhancing economic and financial change, and that these endeavours are inspired by particular types of theories of social capital. We discuss the significance of social capital theorizing in detail in the second part of the chapter.

Having set the context for Third Way policy discourse, we turn to examine Crick's (QCA, 1998) definitions of citizenship to explore how they differ from

Marshall's (1950) classic statement. This raises the central issue of the role of social capital in what we argue is a shift in the nature and direction of citizenship when we compare Marshall to Crick. This will be followed by an analysis of its implication for the projected contribution of CE to Third Way strategies in the UK. Finally, we end by raising some critical questions about the Third Way citizenship model and CE, namely what are the chances of the 'educated citizen' being realized, beyond rhetoric, that is.

THIRD WAY POLITICS AND POLICY

It is by now a commonplace assertion that the political project of the Third Way is concerned with developing an alternative to the social fragmentation and social exclusion produced by eighteen years (1979–97) of Conservative neo-liberal marketization and the earlier bipartisan (1945–79) bureaucratic collectivism and corporatism of the social democratic welfare state (Blair, 1998; Giddens, 1998; Gamarnikow and Green, 1999a, 1999b). The Third Way accepts the economic logic of capitalist globalization, with free markets for goods and services and flexible markets for labour, but recognizes that, because certain individuals and groups were excluded from the 'success' of Tory Britain, the state is required to provide support and opportunities for people to 'help themselves'. The basic ideas entailed in the Third Way focus is on empowering individuals, families and communities to lift themselves out of poverty, unemployment and social exclusion by a combination of individual responsibility, education, social support and welfare to work initiatives (Hayton, 1999; Hodgson and Spours, 1999). Thus, New Labour provides continuity with the Tory idea that the state should not do things *for* people through macroeconomic management and bureaucratic welfare provision. In place of the Conservative preference for a non-interfering state and the old Labour commitment to redistribution and welfare, New Labour ideology constructs the state as partner, enabler and provider of frameworks for opportunities for improved outcomes by regenerating social capital.

Third Way thinking is thus based on two interlocking premises. The first is that the state is relatively impotent in the sphere of economic dynamics in the era of globalization.

> Economic globalisation therefore is a reality . . . Globalisation 'pulls away' from the nation state in the sense that some powers that nations used to possess, including those that underlay Keynesian economic management, have been weakened. (Giddens, 1998, pp. 30, 31)

The second premise follows from the first. If the state cannot intervene directly in the economy, it must therefore focus on changing society, thus approaching the economic indirectly.

> We can only realise ourselves as individuals in a thriving civil society, comprising strong families and civic institutions buttressed by intelligent government ... Whether in education, health, social work, crime prevention or the care of children, *'enabling' government strengthens civil society ... and helps families and communities improve their own performance* ... This is the Third Way – a modernised social democracy for a changing world which will *build its prosperity on human and social capital.* (Blair, 1998, pp. 3, 14, 20; our emphasis)

Therefore, the key notion which the Third Way addresses is society, that aspect of the social world whose existence was specifically denied by Margaret Thatcher in her by now infamous statement made in an interview in *Woman's Own* in 1987: 'There is no society. There are only individuals and families.' The Third Way project adopts an eclectic perspective on society (terms such as 'community', 'stakeholders' or 'partnership' have been used), with the various elements linked to populist notions of social cohesion and a commitment to reducing poverty and social exclusion and promoting social inclusion and social justice. This brings civil society and building its social capital infrastructure into the policy frame.

> A good society depends not just on the economic success of the individual, but on the 'social capital' of the community. Investment in social institutions, including good quality public services, is as important as investment in economic infrastructure. Communities do not become strong because they are rich; they become rich because they are strong. (Commission on Social Justice, 1994, p. 10)

With the demise of Communism from 1989 and the implosion of socialism as a political ideology and theory of social change, with a set of concepts (social class, capitalism), the notions of social justice and social exclusion/inclusion have come to the fore as signifiers of concern about unacceptable inequalities. Thus, social justice, social inclusion and social exclusion have become the Third Way code for talking about social inequalities. These discourses displace notions of structured, systemic economic and social inequalities while locating social exclusion in social capital deficits in individuals, families and communities.

> Exclusion is not about gradations of inequality, but about mechanisms that act to detach groups of people from the social mainstream. (Giddens, 1998, p. 104)

Social capital and social exclusion address opposite themes. A society with high social capital is an inclusive society, whereas at the points when society lacks social capital, it manifests social exclusion:

> Individuals prosper in a strong and active community of citizens. But Britain cannot be a strong community, cannot be one nation, when ... society ... is falling apart ... Worsening inequality, hopelessness, crime and poverty undermine the decency on which any good society rests ... Social exclusion is about income, but is about more. It is about prospects and networks and life-chances. It's a very modern problem, and one that is more harmful to the individual, more damaging to self-

esteem, more corrosive for society as a whole, more likely to be passed down from generation to generation, than material poverty. (Blair, 1997, p. 3)

SOCIAL CAPITAL

The concept of social capital tends to be used loosely and rhetorically in Third Way policy discourse, but in essence it is about the value and power to individuals of participation and social networks. Its attractiveness lies in its appeal to common-sense ideas about the good society of responsible and decent individuals, families and communities, of social cohesion and security, and of the democratic engagement of the citizenry in the communities of civil society and in local and national polities. Social capital is about the multifaceted benefits of 'trust'.

There is also a harder-edged, instrumental aspect to social capital as a strategy for social change. First, it appears to work: education and health research seem to confirm that educational achievement appears to be strongly correlated with family social capital (Furstenberg and Hughes, 1995; Teachman *et al.*, 1996; Wadsworth, 1996; Whitty *et al.*, 1998, 1999; Willms, 1997) and that social groups and societies with high levels of social capital have better outcomes on social indicators, such as education, health, employment, economic development, community involvement and so on (Putnam *et al.*, 1993). Second, we detect a bonus to the state and Third Way policy in social capital theory, in that it appears to deflect responsibility for both social and educational problem identification and solutions from the government and to 'delegate' it to the active citizenry. Key rhetorical terms here are 'partnership' and 'agreements', involved 'participation' rather than 'consumption'.

A closer look at social capital theories shows, however, that there are different formulations with significant tensions between them. We argue that it is essential to explore these to develop an understanding of conflicts and dilemmas at the heart of Third Way policy.

The concept of social capital, as it is currently being deployed, is most commonly associated with three sources: Coleman's (1988, 1990) rational action theory and sociology of education; Putnam, Leonardi and Nanetti's (1993) work on Italian politics; and Fukuyama's (1995) comparative study of national capitalisms. In spite of their different emphases, what all three perspectives share are the links they postulate between successful social outcomes in education, employment, family relationships, health and so on and the presence of social capital. They locate social capital in a pre-economic and pre-political civil society.[1]

The concept of social capital represents the rediscovery of community and of the idea that social relations are an essential resource for people. Unlike physical, financial and human capital which are forms of private property, social capital is a form of public good, available to everybody. Unlike many other public goods which can be reduced or damaged by use (for example, air), using social capital generates more social capital. Capitalizing on this property makes it a magically cost-effective policy resource, as it is produced for free in the day-to-day interactions of social subjects.

So what are the sites for the production of social capital? Here there is some divergence of emphasis between the three main bodies of theory. Coleman (1988, 1990) identified three aspects of social relations which constitute key sources of social capital: obligations, expectations and trustworthiness of structures; networks and information channels; and norms and effective sanctions. The most important of these are trust, shared norms and effective sanctions. Putnam, Leonardi and Nanetti (1993) argue that social trust, norms of reciprocity, networks and civic engagement are key sources of social capital. Here thriving civil societies impact positively on democratization and effectiveness of institutions. This variant of social capital theorization is derived from de Tocqueville's claims in his classic *Democracy in America*, about the educative nature of civic participation and its link to democratic governance. Fukuyama (1995) defines social capital as trust and a thriving civil society. Trust is developed initially in traditional nuclear families. It is oriented towards children's educational achievement, within communities embodying strong norms, values and sanctions which, in turn, provide the cultural framework for co-operation and trust among non-kin in civil society.

All agree that the most important way of generating social capital is to use it: relying and acting on the trustworthiness of networks and structures increases their trustworthiness. They all also agree that social capital has to be introduced to each new generation and that this occurs in families when, as Coleman and Fukuyama argue, parents invest in their children's education through involved parenting and participation in school–community networks. Building social capital begins with the intra-family social capital of parent–child relationships, moves to interfamily social capital in communities, which leads to developing networks linking both individuals and communities, to produce finally, as Putnam *et al.* argue, an engaged, active civil society which invests in, and benefits from, the collective goods produced by institutions in civil society and effective, democratic government.

In the dominant contemporary reading, social capital theories share two further features: the normative status of social capital and its seemingly benign nature (Gamarnikow and Green, 1999a, 1999b). With regard to the former, only specific forms of social relations constitute sources of social capital. There is a curious ambiguity in Coleman's writing concerning the normative status of social capital. In his more abstract, theoretical discussions social capital is neutral in terms of the purposes for which it is used (Foley and Edwards, 1997). For example, trust is as important in legitimate as it is for illicit purposes, organizations and institutions. However, in his empirical work on links between social capital and human capital, or family and education, social capital acquires a normative edge and a specified, desirable institutional form, the traditional nuclear family. Fukuyama's arguments about the fundamental role of the two-parent family resemble Coleman's. Focusing on networks, rather than families, Putnam *et al.* agree with Fukuyama that, while all communities have networks, not all of these networks are productive in terms of social capital. Social networks can be vertical/hierarchical or horizontal/egalitarian, but only the latter are perceived to generate social capital. Horizontal networks, or networks of civic engagement, foster trust and reciprocity for Putnam *et al.*, or trust in and co-operation with non-kin for Fukuyama. Social capital is thus a normative concept in that it distinguishes between different forms of social relationships and institutions and claims social capital building status for some (horizontal networks), but not for others. These considerations are critical to the potential effectivity of social capital as a policy instrument.

The second shared feature of current theories of social capital, namely its apparently benign nature, is linked to its normative status. While it is clear from parts of Coleman's work that social capital is the foundation for all social activities and relations, whether legal or criminal, Putnam *et al.* and Fukuyama argue that, by definition, forms of social capital which encourage and promote nonconformist, undesirable or illegal social activities and relations do not, in fact, constitute social capital. Thus vertical/hierarchical exclusionary networks (possibly the most common structures in unequal societies!) are not a source of social capital; criminal activity as an alternative form of association, as in Colombia, acquires the label of 'perverse social capital' (Rubio, 1997); and excessively familistic societies which do not trust non-kin can fall into nepotism or the *amoral familism* of, for example, Southern Italy (Putnam with Leonardi and Nanetti, 1993; Leonardi, 1995). Real social capital can thus be recognized *ex post facto* by virtue of its benign and beneficial effects

To sum up, trust is the constitutive element at the centre of current conceptualizations of social capital. The key social locations for its development are in the interconnected social institutions of: families, particularly in parent–child and family–school relations; communities with strong norms, values and sanctions; generalized cultural norms of reliability, reciprocity and accountability; dense social networks; and civic engagement (Hall, 1997). Their connectedness may take the form of benign spirals of reinforcement of social capital resources, or become unravelled as vicious circles of deteriorating stocks of social capital and accompanying social disintegration.

However, such formal accounts of current social capital orthodoxy provide only part of the story and ignore significant tensions between different formulations along other dimensions of social capital formation. We claim that current conceptualizations of social capital can be represented as a continuum of social capital manifestations. At one end of the continuum, social capital embraces progressive, liberal and civic notions of co-operation, empowerment, participation and community action in the construction of needs and priorities. Here there is space for an active, confident and empowered citizenry, and civic engagement and political participation thrive. At the other extreme, social capital may be realized in a normative order of traditional institutional forms, for instance, favouring two-parent nuclear families; locating the 'parenting deficit' in women's increased labour market activity and linking this to educational failure; and arguing for a collective non-relativist moral regime of duties and responsibilities to which all are expected to conform, particularly those least well placed in the system. This may be reinforced by much hardened sanctions, 'tough love', 'tough on crime and tough on the causes of crime', 'three strikes and you're out', 'naming and shaming' and 'workfare not welfare' to put metal into social capital processes. At this end of the continuum, traditional forms of political, economic and cultural power relations, although invisible in the accounts, appear to form essential background features of social capital formation, rendering citizenship ambiguous in relation to responsible and 'decent' subjecthood, potentially undermining the project of developing critical civic engagement and revitalizing civil society.

While the social capital continuum clearly signposts the nature of the political tensions concerning the connections between the idea of citizenship and social capital, there is another difficulty embedded in current social capital theorizations. This relates to our earlier point about social capital representing the rediscovery of community, albeit in a pre or non-sociological form. Portes (1998), for instance, points out that the social capital claim that forms and patterns of sociability, association and participation have social consequences has always been at the heart of the sociological enterprise. Concerns about social capital thus represent a return to classical sociological preoccupations with community as the foundation for social solidarity and social cohesion. The journey from sociology to social capital does, however, indicate a key shift in discursive causal trajectories. Sociological explanations tend to incorporate, to varying degrees, the articulation of economic considerations with social structures and relations. By contrast, contemporary social capital theories tend to view society as pre-existing the economy and being causally implicated in its production. This sidelining of economic, material and structural effects or determinations opens the space for policy interventions in the realm of the social, political and cultural, so crucial to Third Way politics.

In view of this shift from sociology to social capital it is perhaps not surprising that Bourdieu's contribution to social capital theory is often overlooked in current discussions (Portes, 1998). Bourdieu (1986, p. 248) argued that social capital is formed through horizontal and vertical networks 'of more or less institutionalised relationships of mutual acquaintance and recognition'. Unlike cultural and economic capitals which are distributed unequally, social capital is ubiquitous, but class-specific forms of sociability and networks make social capital intrinsically unequal. Thus the universality of sociability and networks obscures their differential effectiveness: lower-class networks are as plentiful and varied as middle-class ones, but less productive of socially and economically successful outcomes (Portes, 1998). By contrast, current social capital orthodoxy, in line with Third Way thinking, abstracts society from economy and assumes a universal and undifferentiated form for social capital, potentially equally available to and effective for all. The effect is to link outcomes to the presence or absence of social capital, rather than to the unequal productiveness of different social capitals.

As we have argued elsewhere in relation to the Education Action Zones (Gamarnikow and Green, 1999a, 1999b), there is an important affinity between the Third Way and current social capital theories. Both are preoccupied with social cohesion which is constituted as the foundation for and cause of economic productivity and well-being, and social inclusion. It is in this arena that they differ significantly from both social democracy and neo-liberalism. In diametrically opposed ways, both of these political projects emphasized the centrality of economic considerations. The social democratic state was committed to economic intervention, full employment and the demarketization of welfare as strategies for securing social justice. By contrast, the neo-liberal state regarded marketization and competitive, flexible labour markets as the foundation for a society of citizen-consumers, whose economic well-being was secured by the incentives of economic inequality and the trickle-down effect of growing national prosperity. Society was transformed into an individualistic collection of consumers entitled to quality products and services guaranteed by an ever-widening variety of charters and Kitemarks. The Third Way state, by contrast, positions itself as relatively economically impotent and locates responsibility for successful economic outcomes in a cohesive, responsible and active civil society.

SOCIAL CAPITAL, CITIZENSHIP AND CITIZENSHIP EDUCATION: FROM MARSHALL TO CRICK

The publication of both the Crick Report (QCA, 1998) and the National Curriculum Review (QCA, 1999), which has added CE to the revised National Curriculum, signals a profound policy concern with issues of citizenship and citizenship education in Britain. At the same time, we argue, there is currently a renewed interest in social capital, generally focused around policy concerns of social inclusion/exclusion, poverty and the disintegration of communities, education and health inequalities, and a retreat to a moral order of civic and family responsibilities as against rights. The Crick Report similarly locates itself in and engages with these social policy concerns. Drawing on Putnam, Leonardi and Nanetti's (1993) version of social capital theory, it argues that the parameters and content of its proposals for CE will enable education to contribute to the development of citizens and citizenship in these 'New Times' of global economic, political, social and cultural change (Hall and Jacques, 1989). These multiple overlaps suggest that there are important links between the current concerns about declining social capital and the modernized ideas of citizenship in the Crick Report.

The classical theorization of democratic citizenship is found in Marshall's famous modelling of three forms of citizenship: civil, political and social. Civil citizenship is concerned with individual liberty of the person; political citizenship focuses on democratic rights of participation and representation; and social citizenship is located in the responsibilities of the welfare state to enable people to 'live the life of a civilised being according to the standards prevailing in the society' (Marshall, 1950, 1992, p. 8). Marshall argued that these three forms of citizenship developed sequentially. The eighteenth century saw the rise of civil citizenship with the destruction of feudal statuses and the protection of individual liberties in the courts. In the nineteenth century free individuals fought for the right to political representation and participation. In the twentieth century the creation of the welfare state extended the equality inherent in the idea of democracy to include the processes which attenuate economic inequality.

Marshall claimed that citizenship conferred universal, equal rights upon all citizens, and the progress of citizenship extended this universal equality from liberty (civil citizenship) to democracy (political citizenship), and then to economic condition (social citizenship). The welfare state, or rather, the hyphenated new society of capitalism-democracy-welfare, represented the use of democratic institutions of the state to create a more equal society with a focus on social justice. From today's vantage point we can view this theorization as reflecting post-war high modernity, characterized by a mass production, full employment society with an interventionist state committed to collective forms of non-market welfare and universal citizenship. Remaining inequalities became legitimated by the ideology and educational practices of equality of opportunity whereby merit and effort were rewarded, rather than advantaged class and social position. Marshall's concept of social citizenship thus appears to be a celebration of rights won by citizens from the state in the context of structured economic inequalities, in support of the 'empowered citizen'.

The main critiques of Marshall rest upon interrogating the assumption of universality of citizenship and point to continuing specific forms of exclusion and contestation of the boundaries of the community of equal citizens. Marxist critiques (Hall and Held, 1989; Andrews, 1991) highlight the continuing persistence of 'inherited' class inequalities: although social mobility is technically available to all through education, in practice working-class children continue to underachieve and to undertake working-class jobs, while middle and upper-class children inherit privileged educational, occupational and social positions (Centre for Contemporary Cultural Studies, 1981). Theorists of 'race' and racism demonstrate how the legal racism of immigration legislation (Layton-Henry, 1992; Solomos, 1993) and the institutional racism (Macpherson, 1999) of education (Gillborn, 1999) and employment (Modood *et al.*, 1997) exclude Black and ethnic minority people from the universality of citizenship. Thus citizenship has become an increasingly racialized and nationalist concept. Feminist critiques (Pateman, 1988; Lister, 1997; Walby, 1997) point out that Marshall's universal citizenship and its chronology apply to male citizens in the public sphere, while women are located in the private sphere of the family as economically dependent and subordinated wives, housewives and mothers whose labour in the family facilitates and nurtures male citizenship. These critiques demonstrate that the formal universality of citizenship, according to Marshall's formulation, was in fact built upon continuing substantive and fundamental inequalities and discrimination around the social divisions of class, gender and 'race'/ethnicity. The universal citizen was clearly a minority: white middle-class males.

Marshall's model of social citizenship eventually imploded, along with the tripartite compromise capitalism-democracy-welfare state, under the impact of the economic crises of the 1970s–1990s, associated with the globalization of capitalist markets and the ending of full employment for male breadwinners; the political and ideological crises linked to the fall of Communism, the failures of social democracy and the globalization of neo-liberalism; and the social crises precipitated by the rise of feminism, multiculturalism and anti-racism. In place of the social democratic, collectivist welfare state and Marshall's citizenship came the neo-liberal individualism of the citizen as consumer, the negation of society and the elevation of markets to the status of liberators of individuals and families. The social destructiveness of the neo-liberal era has been well documented in the huge rise in inequality, poverty and social exclusion, perhaps best represented here by one stark statistic: in the decade between 1979 and 1989 the proportion of children and the population living in poverty increased from 10 per cent and 9 per cent to 33 per cent and 25 per cent respectively (Oppenheim and Harker, 1996, p. 37).

However, theorizations of post/late modernity also point to other changes brought about by the shift from traditional class allegiances and politics: a greater focus on and legitimacy of the politics of identity and difference. The collapse of social democracy created spaces for social groups and identities previously excluded from Marshall's citizenship, women, and ethnic and sexual minorities. According to Giddens (1998, 1999), the fracturing of the modernist universality of citizenship and identity is the result of three major changes. First, globalization has significantly reduced the economic, political and social effectiveness of the nation state. Increasingly, structures of governance are either devolved down to lower levels, or delegated to supranational institutions. This results in loss of legitimacy for the state and the development of 'fuzzy' sovereignty on the one hand, and a greater potential for democratization of public life on the other. Second, there is the impact of rapid technological change and the explosion of science in everyday life. The former has fundamentally affected social class, the occupational structure and the nature of employment, and with it social democratic class-based political allegiances. The latter has invaded life through the politics, economics and identities of risk society, where science produces ever more risks and has thus lost its ability to deliver security and progress (Beck, 1992). Third, there has been a significant movement away from tradition and custom as sources of everyday life and identity. This includes the democratization of family life, growing reflexivity, pluralism and multiculturalism. While these changes have created cultural spaces for developing complex, shifting and multi-layered identities and changing relationships, they have also brought to the surface tensions around questions of class, gender, sexuality, race/ethnicity and the politics of difference in the unitary state.

The key problems for citizenship under conditions of late modernity, therefore, lie in addressing the splintering of modernist universality and developing narratives and strategies for the inclusion of identity and difference. In this context the Crick Report offers an interesting reorientation of citizenship which attempts to square the circle of universality by encompassing difference.

The Report divides citizenship into three aspects: social and moral responsibility, community involvement and political literacy.

> Our understanding of citizenship education in a parliamentary democracy finds three heads on one body: *social and moral responsibility, community involvement and political literacy*. (QCA, 1998, p. 13)

Social and moral responsibility do not dictate the precise nature of the moral regime, but indicate that the late modern citizen is expected to foreground the values, identities and practices of responsible sociability and civility. Community involvement is concerned with civic engagement and building the multiple loose networks of civil society. This constitutes an attempt both to revitalize civil society and to legitimate decreasing state intervention. Political literacy is concerned with effective participation, but in circumstances of increasing alienation and abstention from political life and lack of trust in politics and politicians.

If we compare Marshall and Crick it is possible to chart significant shifts in the definitions of citizenship (see Table 9.1). This Table shows quite clearly how far the conceptualization of citizenship has shifted, as well as indicating the direction of this trajectory. Whereas Marshall viewed civil citizenship as the foundation of individual rights and freedoms, the Crick Report sees this level as the exercise of social and moral responsibilities of reciprocity and social trust as a foundation for sociability.

Table 9.1 Definitions of citizenship: Marshall and Crick

Marshall	Crick
Civil Citizenship Personal liberty and a regime of individual rights	*Social and Moral Responsibility* Social virtues and a regime of individual responsibilities
Political Citizenship Political participation and democratic representation	*Political Literacy* Effective participation in public life and the public sphere
Social Citizenship State intervention/Welfare State to reduce economic inequalities and increase social justice	*Community Involvement* Active involvement in the community to revitalize civic networks and associations, in part to offset reduced state involvement

> 'Responsibility' is an essential political as well as moral virtue, for it implies (a) care for others; (b) premeditation and calculation about what effect actions are likely to have on others; and (c) understanding and care for the consequences. (QCA, 1998, p. 13)

Many commentators (Giddens, 1998; Oppenheim, 1998) have noted this movement from rights to responsibilities, locating it in the politics of the Third Way and its critique of the neo-liberal, individualistic, utility-maximizing citizen-consumer. Others (Driver and Martell, 1998) have argued that, in this area, there is also a crucial overlap between Third Way thinking and right-wing communitarianism (Etzioni, 1995), both of which argue that many modern social problems, such as high divorce levels or rising crime, are the detritus of social forms based on principles of rights at the expense of duties. Third Way policy rhetoric views this shift from rights to duties as merely a technical corrective manoeuvre within rights discourse, where rights and duties are inextricably linked. In our view, there is a huge conceptual and policy break here: rights discourse views duties arising out of pre-existing rights, which, according to the Universal Declaration of Human Rights, are 'equal and inalienable' and inhere 'in all members of the human family' (Cassese, 1990; Bobbio, 1996). Third Way policy rhetoric talks about responsibilities, obligations and duties and constructs these as the essential building blocks of sociability and social cohesion. The image here is one of society as bound together by multiple and interlocking networks of responsibilities and obligations from which rights arise: Third Way citizens have to demonstrate that they can exercise their rights responsibly.

Equally large shifts are discernible at the level of political citizenship. Marshall's political citizenship celebrated growing democratization as evidenced in the creation of a welfare state committed to social justice for its citizens, as well as the apparently unproblematic inclusiveness of the structures of governance of nation states. The Crick Report (QCA 1998), by contrast, presents a curious paradox: democracy disappears as a unique power resource for citizens, while reappearing as vulnerable, 'our democracy is not secure' (p. 8), as a set of iconic, binary concepts, 'democracy and autocracy' (p. 44), and as taken-for-granted institutions and practices, Britain's parliamentary political and legal systems at local, national, European, Commonwealth and international level (p. 44). The aim of political literacy would appear to be to reconsolidate the democratic nation state whose value and significance remain unnamed but assumed, in the context of growing political apathy, mistrust and loss of legitimacy of traditional political structures.

The term 'literacy' also requires exploration. Literacy is very properly the stuff of education, rendering its location in a text about CE apparently unproblematic. However, one can distinguish between an instrumental literacy, consisting of the ability to decipher and discuss given texts, and a more critical literacy which enables interrogating the legitimacy and value of the texts themselves. There is an interesting tension here in the Crick Report between instrumental literacy which requires that 'democratic institutions, practices and processes must be understood' (p. 40) and a critical literacy which seems to apply to evidence for arguments alone, 'critical approach to evidence put before one' (p. 44). Thus political literacy appears to be primarily instrumental, 'pupils learning about and how to make themselves effective in public life' (p. 41). Alienation and political abstentionism are thus constructed as deficits of knowledge, understanding and skills, rather than as engendered by institutional inadequacies. Given New Labour's high profile constitutional agenda (Welsh and Scottish devolution, the Northern Ireland peace process, reform of the House of Lords, 'modernization' of the monarchy and the integration of the European Convention on Human Rights into the legal system) which has altered, and continues to alter, the institutional landscape of UK politics, Crick's political literacy is surprisingly timid.

There is also a seismic shift in the social form of citizenship. While recognizing the importance of voluntary associations and a mixed economy of welfare, Marshall's social citizenship located moral and political responsibility for welfare and social justice in the nation state. It was social citizenship and the rights of social justice which 'civilized' society. By contrast, the Crick Report locates the argument for community involvement in the changing balance between state provision of welfare and community and individual responsibility. In other words, Marshall's social citizenship as a site for welfare rights disappears and its place is now occupied by the duties of volunteering and community involvement. The Crick Report constructs the Third Way citizen whose individual and civic responsibility enables the Third Way state to provide opportunities rather than services. Here there is a clear link with the

Conservative 'active citizen', a term first used in 1988 by the then Home Secretary, Douglas Hurd, and taken up by Margaret Thatcher to encourage (unpaid) civic involvement in the community, as a way of mitigating the socially and economically devastating effects of individualism and the citizen-consumer (Andrews, 1991; Hall and Jacques, 1989). Crick's orientation to community involvement appears likewise to represent a deflection of state responsibility for welfare onto civil society.

THIRD WAY CITIZENSHIP, SOCIAL CAPITAL AND THE 'EDUCATED CITIZEN'

Although the Crick Report develops a narrative which links its own conceptions to those of Marshall, we believe that its key formulations owe more to current social capital theories than to citizenship rights discourse. In particular, the interrelationships developed in the Crick Report between norms and values, community, networks, civic engagement and democratization constitute a specific reworking of social capital themes.

> Socially and morally responsible behaviour . . . both towards those in authority and towards each other . . . are essential preconditions of citizenship . . . Volunteering and community involvement are necessary conditions of civil society and democracy . . . Freedom and full citizenship in the political arena itself depends on a society with a rich variety of non-political associations and voluntary groups – what some have called civil society. (QCA, 1998, pp. 10, 11)

It is our contention that the Third Way state constructs the social capital of civil society as the engine of economic renewal, while the Crick Report, following de Toqueville, regards it as the source of political renewal. Our analysis of current approaches to social capital identified norms and values, traditional families, communities, social networks and civic engagement as key sources for building social capital (Gamarnikow and Green, 1999a, 1999b). This list bears a strong resemblance to the links developed in the Crick Report between social and moral responsibilities, networks, civic engagement and democratization (Table 9.2).

Current social capital theorizations and the Crick Report also share other key features. These include an almost total absence of concern for structured inequalities, especially economic ones; a misrecognition of the political, social and educational hierarchies embedded in social relationships, networks and associations; and the invisibility of inequalities of power as an issue for social justice. What has disappeared from the social democratic agenda in Marshall when we examine Crick's formulation of citizenship is any notion of citizenship as a struggle for rights in relation to both the state and other structures of power; citizenship as changing relations of power; and citizenship as fundamentally

Table 9.2 Crick's citizenship and social capital

Crick's citizenship	Social capital
Social and moral responsibility	Norms of trust and social reciprocity; sociability and community sanctions
Community involvement	Families, networks and communities as the revitalization of civil society; networks and civic engagement as a means to/education for democratization
Political literacy	*Making Democracy Work* (Putnam, Leonardi and Nanetti, 1993)

compromised by systemic, structured inequalities. Thus Crick's concept of citizenship is ambivalent in relation to the 'empowered citizen'. Instead we have the 'educated citizen' who is decent and responsible; involved and networked in the community; has concepts, values and dispositions appropriate to, and knowledge and understanding of, existing political institutions; and possesses skills and aptitudes to enable effective engagement with the public sphere.

This displacement of economic effects or determinations in society and social justice concerns parallels, paradoxically, the omnipresent construction of the Third Way state as economically impotent in these globalized times. This relocates responsibility for particular dimensions of economic renewal from the state to civil society and its capacity for building social capital, developing social cohesion and revitalizing citizenship: citizens are constructed as those with responsibility for economic prosperity.

None the less, there are some very attractive and engaging rhetorical features in both social capital theories and the Crick Report's concept of citizenship. They reside primarily in the focus on empowerment through participation, civic engagement and democratization, the progressive end of the social capital continuum discussed earlier. These terms tend to occupy key spaces in discourses on democracy and the right to self-determination and autonomy. It is therefore easy to overlook that both social capital theories and the Crick Report's concept of citizenship are built on foundations that can be problematic in a society structured around polarizing differences rather than universality. The proposed consensus is around a moral regime of values, duties and responsibilities, a commitment to the nuclear family and an emphasis on social cohesion and social solidarity in the absence of a commitment to social justice.

These give rise to critical tensions for the Third Way. In the context of globalization and polarizing social inequalities, building social capital and implementing the citizenship model of the Crick Report could contribute to an authoritarian populism, drawing on ideas of an apparently benign communitarianism. Both social capital and citizenship formulations appear to claim that if parents 'ensure that their children ... behave properly' (Home Secretary, 1998, p. 15), if everyone is educated (Secretary of State for Education, 1997), if everyone is networked (Perri 6, 1997), then a strong civil society will ensue and ensure economic prosperity and democratization. Each in its own way articulates with powerful ideologies of social control in nation states which position themselves as having little influence over economic institutions and practices to engage with problems of social justice. Individuals, families and communities become key players who bear the responsibility for their own successes and failures. Social and moral responsibility of citizenship or generalized norms of reciprocity and social trust of social capital become the main ingredients in this recipe for social progress.

These tensions between democratization and authoritarian/communitarian populism also have a bearing on the contradiction between universality and difference in theories of citizenship. As we mentioned previously, one of the key social changes which produced serious challenges to the Marshall model of citizenship was the development of a reflexive society of agency and multiple identities organized around difference. Families, communities, networks and associations constitute the fabric of an autonomous civil society and are the sites for producing identities and differences. It is this late modern pluralism of civil society which creates its strength and vitality, but which is also a challenge to universal citizenship. Third Way citizenship attempts to resolve, in appearance only, this essential ambiguity by drawing on social capital theories. Political and economic structural differences within and between communities are possible in a generalized social and moral order of pre-political responsibility and rhetorically articulated overarching norms and values of generalized reciprocity and social trust. Third Way citizenship relies on providing a universal normative framework of sociability for the exercise of such differences.

CONCLUSION

Can the 'educated' citizen save democracy and promote social inclusion in the UK? Our argument in this chapter points to serious questions that must be addressed if CE is to contribute to accomplishing these aims. Poverty, social exclusion and the education gap discussed in the Introduction are all closely tied to economic inequality. It is an open question whether building social capital, as currently conceived, through CE policy will succeed. We have serious doubts and have attempted to show that the key conceptualizations of social capital, running below the surface of much of the Crick Report, embody dominant cultural and political tendencies to disarticulate the relations between social capital and cultural, economic and symbolic capitals. Moreover, they tend to abstract and treat social capital as an unproblematically egalitarian social glue, rather than as imbued with social inequalities and differential effectiveness (Bourdieu, 1986). This opens up a potentially dangerous space for the deepening of political complacency, absolving the state from responsibility for economic and political regeneration, while locating the socially well-placed as resources with obligations for renewing civil society and its capacity for social capital building. We have referred to this elsewhere as a species of professionalization of *noblesse oblige* (Gamarnikow and Green, 1999a, p. 60). The Crick Report, unlike Marshall's approach, symbolizes the loss of this passion for combating inequalities. It reproduces a version of educated citizenship unlikely to challenge social mechanisms of inequality reproduction. Instead the aim is to regenerate social capital in the hope that a flourishing civil society will bring about social inclusion where, in the words of the Commission on Social Justice (1994, p. 10) 'Communities . . . become rich because they are strong.' The forces for social and economic polarization may well prove to be tougher nuts to crack than is acknowledged by the policy proposals for CE. Such policies set low targets for citizens' social equity expectations and outcomes. These targets are, of course, very likely to be achieved but with precious little benefit to either citizenship or education.

NOTE

1. We have explored these three theorizations of social capital in detail in our earlier work on social capital and the Education Action Zones (Gamarnikow and Green, 1999a, 1999b). Here we limit our discussion to summarizing our main points.

REFERENCES

Acheson, Sir D. (1998) *Independent Inquiry into Inequalities in Health: Report*. London: Stationery Office.
Andrews, G. (1991) *Citizenship*. London: Lawrence and Wishart.
Atkinson, T. (1998) Social exclusion, poverty and unemployment. In A. B. Atkinson and J. Hills (eds) *Exclusion, Employment and Opportunity*. CASE paper 4 London: LSE Centre for the Analysis of Social Exclusion.
Beck, U. (1992) *Risk Society: Towards a New Modernity*. London: Sage.
Bentley, T. (1998) *Learning Beyond the Classroom: Education for a Changing World*. London: Routledge.
Blair, T. (1997) *Bringing Britain Together*. Speech by the Prime Minister, The Right Honourable Tony Blair MP, for the Social Exclusion Unit Launch. London: SEU.
Blair, T. (1998) *The Third Way: New Politics for the New Century*. Fabian Pamphlet 588.

London: Fabian Society.

Bobbio, N. (1996) *The Age of Rights*. Cambridge: Polity Press.

Bourdieu, P. (1986) The forms of capital. In J. G. Richardson (ed.) *Handbook of Theory and Research for the Sociology of Education*. New York: Greenwood Press.

Cassese, A. (1990) *Human Rights in a Changing World*. Cambridge: Polity Press.

Centre for Contemporary Cultural Studies (1981) *Unpopular Education: Schooling and Social Democracy in England since 1944*. London: Hutchinson.

Coleman, J. S. (1988) Social capital in the creation of human capital. *American Journal of Sociology*, **94** (Suppl. 95): S95–S120.

Coleman, J. S. (1990) *Foundations of Social Theory*. Cambridge, MA: Harvard University Press.

Commission on Social Justice (1994) *Social Justice: Strategies for National Renewal*. London: Vintage Books.

Driver, S. and Martell, L. (1998) *New Labour: Politics after Thatcherism*. Cambridge: Polity Press.

Etzioni, A. (1995) *The Spirit of Community*. London: Fontana Press.

Foley, M. W. and Edwards, B. (1997) Editors' Introduction: escape from politics? Social theory and the social capital debate. *American Behavioral Scientist*, **40** (5): March/April: 550–61.

Fukuyama, F. (1995) *Trust: The Social Virtues and the Creation of Prosperity*. London: Hamish Hamilton.

Furstenberg Jr, F. F. and Hughes, M. E. (1995) Social capital and successful development among at-risk youth. *Journal of Marriage and the Family*, **57**: 580–92.

Gamarnikow, E. and Green, A. (1999a) Developing social capital: dilemmas, possibilities and limitations in education. In A. Hayton (ed.) *Tackling Disaffection and Social Exclusion: Issues for Education Policy*. London: Kogan Page.

Gamarnikow, E. and Green, A (1999b) The Third Way and social capital: Education Action Zones and a new agenda for education, parents and community? *International Studies in Sociology of Education*, **9** (1): 3–22.

Giddens, A. (1998) *The Third Way: The Renewal of Social Democracy*. Cambridge: Polity Press.

Giddens, A. (1999) The way beyond. *LSE Magazine*, **11** (1) Summer: 16–17.

Gillborn, D. (1999) Fifty years of failure: 'race' and education policy in Britain. In A. Hayton (ed.) *Tackling Disaffection and Social Exclusion: Issues for Education Policy*. London: Kogan Page.

Hall, P. A. (1997) Social capital: a fragile asset. In Demos *The Wealth and Poverty of Networks*. Demos Collection issue 12. London: Demos.

Hall, S. and Held, D. (1989) Citizens and citizenship. In S. Hall and M. Jacques (eds) *New Times: The Changing Face of Politics in the 1990s*. London: Lawrence and Wishart.

Hall, S. and Jacques, M. (eds) (1989) *New Times: The Changing Face of Politics in the 1990s*. London: Lawrence and Wishart.

Hayton, A. (ed.) (1999) *Tackling Disaffection and Social Exclusion: Issues for Education Policy*. London: Kogan Page.

HM Treasury (1999) *Modernisation of Britain's Tax and Benefit System: Tackling Poverty and Extending Opportunity*. London: Treasury.

Hodgson, A. and Spours, K. (1999) *New Labour's Educational Agenda: Issues and Policies for Education and Training from 14+*. London: Kogan Page.

Home Secretary (1998) *Supporting Families: A Consultation Document*. London: Stationery Office.

Layton-Henry, Z. (1992) *The Politics of Immigration*. Oxford: Blackwell.

Leonardi, R. (1995) Regional development in Italy: social capital and the Mezzogiorno.

Oxford Review of Economic Policy, **11** (2): 165–79.

Lister, R. (1997) Citizenship: towards a feminist synthesis. *Feminist Review* (57), Autumn: 28–48.

Macpherson, Sir W. (1999) *The Stephen Lawrence Inquiry – Report*. CM 4262–I. London: Stationery Office.

Marshall, T. H. (1950) In T. Bottomore (1992) *Citizenship and Social Class*. London: Pluto Press (originally published 1950).

Modood, T., Berthod, R., Lakey, J., Smith, P., Virdee, S. and Beishon, S. (1997) *Ethnic Minorities in Britain: Diversity and Disadvantage*. London: Policy Studies Institute.

Mortimore, P. and Whitty, G. (1999) School improvement: a remedy for social exclusion? In A. Hayton (ed.) *Tackling Disaffection and Social Exclusion: Issues for Education Policy*. London: Kogan Page.

Office for Standards in Education (OFSTED) (1998) *Secondary Education 1993–97: A Review of Secondary Schools in England*. London: Stationery Office.

Oppenheim, C. (ed.) (1998) *An Inclusive Society: Strategies for Tackling Poverty*. London: Institute of Public Policy Research.

Oppenheim, C. and Harker, L. (1996) *Poverty: The Facts* (3rd edn). London: Child Poverty Action Group.

Pateman, C. (1988) *The Sexual Contract*. Cambridge: Polity Press.

Perri 6 (1997) *Escaping Poverty: From Safety Nets to Networks of Opportunity*. London: Demos.

Portes, A. (1998) Social capital: its origins and applications in modern sociology. *Annual Review of Sociology*, **24**: 1–24, http://social. annualreviews.org/c.

Putnam, R. D. with Leonardi, R. and Nanetti, R. (1993) *Making Democracy Work: Civic Traditions in Modern Italy*. Princeton, NJ: Princeton University Press.

QCA (1998) *Education for Citizenship and the Teaching of Democracy in Schools*, Final Report of the Advisory Group on Citizenship (Crick Report). London: QCA.

QCA (1999) *The Review of the National Curriculum in England: The Secretary of State's Proposals*. London: QCA.

Roberts, H. and Sachdev, D. (eds) (1996) *Young People's Social Attitudes: The Views of 12–19 Year Olds*. Ilford: Barnardos.

Rubio, M. (1997) Perverse social capital: some evidence from Colombia. *Journal of Economic Issues*, **31** (3) September: 805–16.

Secretary of State for Education (1997) *Excellence in Schools*. Cm 3681. London: Department for Education and Employment.

Social and Community Planning Research (1997) *British Social Attitudes*, the Thirteenth Report. London: SCPR.

Social Exclusion Unit (1997) *Social Exclusion Unit: Purpose, Work Priorities and Working Methods*. London: SEU.

Social Exclusion Unit (1998a) *Truancy and School Exclusion*. Cm 3957. London: Stationery Office.

Social Exclusion Unit (1998b) *Bringing Britain Together: A National Strategy for Neighbourhood Renewal*. Cm 4045. London: Stationery Office.

Solomos, J. (1993) *Race and Racism in Contemporary Britain* (2nd edn). Basingstoke: Macmillan.

Teachman, J. D., Paasch, K. and Carver, K. (1996) Social capital and dropping out of school early. *Journal of Marriage and the Family*, **58**: 773–83.

Wadsworth, M. (1996) Family and education as determinants of health. In D. Blane, E. Brunner and R. Wilkinson (eds) *Health and Social Organisation: Towards a Health Policy for the 21st Century*. London: Routledge.

Walby, S. (1997) Is citizenship gendered? In *Gender Transformations*. London: Routledge.

Whitty, G., Aggleton, P., Gamarnikow, E. and Tyrer, P. (1998) Education and health inequalities: Input Paper 10 to the Independent Inquiry into Inequalities in Health, January 1998. *Journal of Education Policy*, **13** (5): 641–52.

Whitty, G., Power, S., Gamarnikow, E., Aggleton, P., Tyrer, P. and Youdell, D. (1999) Health, housing and education: tackling multiple disadvantage. In A. Hayton (ed.) *Tackling Disaffection and Social Exclusion: Issues for Education Policy*. London: Kogan Page.

Wilkinson, H. and Mulgan, G. (1995) *Freedom's Children: Work, Relationships and Politics for 18–34 Year Olds in Britain Today*. London: Demos.

Willms, J. D. (1997) *Quality and Inequality in Children's Literacy: The Effects of Families, Schools and Communities*. Mimeo, Faculty of Education, University of New Brunswick.

Chapter 10

Citizenship in Theory and Practice: Being or Becoming Citizens with Rights

Priscilla Alderson

INTRODUCTION

The growing interest in citizenship education is linked in this chapter to the UN Convention on the Rights of the Child – CRC – (UN, 1989). The CRC is briefly described, followed by a note about connections between democracy, rights and citizenship, and a review of the related literature. British students' views about their rights in schools were researched through a national survey, and the survey methods, its links to the CRC and some of the age-related findings are summarized. Reported disaffection about several aspects of school life increased with age.

Two contrasting ways of interpreting the survey findings are discussed, one based on child and adolescent development theories, the other drawn from newer ideas about children as competent moral agents. Ambiguities between whether children are present, or only future, citizens are further considered in relation to the Qualifications and Curriculum Authority's (QCA's) assumptions that skill and knowledge develop through distinctive age-linked stages, with explicit and implicit theories of children as not yet competent citizens. These assumptions support pedagogic trends in schools which split the theory from the practice of citizenship, seeing citizenship as a set of ideas which adults instruct children about, not as relationships which children already experience in schools. The trends lead on to more abstracted and evasive approaches to teaching citizenship, and these may alienate young people when schools do not practise the respect for rights which they preach. In contrast, the minority of democratic schools show the importance of practical citizenship education which honours the CRC rights. If they are to adopt these standards, staff and students have to engage in critical reconsideration of common assumptions about childhood, education and rights.

THE 1989 UN CONVENTION ON THE RIGHTS OF THE CHILD – CRC

The CRC has been ratified by every nation except two, and is therefore by far the most widely agreed international human rights treaty. A Convention is stronger than a Declaration and, in ratifying the CRC in 1991, the British government undertook to implement it in law, policy and practice. The CRC covers three partly overlapping kinds of rights: *provision* rights such as to education or health care; *protection* rights from neglect, abuse or discrimination; and, an innovation for official children's rights, *participation or civil* rights which adults who live in democracies can take for granted.

The CRC repeatedly qualifies children's rights, for example, when 'the best interests of the child shall be a primary consideration' (Articles 1, 3, 21). Rights are affected by the 'evolving capacities of the child', the 'responsibilities, rights and duties of parents' (Art. 5) and the national law (Art. 31). Rights cannot be exercised in ways which would harm the child or other people and right holders must 'respect the rights and reputations of others', as well as 'national security and public order, health and morals' (Art. 13). The CRC sees rights not as endorsing selfish individualism, but as increasing mutual respect for everyone's equal claim, dignity and worth; rights are collective concepts. The CRC includes aspirational rights to further children's interests, and to promote 'social progress and better standards of life in larger freedom, in the spirit of peace, dignity, tolerance, freedom, equality and solidarity' (Preamble).

Governments undertake to report regularly to the UN Committee on the Rights of the Child on their progress in implementing the CRC which is a tool for raising standards for all children. Before the UK's first report to the UN in 1995, a long, very critical report was published of the UK government's general lack of progress (Lansdown and Newell, 1994). Later, the UN Committee published its concerns that the UK government should establish a legal right for children to be heard before school exclusion, and should introduce procedures 'to ensure that children are provided with the opportunity to express their views on matters of concern to them in the running of the schools ... The training curricula of teachers should incorporate education about the Convention on the Rights of the Child. It is recommended that teaching methods should be inspired by and reflect the spirit and philosophy of the Convention and the provisions of its article 29' (UN, 1995).

The CRC is an ideal basis for citizenship education but, although ratification involves governments undertaking actively to inform 'adults and children alike' about the CRC (Art. 42), the CRC is little known in the UK. In the British survey described later, over 75 per cent of the pupils said they had not heard about the CRC, and only 5 per cent had heard more than 'a bit about it'.

EDUCATION AND RIGHTS

After a note about links between democracy, rights and citizenship, this section reviews some of the relevant education literature. A democratic community is broadly understood, in this chapter, as a community where citizens have agreed rights which they understand and can rightfully claim to enjoy. Examples include a free press, freedom from assault, from arbitrary arrest or from attacks on their honour and reputation, and the right to express a view in matters which affect them. Democracy means that the citizens value and respect one another's rights, and the authorities actively defend these rights. Rights are central to concepts of citizenship and democracy in clarifying the standards which the citizens agree to share. The place of these democratic rights in schools is discussed later.

A typical example of the approach to rights among professionals and policy-makers in education is the Commonwealth Teachers' Report (NUT, 1997) on Education and Human Rights. The report mentions only provision and protection rights for children in its eight sections. In marked contrast, Section 4 speaks of teachers' rights, with 'every other citizen', to vote, contest elections, join political organizations and trade unions, speak and write on political issues and be free from victimization. Teachers (but not students) 'should be involved through consultation and negotiation in forming educational policies at every level' (NUT, 1997). Academics in psychology, philosophy and law tend similarly to be sceptical or cautious about children's participation rights (for example, Eekelaar, 1986; Buchanan and Brock, 1989). In contrast, writers who view education from a rights perspective are more critical about schools which deny rights (Freeman, 1983; Newell, 1989; Lansdown and Newell, 1994; Franklin, 1995; Jeffs, 1995; John, 1996; Hammarberg, 1997; Trafford, 1997; Verhellen, 1997; PEG, 1998; Alderson and Goodey, 1998; Cockburn, 1998; Griffith, 1998; Hannam, 1998). Little research has been conducted about young people's views of their rights, how they define and regard them, and how practical or relevant they consider that concepts of rights are in their daily lives. Hart *et al.* (1997) conducted repeated international surveys, although they use a developmental age-based framework which raises problems discussed later.

An important recent example of official policy is Education for Citizenship (QCA, 1998). The Report acknowledges:

> increasing recognition that the ethos, organisation, structures and daily practices of schools including whole school activities and assemblies have a significant impact on the effectiveness of citizenship education. Through such climate and practices schools provide implicit and explicit messages which can have a considerable influence, both positive and negative, on pupils' learning and development. Schools need to consider how far their ethos, organisation and daily practices are consistent with the aim and purpose of citizenship education and affirm and extend the development of pupils into active citizens. In particular, schools should make every effort to engage pupils in discussion and consultation about all aspects of school life

on which pupils might reasonably be expected to have a view, and whenever possible to give pupils responsibility and experience in helping to run parts of the school. This might include school facilities, organisation, rules, relationships and matters relating to teaching and learning. Such engagement can be through both formal structures such as school and class councils and informal channels in pupils' daily encounters with aspects of school life. To create a feeling that it is 'our school' can increase pupils' motivation to learn in all subjects. (QCA, 1998, pp. 36,57)

However, this clear linking of formal and informal education is not mentioned in the Report's detailed curriculum proposals (pp. 39–55); neither are school councils mentioned there, nor the possibility that students might apply to their schooling their prescribed citizenship education skills to argue and criticize, to recognize forms of manipulation and influence social, moral and political challenges and situations (p. 44). The Report does not mention what staff should do if this happens. Involving pupils in helping 'to run parts of the school' such as making rules may mean little more than complying with teachers' instructions. Then, teachers who believe that students have had a real chance to set the rules might blame them more severely if they default on standards they are supposed to 'own'. Some common rules are 'do not run, keep hands and feet to yourself, always obey members of staff'. Yet 'be kind to everyone' and 'do not throw the books' sound more authentically set by pupils (Cleves School, 1999).

The QCA Report often refers, appropriately, to responsibilities, but very seldom to rights. The first mention of rights comes in a quotation from the National Youth Council which is in contrast to much of the Report that has no young members among the authors. The right to be heard and to freedom of expression are mentioned twice, but they are not strongly stated as articles in the CRC which the government has promised to implement. The CRC is simply mentioned twice, whereas it could have been the basis and justification of much of the Report.

THE SURVEY OF SCHOOL STUDENTS' VIEWS ABOUT RIGHTS

Plans for citizenship education can be improved by knowledge about pupils' views of the relevant topics such as civil rights in two main ways. First, planners and teachers have better understanding of where instruction can begin when they have some idea of pupils' current knowledge. Second, theory and practice are inseparable in such practical matters as citizenship which weave through curricular and extra- curricular schooling, so that teachers also need to know about pupils' attitudes, experiences, values and expectations, if the learning about citizenship is to be authentic, relevant and valued by all concerned. This section outlines the methods of a survey of British school pupils' views about their civil rights in schools, conducted in 1997–1998.

The research developed through multidisciplinary meetings of the Education

Group at the Children's Rights Office in the mid–1990s. The survey began by contacting every local education authority and scanning schools listed on the Internet to compile a purposive sample of 250 schools; primary school deputy heads and secondary school personal education teachers were invited to take part in the survey. Only 58 teachers replied to the single-sheet teachers' survey, and only 49 agreed to conduct the pupils' survey, which yielded 2272 completed questionnaires. The low response rate, less than one-fifth, may reflect how pressured teachers feel or, possibly, their lack of interest in children's rights. Some teachers told us they would like to take part but their head teacher had refused permission. However, the 49 schools provided a wide-ranging sample, including primary, middle and secondary schools, comprehensive, selective and special, local authority, grant-maintained and private, mixed and single sex, secular and religious, and schools in cities, towns and semi- rural areas with pupils from a range of socio-economic and ethnic backgrounds, across the UK.

Questionnaire booklets and explanation sheets were designed to make taking part in the survey as easy and enjoyable as possible. Two main aims in the 24-page booklet questionnaire were to give out information about the 1989 UN CRC to schools, and to collect evidence about young people's views about rights in the CRC, and how these are respected in British schools. A shiny green cover, for each student to detach and keep, briefly explained the CRC and the research. The survey concentrated on the CRC's civil rights, the most abstract type of rights, which were paraphrased on the survey booklet cover as the rights:

> to respect for your worth and dignity (Preamble, 3, 12, 13, 14,15, 16, 17);
>
> to express yourself and to develop your skills and talents fully (6, 13, 23, 27, 28, 29, 31);
>
> to be heard and to have your views taken seriously in matters which affect you (12);
>
> to share in making decisions about your life (12);
>
> to have all kinds of useful information and ideas (13, 17);
>
> to freedom of thought, conscience and religion (14);
>
> to learn to live in peace, tolerance, equality and friendship (29);
>
> to privacy and respect and to fair discipline (2, 16, 19, 37, 39, 40);
>
> to work together for rights and to see that these are shared fairly in your school. (2, 3, 4, 12, 13, 14, 15, 19, 27, 28, 29, 31, 39, 40, 42).

(The relevant article numbers of the CRC added here were not on the survey cover.)

These headings were broken down into many daily details of school life, in order to show the breadth, richness and practical relevance of the CRC in schools, and to gather informed views from students on matters of direct interest to them. There were questions, for example, on which activities pupils enjoy when developing their skills and talents, or their views on the right to express religious beliefs by wearing a turban or scarf. Not all the topics are reported in this chapter. The questions were designed to be independent of pupils' knowledge (if any) of the CRC. The returns were analysed by spss.pc computer package. A single questionnaire for all age groups worked well, with the youngest group being most likely to say that the questionnaire was interesting or very interesting, 88 per cent, with 84 per cent of the middle group and 80 per cent of the eldest ones.

The survey included visits to schools for 34 group discussions, each with six pupils, usually lasting half an hour, and a few illustrative comments from the groups will be given later. Linked and more intensive research, before and during the survey project, in certain other schools was valuable in designing and piloting the survey, and interpreting the replies through detailed knowledge of actual practices in schools (Highfield, 1997; Alderson and Goodey, 1998; Cleves, 1999). In 1997, a short report was sent to every school as a wall display, showing some of the school's own results compared with the overall results, with some teaching materials about the CRC.

EXAMPLES OF AGE-RELATED RESPONSES TO THE SURVEY

This section shows replies to some of the questions, set out in graphs linked to the relevant survey questions. Most of the questions were closed, and pupils were asked to ring their selected reply, usually including 'yes', 'no', 'not sure', 'it varies', in order to avoid forcing people to give definite replies when they felt ambiguous. For clarity, most of the figures in this chapter show only the 'yes' replies. The data are analysed here by age groups: 7–10, 11–13, 14–17 years. Figure 10.1 shows the numbers of students in each age group. On 'the right to develop your skills and talents', the survey asked students to ring 'as many of these thing as you enjoy doing in or out of school' and offered 11 options. Figure 10.2 indicates that reported enjoyment falls with age, although the more skilful students become, the more they might be expected to enjoy creative activities. The same decline with age in reported satisfaction is shown in: views on the fairness of school rules about appearance (question 3) (Britain and Malta are the only European countries to have school uniform); school assemblies (question 4) (Figure 10.3); trusting 'your teachers to keep a secret if you tell them' (question 5); confidence in teachers being 'fair when they talk about their pupils' (question 6); confidence in fair discipline that teachers will listen to students before deciding who is at fault (question 7) and that sometimes they punish the whole class when a few people do something wrong (question 8); having 'somewhere safe to keep your things' (question 9) (Figure 10.4); and having adults to help at break times if needed (question 10) (Figure 10.5).

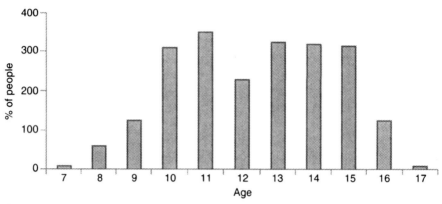

Figure 10.1 The age range

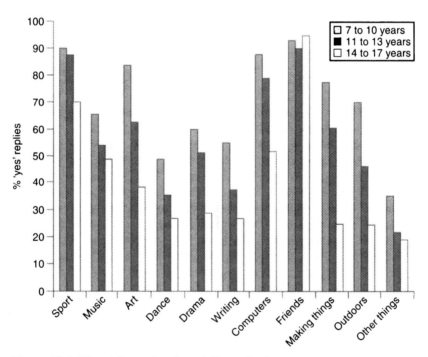

Figure 10.2 The right to develop skills and talents

Question 2. The right to develop skills and talents: Please ring as many of these things as you enjoy doing in your school

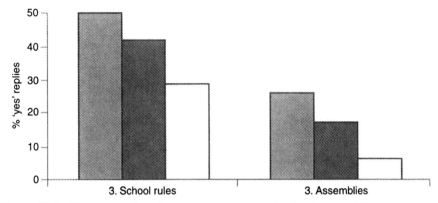

Figure 10.3 Views on rules about appearance and school assemblies

Question 3. What do you think about your school's rules about what you can wear and how you can look?

Question 4. Do you like school assemblies?

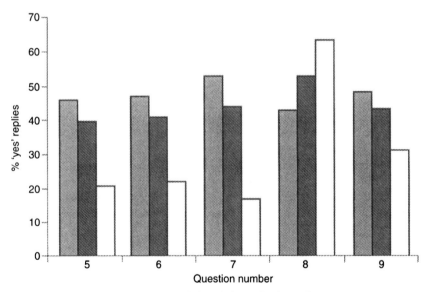

Figure 10.4 Privacy, respect and the right to be heard

Question 5. The right to privacy: If you write or say anything, which you want to be kept private, people should keep your secret, unless they think someone might get hurt. Do you trust your teachers to keep a secret if you tell them?

Question 6. The right to justice and respect: Do you think your teachers are careful to be fair when they talk about their pupils?

Question 7. The right to be heard: If they think someone might have done something wrong, do the teachers listen to that person's view, before they decide whose fault it was?

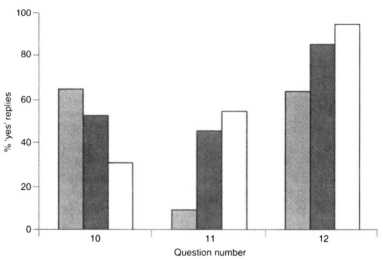

Figure 10.5 Break times

Question 10. At lunch times, are the adults ready to help anyone who needs them?
Question 11. Can you choose whether you stay inside or go out during break times?
Question 12. Do you think you should be allowed to choose whether you stay inside or go out during break times?

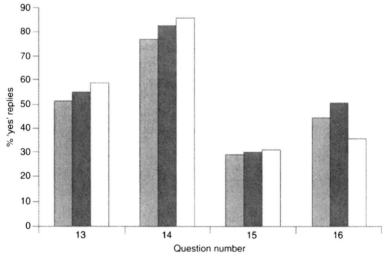

Figure 10.6 Freedom and discipline

Question 13. Do you think girls and boys should be able to choose if they go to assemblies?
Question 14. Do you think you and your friends should be allowed to arrange meetings in school, such as to have a music group or plan an outing?
Question 15. Can boys and girls arrange meetings in your school?
Question 16. Do you think there is the right amount of discipline to keep your school running well?

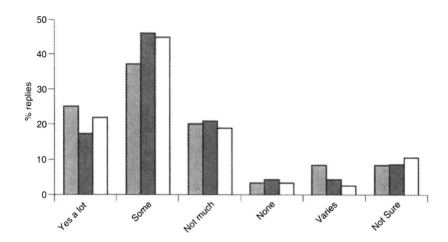

Figure 10.7 Is there any bullying at your school?

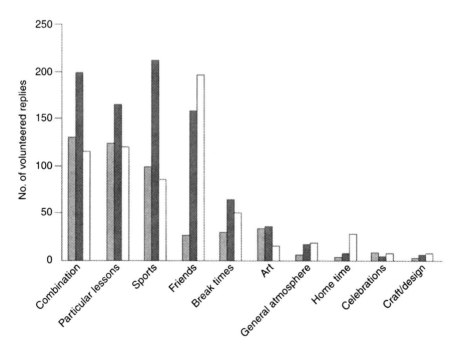

Figure 10.8 What do you enjoy most at school? (question 18)

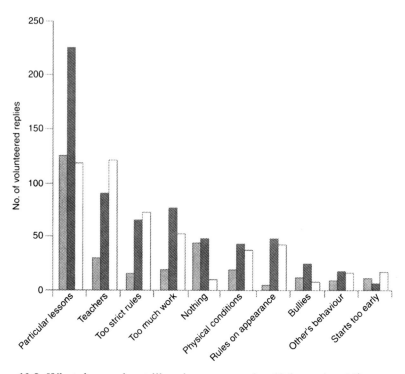

Figure 10.9 What do you least like about your school? (question 19)

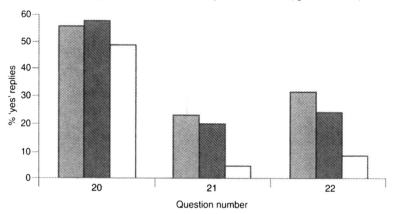

Figure 10.10 Positive replies to questions 20 to 22

Question 20. Working together for rights and how these are shared in your school: Does your school have a council, where pupils and teachers meet to decide about things that happen in the school?

Question 21. Is the council good at sorting out problems? % replies from 55%

Question 22. Does the council help to make the school a better place to be in? %replies from 55%

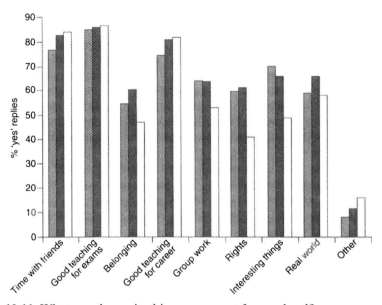

Figure 10.11 What are the main things you want from school?

Question 23. What are the main things you want from school? (please ring all the things that matter most to you): time to be with friends; good teaching to help me to pass tests and exams; the feeling that I belong to my class or to the school; good teaching to help me to get into the job/career I will want to do; learning to be part of a group and to get on with other people; learning about my rights; getting ideas about interesting new things I could try; learning about the real world, such as that I might be unemployed; other main things (please describe).

Figure 10.5 also shows marked discrepancies in all age groups between students being allowed to choose (question 11), and wanting to choose (question 12), whether to 'stay inside or go out during break times'. A majority in all groups thought they should be allowed to choose whether to attend assemblies (question 13), and to hold peaceful meetings (question 14), whereas only a minority said they were allowed to do so (questions 15, 16) (Figure 10.6). Only 16 per cent of all respondents said they 'liked assemblies'. An example of how even the youngest ones thought they should have more freedom was given by 8-year-olds who believed that, when their tradition of going out of school into their safe estate at break times was stopped, the corner shop which benefited the whole community closed for lack of their trade. The middle group was most likely to think 'there is the right amount of discipline to keep the school running well' and was least likely to say there is 'a lot of bullying' is response to a closed question (Figure 10.7).

The booklet asked open questions about what students most enjoy and least enjoy at school, and their top ten most frequently volunteered replies are shown in Figures 10.8 and 10.9. Named lessons and sports were most popular, with friends (top for the oldest group) and break times. The replies show rising ratings with age for friends and home time as most enjoyed aspects of school. Among the main dislikes (Figure 10.9), bullying came seventh for the youngest ones, eighth for the middle group and tenth for the oldest group. This sets bullying in context. It is very serious for many students, but not among the main problems for the majority. Whereas the ten most liked items involved teachers (combination, named lessons) and peers, the top five specific dislikes all involved teachers – named lessons, teachers, rules and conditions for which adults are responsible. To dislike 'nothing' was the second most common reply from the youngest ones and the second least common reply in the top ten from the oldest ones.

To achieve the aim of involving a wide age and ability range among respondents, the questions were very simply and clearly worded. So, for example, although school councils vary widely, the types of council could not be overly defined because this could confuse the readers and complicate the responses. The question simply asked 'Does your school have a council where pupils and teachers meet to decide about things that happen in the school?' This may have excluded schools with pupil-only councils, but these are unlikely to be effective when the staff are not involved. It may also have excluded councils which the students thought did not make decisions. Figure 10.10 shows that around half of the students said they had a council, and that the youngest group gave the clearest views on whether their council was either 'good at sorting out problems' or not. The oldest group was by far the least likely to say that their council sorted problems (5 per cent) or made 'the school a better place to be in' (9 per cent). The most critical students may have held unfairly negative views about their rights in schools. Yet, in practice, their perceptions matter more than what other observers might believe is 'really going on' in the schools, because their perceptions are likely strongly to influence and be influenced by their interest and enthusiasm for their school work, their ambitions and their relationships with staff and peers.

The survey asked 'what are the main things you want from your school?' and offered eight options, for people to ring as many as they liked (Figure 10.11). The order of priorities was almost the same across the age groups, except that the middle and older groups were more likely to say 'learning about the real world', and slightly less likely to say 'learning about my rights'. One important aspect of the replies is the balance between academic and social concerns, between good teaching and passing exams with time to be with friends (second for all groups). The next section reviews the survey findings in relation to two contrasting views of children, education and citizenship.

INTERPRETING THE SURVEY REPLIES: TWO CONTRASTING VIEWS

The survey replies raise urgent questions about why reported disaffection increases for older students. Visits during the survey to meet expert primary school council members (Highfield, 1997) and confident children discussing non-discrimination (Cleves School, 1999), and to talk with friendly lively groups of children and teenagers, as well as my research about competent, wise children aged 0 to 8 years (Alderson, 2000), all provide a stark contrast with the discouraging age group comparisons in the survey replies. How might experienced older students offer much more to their schools, if the promising work in some primary schools could be continued in many more secondary schools? And how much potential is being wasted?

Two possible ways of interpreting the survey responses have been expressed by adults at conferences where the survey has been reported. Their responses align with the markedly contrasting approaches to childhood also found in the education and research literature. The first way accepts the results as unsurprising, even predictable, and criticizes teenagers with resignation, hostility or derision: 'adolescents are like that, what else can you expect?' This response, like racism, picks a biological feature, in this case age, and uses it to attribute many assumed characteristics to teenagers. Such explanations are offered as 'puberty', or the 'crisis' of adolescence, or theories of 'slowly maturing cognitive and moral development'. It is assumed that young people are the problem and adults provide the solution. The report *Wasted Youth* (Pearce and Hillman, 1998) illustrates such victim blaming, as do current efforts to return truants to school which do not also consider how schools must improve if young people's wish to stay away, sometimes in self-defence, is to be addressed. This first view, and its arguments against children's rights, are summarized in column 1 of Table 10.1.

The alternative approach in column 2 sees no single explanation for disaffection. Problems are not seen as intrinsic to youth, but as constructed through relationships, which are shaped by expectations about young people. Adults' high or low expectations can become self-fulfilling; teenagers' rising expectations about how independent and responsible they could be lead to satisfaction or frustration, depending on how much they are trusted and respected. Besides expectations, many contingent factors inside and outside school are also seen as relevant. Similar schools with contrasting policies illustrate this, when one school excludes many students and another none. A climate of mistrust, injustice and the lack of safe personal space reported in the survey do not help. Schools are inevitably political communities where interest groups negotiate the sharing of power and resources, and there are varying degrees of democratic consultation, accountability and respect for everyone's rights.

The approach in column 2 of Table 10.1 recognizes that young children can be competent people with many underappreciated abilities which expand and deepen but do not necessarily change in essence over the years. Their work is accepted as valid and not simply practising (Morrow, 1994). This second approach supports mutual respect and trust between people of any age, as moral agents, who share strengths and weaknesses, who teach and learn, and value one

Table 10.1 Alternative views of citizenship education, democracy, morality and rights

View 1. *'Children' means people up to 19 years*	View 2. *'Children' means people aged up to 11, and implies here that teenagers are as able or more so than children*
Children are ignorant and need to be told about morality and democracy by adults	From their first years, children actively experience and discuss care and justice
The curriculum is 'delivered' by active adults to relatively passive children, a mainly one-way process	Teaching and learning are two-way interactions; children have much to offer to adults and to one another
Children cannot do real work, they practise and develop skills	Children do real work, at home, at school and often for their neighbours and communities
Children learn to contribute to their community outside school by doing voluntary work	Children's immeasurable contributions are undervalued and unpaid (Morrow, 1994), including school work on which society's future depends. Schools are part of the community, and are political communities
Children cannot be really responsible; they need care and examples set by responsible adults	Many young children are responsible, and learn to be more so through being trusted. Adults are sometimes irresponsible. Adults and children care for and set examples for one another
Children must be protected from themselves and others, by firm adult control	Adult control too easily becomes unjust coercion if adults do not have to justify and account for their behaviour
When rights conflict with responsibilities, allowing rights to children undermines their moral education	The CRC rights involve responsibilities. Respecting children's rights and responsibilities is an integral part of moral education; and disregarding them undermines schools' morality and discipline
If rights accompany responsibilities, children cannot be rights holders because, cognitively and emotionally, they cannot yet be responsible. One cannot have power without responsibility	People cannot be responsible without having some power

Table 10.1 *contd*

View 1. *'Children' means people up to 19 years*	View 2. *'Children' means people aged up to 11, and implies here that teenagers are as able or more so than children*
Children's rights cannot, therefore, be respected in schools	Practical, mutual respect for children's and adults' rights is noticeable in well-run schools, such as ones which avoid exclusions
Rights and citizenship must be taught as responsibilities which children will have when they become adults	Unless children's rights are respected, contradictions between what schools preach and practise about democracy and citizenship exacerbate students' resistance and disaffection

another's energy and ideas, using them together creatively. The approach acknowledges that power is easily abused, especially by people in authority who are not accountable to those they control, if complacence turns into arrogant dismissal of any questioning of authority. The point of democracy, therefore, is to have agreed rules to help to prevent this. School rules are too often set solely to protect pupils from one another. In the survey, problems are reported which are more often caused by adults than by pupils. If schools rules are fair, they apply equally to everyone, children and adults: rules of politeness, punctuality, respectful listening and aiming for high standards of work and working conditions.

CHILD DEVELOPMENT AND CITIZENSHIP

Developmental beliefs of a gradual ascent towards adult citizenship, as in column 1, (Table 10.1) explicitly or implicitly discourage adults from regarding children as citizens now, as in column 2. The QCA Report (1998), reviewed above, wavers between the two columns in Table 10.1, unclear whether education is 'for (future) citizenship' or 'of (active) citizens', and whether pupils in schools consume a 'delivered' curriculum or contribute to reciprocal learning and democratic activities. 'Learning by doing' is occasionally mentioned, through 'voluntary work in the community', but activities in school seem not to be regarded as 'work' or active citizenship.

The QCA Report assumes that pupils develop through each key stage to increasingly complicated knowledge, values, skills and aptitudes (QCA, 1998, pp. 44–52), in a prescribed 'comprehensive and sequential citizenship teaching . . . advice' (p. 54). One flaw in this assumption is that, in order to demonstrate gradual progress in assessable steps, curricula are often set at too low levels. Despite noting that junior school children competently help to run school councils and a commercial community newspaper (QCA, 1998, p. 37), the Report recommends teaching skills at Key Stage 4 (14–16 years), such as understanding the terms 'interdependence' and 'peace making' (p. 52), which 3-year-old children demonstrate (Miller, 1996). One way to make children appear to be incompetent and in need of these small, testable steps of teaching is to make topics abstract and remote (Donaldson, 1978; Gardner, 1993), as described with rights teaching later. A second flaw in the ascending curriculum is that its basis, developmental psychology, has been thoroughly discredited in its theories (Morss, 1990; Bradley, 1989; Burman, 1994), its scientific research basis (Donaldson, 1978; Siegal, 1997) and its remoteness from children's everyday lives (James and Prout, 1990; Mayall, 1994; Gardner, 1993; Hutchby and Moran-Ellis, 1995; Miller, 1996, Edwards *et al.*, 1998; Alderson, 2000). A third problem with the notions of developing children and developed adults is that they implicitly deny that adults too have to keep refining their citizenship skills of critical self-knowledge, empathy, tolerance and open-mindedness.

Rights are often contrasted with responsibilities. Yet civil rights concern taking on personal and shared responsibility and decision-making, being trusted, helping and respecting one another. To claim the right to express one's own view also claims respect for everyone's equal right to do so. Do pupils want to claim rights? Only 35 per cent of the youngest group said yes, they had 'enough rights' at school, with 37 per cent of 11–13-year-olds, and 21 per cent of 14–16-year-olds. It is often argued that rights can only be granted to groups which struggle for them, and that children do not. Yet many women did not actively campaign for the women's rights which are now generally accepted, and children do campaign to get their rights acknowledged, such as through the groups Article 12, or PEG. Many children and teenagers protest, resist oppressions and say they long to be listened to, respected and involved in decisions affecting them. They are trapped into compliant dependence if their reasonable protests are ignored, or if they try stronger resistance, they are seen as immature, volatile, irresponsible and in need of firmer adult control.

All the groups in the schools talked about wanting to be heard more, to be trusted and respected, not so much to make demands as to contribute ideas and helpful suggestions (and see also Cullingford, 1992; Save the Children, 1999). The groups discussed contradictions that arise when students are taught about democracy, the free press and fair judiciary, in schools with no forum for listening to individual and majority views, or with a rigidly controlled newsletter, or where students cannot appeal about punishments. In contrast, in more democratic schools, at assemblies everyone can enjoy being a contributing citizen-member of a worthwhile community where they are all valued, they celebrate achievements and honour shared values (Highfield, 1997; Cleves, 1999).

TEACHING ABOUT RIGHTS

Some teachers in the survey schools were keen that their school should practise as well as preach democracy and made great efforts with the students for this to happen. Some were frustrated that senior staff prevented them from doing so. Others seemed unaware of contradictions between their words and behaviour. Taking rights and mutual respect seriously appears to happen in a minority of British schools. 'Materials which invite young people to examine critically their own education are very rare' (Osler, 1995). 'Exposure to one's rights, and skills in challenging discrimination are not in the forefront of reasons for increased government expenditure on education . . . It is difficult to reconcile the screening function of schooling with an acceptance of universal rights' (Davies, 1994).

Teachers can avoid addressing democracy and respect for rights in the classroom in several ways. As already mentioned, some teach education for adult citizenship, not of young citizens, as future duties, systems and remote knowledge. They concentrate on the 1948 Universal Declaration of Human Rights, in which the inherent dignity and worth of the human person, the fundamental freedoms and equal and inalienable rights of all members of the human family, the freedom of speech and freedom from fear which is the highest aspiration of the common people, and the 'everyone' in the Declaration who can work and vote, does not exactly refer to legal minors. The Declaration prescribes equality in 'race, colour, sex, language, religion, political or other opinion, national or social origin, property, birth or other status' but omits age. Another avoidance method in teaching emphasizes provision and protection rights, and pupils' good fortune in enjoying compulsory education and the civil rights which most of them do have – a name, a nationality, a family – but ignores other key participation rights. Some teachers who are deeply concerned about justice and rights keep to distant topics like torture in Indonesia, which can imply that abuses do not occur in 'developed' countries. Teaching international human rights instead of, rather than as well as, children's rights diverts attention away from practical rights in schools. Teachers may believe they cover human rights fully, and indeed they cover numerous crucial matters, but many pupils are disconcerted and sceptical about the missing practical issues.

CONCLUSION

It is illogical to expect students to understand lessons about rights and democracy yet expect them not to notice denials of their own rights, or discrepancies between what school staff practise and preach. The survey and discussion group replies show that students increasingly report these discrepancies as they grow older. Councils in undemocratic schools reveal tensions between rhetoric and reality about democracy in the school, tensions which can ferment disaffection and apathy. Working with students to set up a democratic council involves related changes throughout the school in routines and relationships (Trafford, 1997; Highfield, 1997), which further involves rethinking notions of incompetent undeveloped children. The QCA Report was written partly from concern about apathy and non-voting among adults, but it does not mention the challenges for schools which genuine education about democracy presents, or how teachers can respond to these.

If teachers are not to feel forced into the kinds of avoidances in teaching rights described above, if they are freed to discuss the CRC participation rights with students and if causes of student's growing disaffection are to be resolved, then many schools will have to change radically. Radical (root) changes affect people's 'hearts and minds', in the fear and anxiety of relinquishing cherished but misleading old ideas, and the courage (from 'cor' meaning heart) to acknowledge past mistakes and to try new approaches which include sharing power and knowledge more equally between generations. One head teacher graphically described this intellectual and emotional journey (Trafford, 1997).

For well-grounded citizenship education in the twenty-first century, shared work by researchers and educators, children and adults, about the following issues is vital. The public–private divide needs to be reconsidered. The government-sponsored report (QCA, 1998) is based on Marshall's 1950 principles of citizenship, without noting the huge changes over the past 50 years in academic and public thinking. Feminist scholarship shows how researchers who claimed to speak about the whole of society were, until recently, speaking only about men. The assumed division between public and private life ignored women's work in the home and family, in childcare and education. Marshall's assumptions about public citizenship leave many women and especially children in an invidious position. Are children present or only future citizens? Are schools public or private places, inside or outside 'the community and the world of work'? What do childhood, citizenship and democracy which include children, mean? Theoretical and empirical research is needed about these ambiguities, the practical difficulties they raise in many schools, and methods of resolving the tensions.

Lessons from feminism as they apply to discrimination against children also require attention. To ignore gender issues, or to question whether women should have equal human rights with men, is now seen as ignorant and unscholarly, although only after long, slow changes in knowledge and values. Into the 1980s, feminist scholars' work was banned from mainstream academic journals as subjective and lacking in convincing evidence (Spender, 1981), as research on children's rights is now similarly rejected (personal communications and the scarcity of relevant articles). Extending human rights to children involves radical changes in dominant academic and popular understanding about the nature of rights and of childhood, and change in school policies, teaching methods, curricular and teacher training, as officially recommended (UN, 1995). Such changes require comprehensive research evidence about the effectiveness of new approaches and the varied methods of implementing them, which draws on the views of adults and pupils.

Finally, the extensive research about how childhood is constructed and reconstructed, as dependent and incompetent in some cultures (just as women used to be), and as competent and responsible in other contexts, needs to be far more widely publicized. Before attitudes and polices can change, their roots in developmental psychology have to be reconsidered in the light of more realistic theories and evidence of children's abilities. The values and interest groups served while the popularity of development theories outlasts their credibility also need to be researched and publicized. Then children's competencies and their common humanity with adults as rights holders and rights respecters will more fully be appreciated and realized.

REFERENCES

Alderson, P. (2000) *Young Children's Rights*. London: Jessica Kingsley.
Alderson, P. and Goodey, C. (1998) *Enabling Education: Experiences in Special and Ordinary Schools*. London: Tufnell Press.
Bradley, B. (1989) *Visions of Infancy*. Cambridge: Polity Press.
Buchanan, A. and Brock, D. (1989) *Deciding for Others*. New York: Cambridge University Press.
Burman, E. (1994) *Deconstructing Developmental Psychology*. London: Routledge.
Cleves School (ed. P. Alderson) (1999) *Learning and Inclusion: The Cleves School Experience*. London: David Fulton.
Cockburn, T. (1998) Children and citizenship in Britain. *Childhood*, 5 (1): 99–117.
Cullingford, C. (1992) *Children and Society: Children's Attitudes to Politics and Power*. London: Cassell.
Davies, L. (1994) Focusing on equal rights in teacher education. *Educational Review*, 46 (2): 109–20.
Donaldson, M. (1978) *Children's Minds*. Edinburgh: Fontana.
Edwards, C., Gandini, L. and Forman, G. (1998) *The Hundred Languages of Children*. London: Ablex.
Eekelaar, J. (1986) The emergence of children's rights. *Oxford Journal of Legal Studies*, 6 (161).
Franklin, B. (ed.) (1995) *The Handbook of Children's Rights: Comparative Policy and Practice*. London: Routledge.

Freeman, M. (1983) *The Rights and Wrongs of Children*. London: Frances Pinter.

Gardner, H. (1993) *The Unschooled Mind: How Children Think and How Schools Should Teach*. London: Fontana.

Griffith, R. (1998) *Educational Citizenship and Independent Learning*. London: Jessica Kingsley.

Hammarberg, J. (1997) *A School for Children with Rights*. Florence, Italy: Innocenti.

Hannam, D. (1998) *Reports of Effective School Councils*. (some examples were published in the QCA Report, 1998).

Hart, S., Pavlovic, Z. and Zeidner, M. (1997) Cross-national research on children's rights. In E. Verhellen (ed.) *Understanding Children's Rights*. Ghent: Children's Rights Centre.

Highfield School (ed. P. Alderson) (1997) *Changing our School: Promoting Positive Behaviour*. Plymouth: Highfield School/London: Institute of Education.

Hutchby, I. and Moran-Ellis, J. (eds) (1995) *Children and Social Competence: Arenas of Action*. London: Falmer.

James, A. and Prout, A. (eds) (1990) *Constructing and Reconstructing Childhood – New Directions in the Sociological Study of Childhood*. Basingstoke, Hants: Falmer.

Jeffs, T. (1995) Children's educational rights in a new ERA? In B. Franklin (ed.) *The Handbook of Children's Rights*. London: Routledge.

John, M. (1996) *Children in Charge: Children's Rights to a Fair Hearing*. London: Jessica Kingsley.

Lansdown, G. and Newell, P. (eds) (1994) *UK Agenda for Children*. London: Children's Rights Development Office.

Mayall, B. (ed.) (1994) *Children's Childhoods Observed and Experienced*. London: Falmer.

Miller, J. (1996) *Never too Young: How Young Children Can Take Responsibility and Make Decisions*. London: National Early Years Network.

Morrow, V. (1994) Responsible children. In B. Mayall (ed.) *Children's Childhoods Observed and Experienced*. London: Falmer.

Morss, J. (1990) *The Biologising of Childhood*. Hove: Lawrence Erlbaum Associates.

Newell, P. (1989) *Children are People too*. London: Bedford Square Press.

NUT (National Union of Teachers) (1997) *The Stoke Rochford Declaration of Commonwealth Teachers. Education and Human Rights*. Presented to the 13th Commonwealth Conference of Education Ministers, Gaborone, Botswana. London: NUT.

Osler, A. (1995) Urban protest, citizenship and human rights. In A. Osler, A. Rathenow and H. Starkey (eds) *Teaching for Citizenship in Europe*. Stoke on Trent: Trentham, pp. 73–90.

Pearce, N. and Hillman, J. (1998) *Wasted Youth: Raising Achievement and Tackling Social Achievement Amongst 14–19 Year Olds*. London: Institute for Public Policy Research.

PEG (Participation Education Group) (1998) *Celebration Newsletter*. Newcastle: PEG.

QCA (1998) *Education for Citizenship and the Teaching of Democracy in Schools* (Crick Report. Final Report of the Advisory Group on Citizenship). London: DfEE/QCA.

Save the Children (1999) *We have the Rights Okay*. London: Save the Children.

Siegal, M. (1997) *Knowing Children*. Hove: Lawrence Erlbaum Associates.

Spender, D. (1981) The Gatekeepers: a feminist critique of academic publishing. In H. Roberts (ed.) *Doing Feminist Research*. London: Routledge, pp. 186–202.

Trafford, B. (1997) *Participation, Power-sharing and School Improvement*. Nottingham: English Heretics.

UN (1989) *Convention on the Rights of the Child*. Geneva: UN.

UN Committee on the Rights of the Child (1995) *Consideration of Reports Submitted by*

State Parties under Article 44 of the Convention: Concluding Observations: United Kingdom and Northern Ireland. Geneva: UN, CRC/C/15/Add.34.

Verhellen, E. (ed.) (1997) *Understanding Children's Rights.* Ghent: Children's Rights Centre.

Chapter 11

The Moral Agenda of Citizenship Education

Graham Haydon

INTRODUCTION

How should we see the relationship between citizenship education and moral education? It is probable that no single answer to this question would appear evident to every reader. That probability itself reflects a state of affairs which forms the background to my argument in this chapter. In a society like Britain at the beginning of the twenty-first century there might be fairly wide – though probably not unanimous – agreement that there should be *some* relationship between moral education and citizenship education, but this agreement would not rest on any deep shared understanding of the nature of morality or of what it has to do with citizenship.

I shall argue in this chapter that there is a particular way of seeing morality which could be widely shared and which it should be the business of citizenship education to promote. I propose this as a way in which education can respond to the existing diversity – not to say confusion – in ways of seeing morality and its relationship to citizenship. Hence it is important to set out by illustrating this diversity.

Let me start with two extreme positions – one which would see no effective distinction between citizenship education and moral education, and one which would see citizenship education as having nothing to do with moral education. On the first of these views, to be a good citizen is to live according to the norms of one's society – and this is also what it is to be a moral person. So there is no effective distinction between being a good person, morally speaking, and being a good citizen. Hence moral education and citizenship education are the same thing.

This is likely to strike the reader as a simplistic position. I think I have seen it maintained (though not in published work) by individuals from parts of the world in which two separate discourses, of moral education and of citizenship education, have not as yet developed. But I am more likely now to be addressing readers whose thinking is influenced by a background of Western liberalism in which freedom of individual choice itself has moral weight and in which distinctions between the moral and the political and the private and the public are deeply entrenched (albeit problematic).

Against this background one is more likely to encounter the other extreme position – that citizenship education should be conceived as something quite distinct from moral education. On this view, citizenship has to do with the public, political realm, and it recognizes individuals as autonomous participants in democratic processes. Such a view can coexist with a suspicion of the public political realm getting involved with morality at all: for morality may be seen as a matter of individual choice which is inherently personal and private. Hence the very idea of moral education can come under suspicion; it can look like an attempt by teachers, as agents of the state, to impose certain values on individuals.

The combination of support for citizenship education with suspicion of moral education is the second extreme position, at the opposite end of the spectrum from the view which would draw no distinction. It may be difficult to give a coherent defence of the second extreme, once it is spelt out, but that does not stop it having some influence within modern Western culture. At the same time, a more common view would be one which recognizes both moral and citizenship education as being legitimate concerns of schooling, and recognizes that there will inevitably be some interrelationship between them, while not necessarily being very clear as to just what this interrelationship is.

In England most recent official and semi-official policy and documentation on citizenship education would fall somewhere within this middle range. Thus the Crick Report (QCA, 1998) has 'social and moral responsibility' as one strand out of three comprising citizenship education, the other two being 'community involvement' and 'political literacy'. And it recognizes that in primary schools preparation for citizenship will be subsumed under PSHE (personal, social and health education), within which it would be difficult in any case to maintain any clear differentiation between moral education and citizenship education.

Nevertheless, the term 'moral education' itself figures very little in recent discussion of citizenship education, and not much more in discussions of PSHE. It can hardly be said at present that teachers who are likely to be involved in citizenship education are being offered any clear or consistent view of how far and in what ways their concern should include or overlap with moral education.

This state of affairs, I am suggesting, reflects a broader confusion within society about the very idea of morality. Aspects of this confusion are often revealed within public discourse about politics and politicians. For instance, when sexual infidelities of married politicians are revealed, both of two opposing views are often expressed: that matters of personal morality have no bearing on the politician's capacity to do his job; and that someone who does not observe recognized moral norms shows him or herself to be unfit for public office. Two areas of confusion are already implicated here: the problematic distinction between what is of public concern and what is purely a private matter; and the extent to which morality does or does not have something especially to do with sex.

Twice during the summer of 1999 the British Prime Minister was reported as calling for a shared moral purpose for the nation. On one occasion the context was Blair's declared aspiration to end poverty in Britain: without dispute a legitimate concern of politicians, and of the citizens whom politicians are addressing. On the other occasion the context was a number of reported cases of 12-year-old girls becoming pregnant. To some people, the second context obviously raises moral issues, but the first, while clearly being a political issue, is not really a moral matter at all. To other people, a political response is clearly what is needed to both issues, and bringing in morality – making moral judgements, being 'judgemental' or 'moralizing' – might be irrelevant in the first context and possibly counter-productive in the second.[1] So the relation between morality and politics is a further area where people may often be talking at cross-purposes. And in a multi- faith (and not entirely secularized) society the relation between morality and religion is yet another area of conflicting points of view.

It would not be putting it too strongly to say that British society at the beginning of the twenty-first century is confused about morality. Consider the following ideas.[2] Morality consists of ideals as to how every person should live his or her life; these are aspirations for every individual, regardless of whether others are or are not living up to these same ideals, but by the same token we should not worry too much if we do not live up to them. Or, morality is a set of constraints on what each of us in society is allowed to do, and their point is that we should not unduly interfere with each other; these minimal constraints – not killing or injuring each other, not breaking contracts and so on – are not too difficult to live up to, and provided we respect them, we are each of us free to live in whatever way we like. Or, morality consists of those values which an individual takes to be most central and most important in his or her own life – hence my moral values may be quite different from yours, but we should each of us strive to live according to our own moral values. Or, morality is a set of universal truths about what is required if human life is to go well. Or, morality consists of the commands of an omniscient and omnipotent deity, and it is not for mere mortals to ask the reason for these commands. Probably each reader will find some familiarity in all of these ideas, and will be inclined to agree with two or three of them – a different two or three for different readers. But they are by no means all compatible with each other.

WHY EDUCATION SHOULD ADDRESS THE CONFUSION

If I am right that there is this collective confusion about morality, does it matter so far as education is concerned – and citizenship education in particular? What I want to argue in this chapter is, first, that education should address this area of confusion; second, that it is particularly appropriate for citizenship education to do this; and third, and probably most controversially, that there is one particular view of morality which citizenship education can and should seek to promote.

Because the first two points are likely to be less controversial, I shall express the arguments only briefly here. I want to say first that the confusion I have referred to should be of concern to education generally because education has a responsibility to help people to think clearly and to get free of confusions. This does not mean that education itself has to take a stand on – or even encourage individuals to take a stand on – everything where confusion and differences of opinion are possible; on some matters, in a plural society, the existence of all sorts of different views may be something to be tolerated or even celebrated. But there are also some matters on which the conditions of life in a plural society themselves suggest that confusion could have detrimental effects.

This brings me to the reason why confusion on this particular matter is relevant to citizenship. It is a commonplace that citizenship in a plural society has a lot to do with the working out of modes of coexistence and co-operation between adherents of different cultures. And it is another commonplace that one of the differentiating features of different cultures is their differences in values, and that it is such differences – rather than differences in, say, food or music – that sometimes make demands on understanding and toleration. Some of the starkest situations of potential conflict come up on matters where there seem to be directly competing views as to whether some way of behaving or way of life is acceptable or not – these are the kinds of disputes in which we recognize that at least some parties to the dispute see the issues involved as moral ones.

In such matters the differences are often not just differences in the content of people's moral beliefs; they involve different views of what morality is about, what it is for something to be a moral issue. And sometimes these differences will come to the surface in public discourse. In his remarks mentioned above, Tony Blair was implicitly assuming an agreement about morality and the role of morality in public life. But that agreement may not be there: if citizens have not, through their education, been enabled to look at moral discourse and its role, they will hardly know whether they do or do not agree with their fellow citizens.

IS THE TASK ONE FOR CITIZENSHIP EDUCATION?

These points show, I hope, that an education which looks at ideas of morality and at the uses of moral discourse is important for citizenship; but it does not yet show that citizenship education is the part of the curriculum which should be addressing the understanding of morality. Others have argued for the relevance to citizenship of various forms of understanding – such as historical, or mathematical or scientific; but such understanding is likely to be pursued in the appropriate historical, mathematical or scientific parts of the curriculum. Few would argue that citizenship education, as such, should be taking on all these tasks. So it is a further question whether we should see the promotion of an understanding of morality and moral discourse as part of the task of citizenship education.

This question is, I think, one to be approached pragmatically, bearing in mind the practices of a particular education system. In a country which has a part of the curriculum labelled 'ethics' or 'social morality', that would be the place to address the kinds of issues I have in mind. Within the English curriculum there is no such recognized area. The likely candidates we in fact have are Religious Education, Personal Social and Health Education and (within the revised National Curriculum) Citizenship Education. RE has a claim to be considered because historically its practitioners have been trained to deal with moral issues in their teaching; but if there is to be a curriculum area which deals directly with the phenomena of morality, recognizing that to many people these phenomena are of an entirely secular nature, then RE starts under a handicap because, fairly or unfairly, it would often be seen as linking morality to religion and thus as favouring certain conceptions of morality over others.[3]

If RE is put on one side, this leaves PSHE and citizenship education. Since these two are meant to be combined in the primary school, it is only at secondary school that they could be either complementary or alternative routes for an educational focus on the public understanding of morality. This is significant, because it is especially at secondary level, I suggest, that what we might call the ethos of these two areas of concern will begin to diverge.

I referred above to the great diversity in understandings of morality within our society. Within this diversity I think two major and opposing tendencies can be found. One is a tendency towards what I would call the 'personalization' of morality: the idea that ultimately morality – what it requires, and how seriously it is taken – comes down to individual choice and commitment (the term 'relativism' is often used here, but rather misleadingly, because morality might in some respects be relative to cultures without being a matter of individual choice). But coexisting with this is a presupposition – seen for instance in the Prime Minister's remarks – that there is in morality something objective,[4] or at least publicly agreed, that can be appealed to.

I want to suggest (though it involves simplifying at the risk of caricature) that within the school curriculum, the tendency towards personalization is reflected within PSHE. The personal rather than the social is often emphasized: it is seen as overridingly important that individuals make informed choices, realizing the consequences of their actions, and being prepared to live with them. In this ethos, it may be difficult to talk about morality conceived as something more like an impersonal framework to which individuals are expected to conform. But the latter model is one that many people would still subscribe to, and one that needs to be taken seriously in a context of citizenship. It may raise spectres of imposition or indoctrination, but it is (or so I shall argue) possible to interpret morality in a more democratic spirit which respects autonomy. Seen in this way, an understanding of morality will be very much an appropriate concern of citizenship education. (The phrase 'public morality' is sometimes used in this context, but this can also be misleading because it may suggest that a publicly shared understanding of morality has no bearing on people's personal or private lives; and this is something we should not accept without looking very carefully at how we draw the public/private distinction.)

I suggest, in fact, two ways in which citizenship education could and should address issues about morality. The first is to promote an understanding of the diversity in understandings of morality which exists within our society.[5] The second is to promote one particular understanding of morality. The second proposal may look incompatible with the first and will in any case be more controversial, so I need to devote more space to it.

MORALITY IN THE NARROW SENSE

I have said enough about diversity in understandings of morality to show that I do not think it is the role of citizenship education to pick out just one understanding of morality and put it across as the single correct one. On the face of it, this would seem to rule out doing anything other than promoting an understanding of diversity. But there is another possibility, *if different understandings of morality are not necessarily mutually exclusive.* And this is what I think is the case. It should be, I suggest, possible for citizens in a plural and democratic society to agree on one way of seeing morality which can be shared on the level of public discourse, while not having to give up their perhaps more favoured and more deeply held understandings of morality which may stem from cultural tradition or personal reflection.[6]

Is there a conception of morality available which could be publicly agreed? I think that there is, and that it is indeed already likely to be a familiar way of looking at morality to many readers.[7] It is a conception which some philosophers have labelled 'morality in the narrow sense'. Morality in this sense is a system of constraints on people's conduct, which tends to check people's inclinations to act in ways which might be harmful to other people's interests, and thereby serves a social function of protecting people's interests in general. (This is intended as a way of capturing a familiar idea, not as a definition.)

Quite consciously, this account of morality as a social institution makes no attempt to capture many elements which may (in different ways and in different combinations for different people) come into many people's fuller understanding of morality. It says nothing about what you should aim at in life, or even about how you should live your life from day to day provided you respect certain constraints which are publicly acknowledged. In this way the social institution of morality serves a function rather similar to that of the criminal law, but its mode of operation is much less formal: it is not clearly codified, it carries no formal sanctions and there is no mechanism by which its provisions can be changed (nevertheless they can change – a point I shall come back to). Morality in the narrow sense exists primarily in the form of shared ideas – ideas which are part of public discourse, which can be passed on from one generation to another and which can be called to mind and referred to in speech or writing as the occasion demands. When, for instance, people refer to norms such as 'don't tell lies' or 'keep your promises' or 'don't take what doesn't belong to you' they are making use of a stock of ideas which – they assume – is widely shared. (These particular examples may be relatively uncontroversial, but there will be many ideas, even within a shared public understanding of the nature of morality, which can be recognized as open to interpretation and criticism.)

WHAT KIND OF LANGUAGE?

If we think of morality in the narrow sense as being in some ways analogous to law, it is natural to think that its linguistic expression will be (as in the examples above) in terms of norms, that is, prescriptions telling people to do this or not to do that. (I am taking 'norms' here to include both rules and principles, though there is an important distinction that can be marked by these two terms: briefly, rules give us relatively specific instructions; principles pick out broader considerations, such as fairness or consideration of people's interests, which we need to keep in mind in deciding what to do.)[8] But a recent tendency in moral philosophy has challenged the idea that morality is fundamentally a matter of rules and principles; instead, it gives a fundamental place to certain kinds of personal qualities, which it labels by the term 'virtues'. To the non-philosopher this particular word may have an old-fashioned sound, but reference to personal qualities (positive ones such as generosity or kindness, or negative ones such as cruelty and selfishness) is an everyday part of moral discourse.

The philosophical debate is continuing, and it does have implications for how we think about the aims both of moral education and of citizenship education. Some approaches are primarily concerned that people should grow up aware of accepted norms and willing to abide by them; given that, it does not give a central place to the feelings and motivations which lead people to abide by the norms. Other approaches – those advocated now under the heading of 'virtue ethics' – want people to grow up having certain kinds of concern, being motivated in certain ways – in short, being people of one kind rather than another. Some recent work – e.g. White (1996) – has been discussing explicitly the virtues appropriate to the citizens of a democratic society.

In other places (Haydon, 1997, pp. 124–6; 1999, Chapters 5–6) I have gone into this debate at some length; my own position in summary, as it bears on my present topic, is that references to personal qualities are so ingrained in ordinary discourse that there would be little future in trying to restrict ourselves to a language of norms; but that nevertheless, in the articulation of morality in the narrow sense, the language of norms has a certain priority, because this kind of morality does work primarily by influencing, often constraining, people's behaviour, and to some extent it can leave matters of feeling and motivation to a more personal realm. There might be implications here for just where the line is to be drawn between the concerns of PSHE and those of citizenship education, but teachers of both are in any case going to need to be able to work within both sorts of language.

A MORALITY IN WHICH CITIZENS CAN ENGAGE

What is the effect, for citizenship, of looking explicitly at morality in the way I have suggested? It is important that it makes of morality something that is not a mysterious alien force, and something that cannot be purely personal and subjective. It brings morality into the public realm in which citizens can see themselves as participating and exercising influence.

Clearly morality in the narrow sense is not timeless. It does, at least in some aspects, change over time (there are clear examples in the area of sexual behaviour), and the changes can be interpreted in terms of the functions which morality serves. Of course, most citizens, individually, do not exercise very much influence over the changes that may come about; in that sense it may still seem to an individual that morality is like a grid to which his or her behaviour is expected to conform. And in a way it has to be like that, just as the law is; otherwise we are back to the thought that it all comes down to individual choice, in which case morality in the narrow sense cannot serve its function. But the law is susceptible to change, through processes which are intelligible, which individuals can become involved in and which citizenship education can encourage people to become involved in. The processes by which morality, as a social institution, changes are not so very different, though they are not formalized. Consensus has a lot to do with it; morality as a social institution cannot exist without at least some consensus across society (people 'speaking the same language' in the sense of having the same reference points; this is an important function of shared rules and principles), and it also cannot change without consensus. But whereas in the case of law there are formalized processes of change involving voting, there is no such explicit process determining change in morality. While there is consensus on certain moral norms, they remain in force, in the only sort of way that the norms of morality in the narrow sense can have force; where there is no longer consensus, respect for the norms tends to wither away, or they are replaced by others.

By consensus here I do not mean agreement of a majority; I am referring to an ideal which is agreement of everyone concerned. People are often worried by a suggestion that morality – even in its explicitly public aspects – has anything to do with consensus; they think that means that the morality of Nazi Germany was all right. But what is so striking about Nazi morality is that it was emphatically *not* a morality of consensus among all concerned; whole sectors of society were left out of the consensus, treated as non-participants. So at an ideal level, we need not be worried about the idea that morality depends on consensus.[9]

In practice, of course, we cannot expect consensus of everyone – perhaps not even on what might seem to myself or to the reader the most evident of moral principles (such as those often listed under 'human rights'). This might seem to leave us in a moral limbo so far as the social function of morality is concerned. But it does not, because the social reality of morality gives it a certain inertia – it remains in force until changed. Nevertheless it does sometimes change, partly because people can ask questions about whether received ideas actually do tend to serve the function that morality in the narrow sense is supposed to serve. People can express their opinions about this and argue over it; they can discuss the relevance of particular norms in the prevailing circumstances and so on. This sort of thing goes on anyway, and it is not very different from the way in which existing law can be criticized. What I am advocating is that a process which happens anyway should become so far as possible transparent and inclusive – and that citizenship education can help to make it so. Citizenship education can encourage people to see themselves, not as subject to an alien or ideological force labelled 'morality' – it is this sort of view that breeds scepticism or nihilism – but as participants in morality as a shared undertaking.[10]

It may be wondered whether, on this view, morality can be seen by individuals as having any authority over their conduct. If I recognize that prevailing moral ideas are maintained and passed on, within public discourse, by other human beings – fellow citizens – who do not, as individuals, have authority over me, can I see those ideas as having authority? I think the answer to this has to be similar to the answer to the question why anyone should have respect for the law. Of course, not everyone will in fact abide by the law and many people may break certain laws if they think they can get away with it; nevertheless, in a democratic system (with all its real world deficiencies) it is possible to feel a part of the society for which the laws are made and a participant in the processes by which they are made. People who feel themselves in this way to be citizens are more likely to take the law seriously. Something similar can be said about morality as a social institution. It is certainly possible for people to feel alienated from it, and this is all the more likely if their experience of morality is of something handed down, as if on tablets of stone, but actually by other people with power. But it is also possible for people to feel involved in morality (with all its doubts and controversies). So the underlying aim of education for the public understanding of morality, in the sense in which I have discussed it here, has to be the same as the underlying aim of education for democratic citizenship: that people should be able to see themselves as included, not excluded.

MORALITY AND THE TEACHER OF CITIZENSHIP EDUCATION

I want to end with a note on where my suggestions leave the individual teacher. Many teachers already feel both that heavy demands are being made on them as upholders of morality, and that the part they are already playing in this respect is not being recognized. Among other tasks, they are expected to maintain discipline in the classroom and its surroundings, to transmit society's norms, to have some concern for the moral development of individual pupils, to promote respect and tolerance for differences and to encourage understanding and reflectiveness about values. If teachers feel that all these demands are being made on them, then asking them, in their role as teachers of citizenship, to put across some particular understanding of morality could be perceived as just one more demand.

Even as things are, before the statutory introduction of citizenship education, most teachers have little systematic preparation for their role in relation to public perceptions of moral demands. If I am right about the possibilities of confusion and cross-purposes in understandings of morality in the wider society, there is no reason to think that people who go into teaching are immune. Nor is there, at present, any expectation that teachers as they emerge from their professional education will share any particular understanding of morality. Indeed, the majority of teachers in their training are probably given little if any encouragement even to clarify their own understandings in this respect. Individual views about morality may, after all, be considered to be part of teachers' personal life, which it is not for professional training to concern itself with.

Yet even as things are now, these same people will be expected, as part of their professional role – albeit an ill-defined part – to have some dealings with questions of morality in the public context of education. It would not be surprising if many teachers felt even more confused than the representative member of the general public. And it would be still less surprising if many felt, if asked explicitly to promote the public understanding of morality, that they were being asked to impose something alien on pupils, and wished to have nothing to do with it.

Professional education and development – both pre-service and in-service – has not served teachers well as regards the nature and understanding of morality. There is much more that could be done, without crossing any boundary between legitimate public concerns and the personal commitments of teachers.

I have tried to offer, in this and other writings, a way of seeing morality which teachers could feel they can work with without having to subscribe to particular metaphysical or religious commitments, without hypocrisy and without authoritarianism. Seeing their concern with morality as part of their work in citizenship education – in addition to the ways in which it may enter, explicitly or implicitly, into other areas of curriculum and school ethos – could help teachers to see the relationship between the various demands on them. Passing on from one generation to the next a knowledge of and commitment to the norms of society is one of the functions of education, because morality in the narrow sense requires a degree of stability in its norms. But the stability is not absolute and the commitment is provisional. So – in addition to whatever value is assigned to individual autonomy or critical thinking for its own sake – it is important that teachers encourage pupils to think about the point of society's norms. Since the continuing function of morality requires a degree of consensus and the possibility of change through a changing consensus, it is important that teachers initiate pupils into the processes by which criticism can go on and changes can come about. Since all of this happens in a context of considerable diversity of ideas about morality and of values of other kinds, it is important that pupils are made aware of the diversity. And since teachers have to be able to talk to their pupils, and pupils talk to each other, in ways that all can understand and which are not split off from the wider language of public discourse, it is important that teachers can work with the kinds of language – often of rule and principles, but also referring to personal qualities – in which public moral concerns are articulated. None of this will decrease the demands themselves, but it may help to make sense of them.[11]

NOTES

1. Similar differences arise over responses to violence within society. In Haydon (1999) I ask how far moral language is appropriate in relation to such concerns.
2. There is some borrowing in the next few paragraphs from a more extended treatment of diversity in Haydon (2000).
3. There is certainly more to be said on this point, both for and against the role of RE, but I shall not attempt to say it here.
4. There are many pitfalls in the use of this term. See Haydon (1997) pp. 35–37 for a cautionary note.
5. I argued for this in Haydon (1995), though I was not then writing explicitly about citizenship education.
6. My distinction between a shared public conception of morality, and more particular understandings which may, for instance, be rooted in particular traditions, has some (deliberate) parallels with John Rawls's (1993) distinction between political liberalism and comprehensive political and ethical doctrines.
7. Francis Dunlop (1999), reviewing a longer work (Haydon, 1999) in which I made an

earlier, and probably more confused, attempt to argue my position, suggests that I am trying to replace 'our traditional conception of morality with a completely new one'; indeed, he titles his review 'The Abolition of Morality?'. I do not see what I am advocating in this way; not only am I doubtful that there is such a thing as 'our traditional conception of morality' (as opposed to a variety of conceptions), I also do not see the conception I am putting forward as 'completely new' (in fact I think it has been around for a long time). But whether it is unfamiliar to the reader is for the reader to judge.
8. See Haydon (1999) Chapters 8–10 for a much fuller discussion.
9. In a fuller treatment I would refer here to Habermas's conception of communicative ethics.
10. I might have thought that the desirability of people seeing themselves as participants in morality woud be uncontroversial, but it is not. Dunlop (1999) says 'it is better that the whole process [of moral change] . . . is obscure' (p. 483).
11. This chapter is an extended version of a paper presented at the Citizenship Conference at the Institute of Education in July 1999. Even so, many of its arguments need expansion and qualification; to some extent they receive this in Haydon (1999).

REFERENCES

Dunlop, F. (1999) The abolition of morality? *Journal of Philosophy of Education*, **33** (3).
Haydon, G. (1995) Thick or thin? The cognitive content of education in a plural democracy. *Journal of Moral Education*, **24** (1).
Haydon, G. (1997) *Teaching about Values: A New Approach*. London: Cassell.
Haydon, G. (1999) *Values, Virtues and Violence*. Oxford: Blackwell. Also published as special issue of *Journal of Philosophy of Education*, **33** (1).
Haydon, G. (2000) Understanding the diversity of diversity. In M. Leicester, C. Modgil and S. Modgil (eds) *Values, Diversity and Education*. Brighton: Falmer.
QCA (1998) *Education for Citizenship and the Teaching of Democracy in Schools* (Final Report of the Advisory Group on Citizenship). London: QCA.
Rawls, J. (1993) *Political Liberalism*. New York: Columbia University Press.
White, P. (1996) *Civic Virtues and Public Schooling*. New York and London: Teachers College Press.

Part III

Comparative Perspectives

Culture, Community and Curriculum in Wales: Citizenship Education for the New Democracy?

Robert Phillips

INTRODUCTION

Much attention has centred in recent times upon the Crick Report (QCA, 1998) which argues for a citizenship education based upon social and moral responsibility, community involvement and political literacy. Interestingly, debates over nationhood, citizenship education and identity have been prevalent in Wales throughout the 1990s, as a distinctive curricular framework in Wales has emerged. This chapter draws attention to some of these developments, including the emergence of the Curriculum Cymreig which itself mirrors the wider move towards political devolution. It focuses upon the ways in which the Curriculum Cymreig emerged over and above an alternative cross-curricular model namely Community Understanding. The chapter considers whether the current curriculum reflects the needs of Wales in the future and in particular the extent to which the current proposals for reform of the curriculum in Wales (see ACCAC, 1999a) sufficiently prepare Welsh pupils for active participation in the new political culture of the twenty-first century.

'COOL CYMRU': CHANGING TIMES?

At the end of the twentieth century, there was a renewed interest in the ways in which national identity and visions of citizenship were perceived, particularly in Wales (Fevre and Thompson, 1999). Perhaps few things created as much irritation to serious students and observers of political and cultural life at the time than phrases such as 'Cool Britannia' or the much-vaunted 'Cool Cymru'. Often an invention of media and political spin, these sorts of phrases revealed more about the originators of image and power in our society than about the reality of that society. Such images may be interpreted as the apotheosis of what Billig (1995) has usefully referred to as the 'banal' underpinnings of an (imagined) national identity.

Yet at the beginning of the new century, even the deepest sceptic would acknowledge that there is an undoubted vibrancy in Welsh cultural life at present: change is very much in the air. A growing confidence and interest in the Welsh language and contemporary Welsh music is only matched by a corresponding lack of interest in Welsh politics. A recent survey of young people between 18 and 29 for the Welsh BBC current affairs programme *Week In/Week Out* (22 June 1999) revealed some very interesting developments about the ways in which young people perceive their identity and politics. When asked what they associated most with the concept of 'Welshness', most referred to the landscape of Wales, closely followed by Welsh music. More than 50 per cent of the young people surveyed perceived themselves as Welsh first, British second, while the survey showed an overwhelming support for the teaching and learning of the Welsh language. Of even more significance for the purposes of this chapter, however, is that when it came to politics, the survey revealed that only 1 in 3 had voted in the Welsh Assembly elections; two-thirds claimed that they had no interest in politics, with four-fifths claiming that they have no faith in politicians.

This sort of evidence suggests that the new democratic machinery established under the Welsh Assembly has some serious challenges ahead convincing young people that politics is worth bothering about. In this sense, of course, Wales is very little different from other parts of the UK and Europe. The *Week In/Week Out* survey was important not only for correlating the apathy amongst Welsh youth about the importance of political and civic participation but also for confirming a new vibrancy and interest in contemporary Welsh cultural life. This dichotomy between cultural interest and political apathy forms a central theme of my chapter. How can we account for it?

The answer lies partly in contemporary history. Whereas in the late 1970s and early 1980s there was seemingly little interest in distinctively Welsh aspects of culture and heritage (witnessed by the struggles faced by Welsh language campaigners), a number of important developments in the 1980s and 1990s caused a cultural/political shift. As long as the economy and industry were buoyant, the mainly English-speaking and industrial South Wales saw little relevance in the need to preserve Welsh cultural life. Yet the economic downturn of the 1980s, de-industrialization, social dislocation and the perception throughout the decade that Wales was effectively disenfranchised politically, caused a reaction, particularly amongst young people who suffered particularly badly in terms of youth unemployment. The result has been a reawakened interest in Welsh culture and language, often as a reaction against a (perceived) dominant English hegemony (see Thompson and Day, 1999). Parallel with this, of course, has been the move towards political devolution, perceived by some Welsh politicians as a guarantee against the excesses of the Thatcher years.

FORGING THE NATION? THE EVOLUTION OF CURRICULUM CYMREIG

An important point to consider is that political devolution has been mirrored in Wales by educational devolution (see Phillips *et al.*, 1999). It seems extraordinary to consider that, before 1988, apart from the Welsh language (itself taught patchily in schools), Wales did not have a distinctive curricular framework. By contrast, as we approach the new millennium, Wales effectively has its own National Curriculum (NC) with distinctive Statutory Orders in a range of subjects and, perhaps most significantly, its own curricular authorities to oversee it which now come under the auspices of the Welsh Assembly. Equally significantly, each of the NC subjects has a commitment to the promotion of the Curriculum Cymreig. Thus, for example in history, the most recent document under the Wales 2000 reforms requires that:

> Pupils should be given opportunities, where appropriate in their study of history to develop and apply knowledge and understanding of the cultural, economic, environmental, historical and linguistic characteristics of Wales. (ACCAC, 1999b, p. 5)

One of the important things I want to consider is the extent to which the Curriculum Cymreig promotes notions of citizenship. Before doing so, it is important to consider its historical and philosophical roots. The Curriculum Cymreig emerged during the late 1980s and early 1990s, an extraordinarily innovative period for the Welsh curriculum. The 1988 Education Reform Act established the Curriculum Council for Wales (CCW: later renamed Qualifications and Curriculum Authority for Wales: ACCAC) to oversee the implementation of the NC in Wales which also involved developing a cross-curricular framework. In 1993, CCW published *Developing a Curriculum Cymreig* (CCW, 1993), which sought to define the ways Welsh culture, heritage and identity could be promoted through the curriculum. Although it emphasized that the Welsh language could be perceived to be the primary expressive form of 'Welshness', it was not the only form of expression; Welshness, said CCW, could also be cultivated through:

- place and heritage
- a sense of belonging
- literature
- art and religion.

Perhaps mindful of the charges of cultural exclusivity (see below), the documentation also emphasized that Welshness should be explored from different standpoints and that therefore Welshness would inevitably manifest itself differently in each school.

By any standards, this was a remarkable development. Given that for most of the period since 1944 Welsh cultural aspects had been relegated (Jones, 1997), here was a curricular initiative that was actively encouraging schools to promote it. As with all education policy initiatives, when it came to actual implementation, there was a gap between what CCW were requiring in theory and what teachers did in practice – what Ball and Bowe (1992) have termed 'slippage' between the statement of intent (text production) and actuality (policy implementation). Nevertheless, as a symbol of the sea change which was beginning to impact upon the other dimensions of Welsh life mentioned at the beginning of this chapter, the Curriculum Cymreig was significant (see Jones and Lewis, 1995).

CURRICULUM, COMMUNITY AND EDUCATION POLICY IN WALES

As I have argued elsewhere (see Phillips, 1996a; 1996b; 1996c), the Curriculum Cymreig was a product of cultural restoration, an attempt by those within the curricular authorities in Wales to restore particular aspects of Welsh aspects of cultural life which had been apparently relegated for so long. Interestingly, an alternative cross-curricular framework had been suggested in the early 1990s, also the product of CCW, namely *Community Understanding* (1991). In many ways, this was a remarkably radical document, produced during a conservative age; its very publication is testament to the degree of institutional educational autonomy that had been built up in Wales since 1988. I want to describe this document in some detail as it contrasts with the Crick Report published nearly a decade later.

Community Understanding offered a useful intellectual justification of 'community': community, it said, can refer to a group of people who occupy the same geographical area, but it can also refer to those who do not necessarily live in the same geographical proximity. In addition, community can be regarded as a close relationship best described by the term 'community spirit'. Second, it stressed the complexity of community:

> Children soon become aware of the ways in which people are grouped in terms of class, gender, race and age. Pupils should recognise that such groupings are based on certain differences between people that raise issues of diversity, inequality and prejudice. (CCW, 1991, p. 6)

The same paragraph went on to stress that pupils should learn to question stereotypes and understand the ways in which cultural diversity can be celebrated and inequality and prejudice combated. Third, the document suggested that pupils should explore what citizenship means at various levels. Interestingly, this involved exploring what it means not only to be a Welsh citizen but a world citizen too. Fourth, it stressed that children at an early age should become aware of human rights:

> They should know of their responsibility in respecting, protecting and promoting the rights of others. (CCW, 1991, p. 7)

Fifth, it emphasized that pupils should be given an awareness of the democratic processes available to them and their future role as decision-makers in society and the ways they can initiate change either as individuals or as members of groups. Sixth, in a remarkably frank paragraph reflecting the stark reality of economic and social life in Wales at the end of the twentieth century, the document stated that 'pupils should know how and why wealth and resources are distributed unevenly between individuals, groups, nations and continents' (CCW, 1991, p. 9). Finally, the document called for pupils to be 'aware of the diversity of races, faiths and languages, within Wales and beyond' (CCW, 1991, p. 9).

Clearly, Community Understanding reflected apparently moribund concepts in Welsh cultural and national life, namely locality, community and territoriality (see Roberts, 1999). For those who believe that Crick places too much emphasis upon civic action at the parliamentary political level and perhaps not enough upon social justice, Community Understanding provides an interesting alternative. It placed attention not only upon the school as a focal point of civic education, but also defined the ways in which society at large is crucial in this process. After all, as Hall *et al.* (1999) have recently reminded us 'there are many aspects of identity encompassed by a broad notion of citizenship which young people encounter, engage with and learn about away from school' (p. 512).

A clear distinction can be made between the 'Curriculum Cymreig' and 'Community Understanding'. The former views identity and a sense of citizenship in terms of cultural heritage and nationhood. The latter also recognizes the vitality of Welshness as an important means of collective identity but elevates the notion of community, and a universal concept of citizenship. As I have suggested elsewhere (Phillips, 1999) this debate reflected a wider historical debate in Wales between what Williams (1985) once referred to as 'the two truths' of Welshness – namely the essentially rural vision of Welshness rooted in ancient language and culture, and the industrial view of Wales which draws upon a turbulent industrial heritage. As the social and economic dislocation of the 1980s and 1990s set in, the latter 'truth' began to fade into a myth; correspondingly, a combination of a culturally aware Welsh HMI and their allies centred at CCW ensured it was the Curriculum Cymreig and not Community Understanding that became statutory in the schools of Wales. In this sense, education policy provided a microcosm of wider debates in Welsh social, cultural and political life. Yet, as we shall see below, the legacy of Community Understanding can be seen in the latest proposals on the curriculum for 2000 in Wales.

TOWARDS 2000: CITIZENSHIP EDUCATION FOR THE NEW DEMOCRACY?

I want to consider, within the context of the debate above, the extent to which present curricular arrangements and proposals in Wales equip Welsh pupils as citizens in the future. Before doing so, I need to clarify the kind of citizenship education I envisage. Here I want to draw upon a previous paper (Phillips, 1996a) in which I argued that I would like to see an education system and a curriculum which seeks to:

- produce citizens who have a properly informed perception of their own identity, as well as those of others
- actively promote an inclusivist as opposed to an exclusivist view of community, society and nation
- cultivate a depth of vision amongst pupils which addresses some universal values such as tolerance, social justice and honesty
- cultivate a view of the world which looks outwards not inwards
- develop an attitude of mind which has confidence to celebrate the familiar and the less familiar
- encourages pupils to recognize and celebrate a multiplicity of potential identities

The above is premised upon a particular perception of identity that views the concept of Welshness as fluid and dynamic, a view which embraces 'several different versions of Welsh identity and a variety of different contests over such identities' (Fevre and Thompson, 1999, p. 22). This recognizes the problematics of defining Welshness in a monolithic fashion, thus asking us not only to recognize 'the existence of variety and difference but (also) the very process of identity construction in which identities are not simply being made and remade all the time but argued and even fought over' (*ibid.*).

An education system which seeks to teach pupils about the importance and relevance of civic awareness and political action, has to be placed within this fluid concept of Welsh identity and construction. This itself envisages not only a comprehensive programme of education which centres upon the teaching of civic rights and responsibilities, particularly within the context of the new political arrangements through political devolution and the Welsh Assembly, but one which encourages pupils to view their identity more reflexively within a complex (postmodern) world.

What potential exists, therefore, within the proposals set out by ACCAC, for these aims and objectives to be met? It needs to be made clear from the outset that the Wales Curriculum 2000 proposals do not, at present, propose the explicit teaching of citizenship as a distinct entity. As well as the common requirements of the Curriculum Cymreig and Skills – Communication, Mathematical, Information Technology, Problem-Solving, Creative – the current proposals encompass Personal and Social Education (ACCAC, 1999c). This latter document emphasizes that pupils should be: -

> encouraged to become active citizens in a local and global context ... considering social and moral responsibility in a democratic society, becoming practically involved in the life and concerns of the community and learning how to be 'literate' in the political and economic realms. (p. 4).

The document claims that such 'active citizenship' implies:

- an understanding of the nature of communities in Wales and beyond and the roles, relationships, conflicts and inequalities that affect the quality of life, including exploring the rights and responsibilities in a democratic society
- encouraging pupils to be committed to community life and participation
- the cultivation of political literacy.

In practical terms, the document spells out, under the title 'Community Aspect', what this implies at each of the key stages:

KS1:
Know about the variety of groups to which they belong and understand the diversity of roles that people play in those groups.
Understand that they can take on some responsibility in their friendship groups.

KS2:
Know about aspects of their cultural heritage in Wales including the multi-cultural dimension.
Understand the importance of democratic decision-making and involvement and how injustice and inequality affect community life.

KS3:
Understand the nature of local, national and international communities with reference to cultural diversity, justice, law and order and interdependence
Understand the issues relating to democracy in Wales and know the rights and responsibilities of a young citizen
Know how representatives (MPs, MEPs, Members of the National Assembly and Councillors) are elected and what their roles are.

In terms of the criteria spelt out earlier – informed identity, inclusiveness, universality, outwardness, tolerance, multiculturalism – as well as the need to promote political literacy, and community awareness, the proposals score quite well. Interestingly, by making reference to the need to explore some of the reasons for social inequality, ACCAC's proposals on Personal and Social Education draw heavily upon the legacy of Community Understanding and reflect Wales' current social and economic complexity. Moreover, in this sense it could be argued that it offers a more radical package than that provided by

Crick, which tends to shy away at times from issues of inequality and their causes.

CITIZENSHIP EDUCATION IN WALES IN THE FUTURE: CAUTION OR OPTIMISM?

On the other hand, there are fundamental challenges ahead in Wales, not least of which, referred to at the beginning of this chapter, involves confronting the perceived apathy amongst pupils for contemporary politics. Therefore, I want to focus more attention upon some of these challenges and consider some of the ways in which they can be met.

In contrast to England, it must be remembered that citizenship education in Wales is not a separate policy proposal, it is one element of the wider package on Personal and Social Education. Moreover, it is not even assigned the term 'Citizenship', it comes instead under the heading 'Community Aspect'. In some senses, this has advantages in terms of curricular coherence and planning, with the 'Community' aspect of PSE sitting conveniently alongside the other aspects, particularly 'Social', 'Moral' and 'Environmental'. On the other hand, in terms of focusing curriculum planners' minds on a specific policy, there is also merit in having a separate set of proposals and, in this sense, citizenship education in England may have advantages over Wales, not least in terms of arousing public attention and interest. Yet, citizenship education in England and in Wales ultimately depends upon effective implementation and, here, it may be that Wales has gone for the wise move of including aspects of citizenship education within a wider coherent programme. Moreover, one of the most characteristic features of the NC in England since its inception is the incoherent means by which policies have been initiated; curriculum policy development has been bedevilled by a multiplicity of working parties offering different things. I fear that some of these lessons have not been learned.

In both England and in Wales, apart from the perennial issue of lack of time, there is also the vitally important need to convince teachers of the merits of promoting citizenship education in the widest sense. Here, there is a danger, particularly in Wales, of the view that citizenship education is a separate entity to be taught only through PSE, a view that has plagued cross-curricular thinking in secondary schools for years. A number of papers at the London Institute of Education Citizenship Conference rightly drew attention to the ways NC subjects can promote effective citizenship education. I would like to draw attention to some of the ways my own subject, history, could promote some of the values, dimensions, skills and traits outlined above.

The development of history in Wales is an interesting story and has focused sharply upon the issues of nationality, identity and citizenship raised in this chapter. The challenge for the architects of the history curriculum in Wales has been – and remains – the need to balance the teaching of a distinctive Welsh history dimension within the wider picture of British, European and world history (see Phillips, 1999, for a wider discussion of this). The most recent proposals maintain these links (ACCAC, 1999b) and can be creatively interpreted to provide opportunities to focus upon fundamental elements of citizenship education. For example, teachers could focus upon:

Community Understanding: by focusing upon the development of industrial and rural communities in Wales and the rest of Britain.

Curriculum Cymreig: which permeates many aspects of the proposals.

Civic Rights: in Wales (e.g. Chartism and Rebecca) and the wider world (e.g. Civil Rights Movement in the USA).

Global Understanding: by focusing upon aspects of world history.

Anti-Racism: in Wales (e.g. reaction to Irish immigrants) and the wider world (e.g. the legacy of the Slave Trade).

Commemoration: e.g. of the First World War.

In this brief summary, it is clear that there are rich opportunities for a positive approach to citizenship education in Wales through a subject like history. Similar potential occurs in geography (see Daugherty and Jones, 1999). Moreover, an important consideration here is the extent to which citizenship education may be a means by which subjects like history are saved from the curriculum broom cupboard (a useful argument to use when arguing citizenship's case).

The brief discussion of the teaching of history illuminates another challenge that faces the curriculum at large in Wales: that is, the need to teach distinctive cultural aspects of Welsh heritage in ways which do not create insularity and cultural exclusivity but instead promote the reflective, varied and dynamic vision of Welsh identity mentioned earlier. Moreover, one of the most depressing features of some aspects of the 'Cool Cymru' media spin and other 'banal' representations (see Billig, 1995) of Welsh national identity is the seemingly nonchalant and unassuming ways in which it has become fashionable to denigrate 'the other' – particularly the English. A challenge for schools in Wales in the future will be to attempt to counteract some of these negative starting points for identity formation. The ways in which the media impact upon children's perception of identity needs further research, particularly within the context of a changing Wales. Yet, it seems clear that a properly informed, serious, objective and balanced approach to issues of identity, nationhood and citizenship education is badly needed in Wales in the new millennium.

More attention should also be given in schools in Wales in the future to an issue that has been effectively brushed under the carpet in recent years, not only in education but in wider political and social life also, namely issues of 'race' and racism. As Williams (1999, p. 84) has rightly pointed out, 'there is no reason for believing that Welsh political consciousness has been immune to the influences of wider British racist ideology.' In 1996, racial violence leapt more sharply in South Wales than in any other part of the UK. Experience suggests that Welsh schools still suffer badly from the 'No Problem Here' syndrome revealed so brilliantly by Chris Gaine in England in the early 1980s (Gaine, 1987).

Finally, perhaps the biggest challenge of all involves convincing pupils in Wales of the importance of politics and political institutions. Efforts have already been made to educate pupils about the role and functions of the Welsh Assembly (Wallace and Johnson, 1999). There is scope for some optimism; the *Week In/Week Out* survey referred to earlier suggests considerably more support for the concept of a Welsh Assembly amongst young people than the population at large. Yet, ultimately, as with so many other aspects of curriculum and education, circumstances may be out of the control of schools. The extent to which young people ultimately see the value and purpose of politics and civic activity ultimately depends upon the ways in which politicians make efforts to connect with their needs. On the other hand, schools, curriculum planners and education policy-makers must also play a part. It is hoped that this chapter has in some small measure contributed to this discourse on citizenship education in Wales which has profoundly important implications for the future.

To summarize, I would argue that if we are to equip pupils in Wales to meet the challenges of life in the next century, civic education has to be based upon the following principles:

- A healthy respect for Welsh culture, heritage and identity but taught in a way that is not exclusive to alternative cultures.
- Full endorsement of the principles outlined in 'Community Aspect' that involves a programme of civic literacy which is taught both within PSE programmes and the existing NC subjects.
- Continuation of explicit education programmes designed to raise pupils' awareness of the workings of political institutions and their implications: here again, NC subjects such as history will have to play an important part.
- A genuine commitment within Wales to face up to and combat the issue of racism in predominantly 'all white' schools.

Perhaps these measures will go some way towards enabling Wales to 'grow up at last' (Jones, 1998) and meet the challenges of the new democracy in the new century.

REFERENCES

ACCAC (1999a) *Wales Curriculum 2000: Summary of the Consultation Proposals. Cardiff:* *ACCAC.*

ACCAC (1999b) *History in the National Curriculum: Proposals for Consultation*. Cardiff: ACCAC.

ACCAC (1999c) *Personal and Social Education Framework: Key Stages 1 to 4 – Consultation Draft*. Cardiff: ACCAC.

Ball, S. and Bowe, R. (1992) Subject departments and the 'implementation' of National Curriculum policy: an overview of the issues. *Journal of Curriculum Studies*, **24** (2): 97–115.

Billig, M. (1995) *Banal Nationalism*. London: Sage.

CCW (1991) *Advisory Paper 2 – Community Understanding – a Framework for the Development of a Cross-Curricular Theme in Wales*. Cardiff: CCW.

CCW (1993) *Advisory Paper 18 – Developing a Curriculum Cymreig*. Cardiff: CCW.

Daugherty, R. and Jones, S. (1999) Community, culture and identity: geography, the National Curriculum and Wales. *The Curriculum Journal*, **10** (3): 443–61.

Fevre, R. and Thompson, A. (eds) (1999) *Nation, Identity and Social Theory: Perspectives from Wales*. Cardiff: University of Wales Press.

Gaine, C. (1987) *No Problem Here: Multicultural Education in Predominantly 'All White' Schools*. London: Hutchinson.

Hall, T., Coffey, A. and Williamson, H. (1999) Self, space and place: youth identities and citizenship. *British Journal of Sociology of Education*, **20** (4): 501–13.

Jones, B. and Lewis, I. (1995) A Curriculum Cymreig. *Welsh Journal of Education*, **4** (2):22–35.

Jones, G. E. (1997) *The Education of a Nation*. Cardiff: University of Wales Press.

Jones, G. E. (1998) *Growing Up At Last: Education & the National Assembly*. Talybont: Lolfa.

Phillips, R. (1996a) Informed citizens: who am I and why are we here? Some Welsh reflections on culture, curriculum and society. Speech given to the SCAA Conference on Culture, Curriculum and Society. *Multicultural Teaching*, **14**: 41–44.

Phillips, R. (1996b) Education policy making in Wales: a research agenda. *Welsh Journal of Education*, **5** (2): 26–42.

Phillips, R. (1996c) History teaching, cultural restorationism and national identity in England and Wales. *Curriculum Studies*, **43**: 385–99.

Phillips, R. (1999) History teaching, nationhood and politics in England and Wales in the late twentieth century: a historical comparison. *History of Education*, **28** (3): 351–63.

Phillips, R., Goalen, P., McCully, A. and Wood, S. (1999) Four histories, one nation? History teaching, nationhood and a British identity. *Compare*, **29**: 153–69.

QCA (1998) *The Final Report of the Advisory Group on Education for Citizenship and the Teaching of Democracy in Schools* (Crick Report). London: QCA.

Roberts, B. (1999) Welsh identity in a former mining valley: social images and imagined communities. In R. Fevre and A. Thompson (eds) *Nation, Identity and Social Theory: Perspectives from Wales*. Cardiff: University of Wales Press.

Thompson, A. and Day, G. (1999) Situating Welshness: local experience and national identity. In R. Fevre and A. Thompson (eds) *National Identity and Social Theory: Perspectives from Wales*. Cardiff: University of Wales Press.

Wallace, T. and Johnson, T. (1999) *National Assembly for Wales Workpack*. Cardiff: Welsh Assembly.

Williams, C. (1999) Passports to Wales? Race, nation and identity. In R. Fevre and A. Thompson (eds) *Nation, Identity and Social Theory: Perspectives from Wales*. Cardiff: University of Wales Press.

Williams, R. (1985) Community. *London Review of Books*, 21 January.

Chapter 13

Thirty Years of Teaching Political Literacy in Scottish Schools: How Effective is Modern Studies?

Henry Maitles

INTRODUCTION

Across Europe there is increased awareness of the need for political education in school, and political literacy amongst young people in general: evidence for this includes the Crick Report, as to why and how citizenship issues for all pupils can be better, or at least formally, introduced into schools, and the National Curriculum Guidelines from the QCA; the establishment in the Republic of Ireland of a compulsory, examined course in Political Education; the continuing research in Europe as a whole of citizenship education involving some 20 countries (East and West) organized by IEA from Berlin; the continuing interest in this area from the newly democratic states of Central and Eastern Europe. International developments in the real world are central, as Harber (1997) has pointed out, to the development of education for democracy; and in Scotland, the formal opening of the Scottish Parliament on 1 July 1999 and the stated aim of the coalition government in Scotland to ensure that the workings of the Parliament are open to full participation from active citizens, suggest that political education in schools will be an important area for the politicians. Indeed, the Scottish Consultative Committee on the Curriculum, which advises the Scottish Executive Education Department, established, late in 1999, a Review Group to develop proposals for education for citizenship and democracy in schools.

The Scottish experience of Modern Studies clearly has an input, both in terms of relating the experiences over the last 30 years and in terms of learning from other experiences. My research since February 1998 has led to a detailed questionnaire to every modern studies department to solicit their views on the value of modern studies. There was a very encouraging response to this (over 50 per cent of schools). This was followed up by representative principal teacher interviews and a political literacy 'test' to representative S3/S4 pupils (Key Stage 4) to elicit the effectiveness of modern studies in delivering political literacy. This chapter will concentrate on the results of 'tests' comparing the political literacy levels of similar ability pupils, some studying modern studies, others not. Overall, the hypothesis that teaching modern studies has an effect on political literacy levels will thus be examined.

BACKGROUND: MODERN STUDIES IN SCOTTISH SECONDARIES

In a relatively short time, some 35 years, modern studies has had a marked effect on the curriculum in most Scottish schools, being seen by educators, pupils and parents as a meaningful addition to social subjects. Modern studies is in many ways a success story. There is little doubt, evidenced especially at election times, that modern studies departments in schools contain many of the most politically literate students in the schools. Sometimes this can be difficult to control, as happened in Glasgow south side schools during the construction of the M77 motorway extension; numbers of pupils truanted from school to participate in pressure group activities to oppose the extension, and some justified this to the media on the basis of their modern studies lessons on the importance of pressure groups! Starting as an amalgam of history and geography in the late 1960s and early 1970s, modern studies has developed into a mainstream subject, taking its intellectual concepts primarily from politics and sociology, taught now in over 80 per cent of schools at some level and accepted academically on a par with the other social subjects; indeed, in most years in the 1990s, there were more presentations at 'Higher' (the university entrance qualification) in modern studies than in history or geography.

AIMS OF MODERN STUDIES

There are three main educational areas developed through modern studies. The first area provides knowledge and understanding. This involves varied content and includes both institutional knowledge, local/Scottish/British/world affairs and knowledge of methods of participating. The content is laid down at Standard Grade (taught in S3/4 (Key Stage 4) of secondary schools) and Higher Grade, although there is scope for choice at Higher. In S1/S2 (the first years of secondary education), though, there is much more scope in the absence of prescription and a recent survey of some 150 modern studies departments in large secondaries in Scotland found the following general areas to be popular amongst teachers:

- representation
- participation
- rights and responsibilities
- the media/bias/exaggeration/opinion
- human rights/racism/multicultural issues
- the gender gap
- USA
- developing world/development issues
- law and order
- Europe
- needs and wants (elderly, housing, employment)
- United Nations
- local comparison with a different country

Most modern studies teachers find the overall content stimulating, and the need to update the material ensures that the subject is constantly challenging, although this can mean a large workload.

The second area is the development of enquiry skills involving evaluating and investigating. Evaluating is the promotion of pupil ability in the critical appraisal and evaluation of information about social and political institutions, processes and issues through:

- recognising lack of objectivity
- making comparisons and drawing conclusions
- expressing support for a personal or given point of view (SQA, 1997, p. 7)

These are clearly central to the development of political literacy at any level; progression from S1 to S6 involves the use of increasingly complex, subtle and abstract sources. For the 'Higher', pupils are expected to analyse critically and evaluate complex sources and to show, through a decision-making exercise, how their evaluating skills can be applied in other specific contexts. Investigating involves the processes of planning, recording, analysing/synthesizing and reporting; again it is a vital skill for political literacy.

Thirdly, modern studies has a distinctive and important role in attempting to develop positive attitudes amongst pupils/students. This should include at all levels:

- respect for truth and reason;
- willingness to accept that other views and beliefs can have validity;
- willingness to accept the possibility of, and limits to, compromise;
- confidence and enterprise in pursuing information and communicating views. (SQA, 1997, p. 8)

The Scottish Consultative Committee on the Curriculum has suggested that modern studies should develop open-mindedness, tolerance and the moral and ethical responsibilities of individuals (SCCC, 1997). This is often seen in pupil activities and course content focusing on issues such as poverty, the elderly, development issues and civil and equal rights. Where dealing with controversial issues, modern studies teachers should be allowing pupils to examine evidence relating to a range of views.

METHODOLOGY IN THE CLASSROOM

This factual summary of what is taught in the subject misses out a central feature of the subject – its dynamism in the classroom. The teaching and learning of modern studies has since its development as a distinctive sociological/political subject been characterized by the enthusiasm of the teachers and novel methodologies. Central to this has been the use of 'dialogue' in the classroom. Indeed, debate, role-play, dialogue, group work, stages work and the varied use of media and IT have been central to its delivery in the classroom, especially around elections and participation. In particular, modern studies teachers are aware that the content of the subject means that many pupils will be coming to the classroom with some experience that they can input to the lesson. As the Scottish Inspectorate noted:

> Most teachers encouraged a classroom atmosphere in which open questioning and challenging of opinion was common-place. (HMI, 1992, p. 31)

Clearly, pupils coming out of schools and able to handle complex skills, with a knowledge of political institutions and able to debate, articulate and discuss political issues would be welcome in any democracy, even if they were sure of their rights and consequently make choices unpalatable to some.

SCOPE AND METHODOLOGY OF THE RESEARCH

The last major research into modern studies teaching was undertaken in the early 1970s. Its findings (Mercer, 1973) suggested that modern studies teaching was not particularly effective in terms of comparing the political/institutional knowledge of students studying modern studies and those not. In this, it was similar in overall findings to the 1970s evidence of political education teaching in England (Stradling, 1977). This current new research, attempting both to reassess and further develop our knowledge of the effectiveness of modern studies, can be encapsulated in the following four stages:

Stage 1: A questionnaire was sent to all known modern studies departments in Scotland. It asked a number of general questions relating to the subject and some specific ones on the values developed through the subject. The return was exceptionally high, with over 50 per cent of all departments returning the questionnaire.

Stage 2: There were 30 interviews conducted with a representative sample of principal teachers to develop the answers from the questionnaires. They were picked from those returned and included schools in different socio-economic areas, from the denominational and non-denominational sectors and from all areas of Scotland.

Stage 3: A 'test', designed to fit in with the IEA study in Europe, which the last government declined to let Scotland join, was given to two distinct groups of S3/4 pupils (Key Stage 4). First, the 30 principal teachers interviewed were asked to administer the test, and there were approximately 900 returns; second, principal teachers of joint departments (either history/modern studies or geography/modern studies) were asked to give the 'test' under exam conditions to groups of similar ability pupils in both subjects at the same time.

Stage 4: This stage is designed to allow the pupils to give their opinions of modern studies through detailed interviews and has not yet been undertaken, itself a reflection of the large number of interviews and tests that came from the unusually high Stage 1 return. However, this stage is now a priority.

This chapter will describe and tentatively analyse Stage 3 and, in particular, the 'tests' given to the modern studies and non-modern studies pupils in the joint departments. This stage is undoubtedly the key way of checking whether modern studies teaching is effective. To ensure objectivity, joint department principal teachers were asked to ensure both that the test was given to pupils of similar ability, and was given under formal conditions, with no colluding.

Of the three main aims of modern studies teaching outlined above, the 'test' was designed to examine political literacy in terms of institutional knowledge and the development of positive political attitudes. Although, as outlined above, enquiry skills are important components of modern studies development, it was felt in discussion with principal teachers that this area, generally thought by the Scottish Examination Board to be well taught, could not be properly assessed in this study without giving examination questions similar to existing course assessments. Methods of assessing this area needs further development, especially as it can be argued that a politically literate citizenry needs these transferable skills as much, if not more than, knowledge per se (Maitles, 1999).

The positive attitudes section of the test was hard to devise and to analyse, especially as 'positive' itself has such value connotations. To give two examples of the difficulty, pupils who suggest that the police should have more power to deal with crime were considered not to have developed positive attitudes in this question, but there is little doubt that more police powers might be seen as positive by many people. Similarly, the question which asked whether there should be a European army to intervene in European 'trouble spots' is equally problematic. None the less, there has been an attempt to ensure a similar 'positive' perspective to that developed for the IEA civics survey and this Scottish research thus pushed on with our, admittedly sometimes subjective, criteria of positiveness in terms of values.

POLITICAL/INSTITUTIONAL KNOWLEDGE

This section of the test was divided into four subsections of Scottish Issues, British Issues, European Issues and International Issues. There is clear evidence (see Table 13.1 showing the overall percentages of modern studies pupils throughout Scotland and Table 13.3 showing modern studies/non-modern studies from the joint department control groups) that modern studies students were significantly more knowledgeable in terms of political/institutional affairs than their non-modern studies counterparts. In terms of Scottish, British and International issues there were overall significant differences (14.5 per cent, 18.7 per cent and 14.4 per cent respectively) and in the European section, a question relating to footballer John Collins (answered well by the non-modern studies group) ensured a much closer overall result in that section.

In particular, as the tables show, in questions, such as the parliamentary constituency of the school, the leader of the Liberal Democrats, the city(ies) of the European parliament, the residence of the US President and the Secretary-General of the UN, there was a large difference between the modern studies and non-modern studies groups. Sometimes, for example in questions on the two parties likely to dominate the Scottish Parliament, the leader of the Liberal Democrats and the President of Iraq, the knowledge of modern studies pupils is impressive. In other areas, such as knowing the local MEP and about the Snowdrop campaign, the results are less impressive. In particular, the section on Europe suggests some significant gaps and in the new millennium teachers are going to have to consider either how to start teaching this area (as opposed to seeing it as 'boring') or, if they are already doing so, teach it more imaginatively.

POLITICAL ATTITUDES

This part of the test proved to be far more problematic. Tables 13.2 and 13.4 suggest that there is much less difference between the modern studies and non-modern studies groups. In the result of attitudes towards voting rights for immigrants (Table 13.4 section 1), it might have been reasonable to expect that there would have been a more enlightened, positive attitude from modern studies pupils than the results show. In particular, the question suggested, and we

Table 13.1 Findings from modern studies national 'test': knowledge/political literacy

Knowledge/political literacy	Modern Studies pupils % correct
A. Scottish Issues	
Overall	68.8
1a. Local MP	70.7
1b. Parliamentary constituency	24.8
1c. MP's political party	73.2
2. Leader of SNP	60.6
3. Two services from local council	68.7
4. City of Scottish Parliament	92.3
5. Two parties likely to dominate Scottish Parliament	90.3
B. British Issues	
Overall	55.2
1. Snowdrop campaign wanted what?	47.7
2. Her Majesty's Opposition	50.3
3. Name of Foreign Secretary	60.0
4. Leader of Liberal Democrats	68.4
5. Who delivers the Budget?	49.7
C. European Issues	
Overall	32.7
1. European Parliament city	49.4
2. Spot non-member EU	41.3
3. Who is Helmut Kohl?	26.5
4. Local MEP	13.9
5. John Collins' football club	64.5
D. International Issues	
Overall	50.9
1. Who lives 1600 Pennsylvania Ave?	53.6
2. Secretary-General UN	19.4
3. President of Iraq	58.1
4. Who is Nelson Mandela?	72.6
5. Where will the next Olympics be?	50.9

Table 13.2 Findings from modern studies national 'test': attitudes/opinions

Attitudes/opinions	Modern Studies pupils %
1. *Voting rights for immigrants*	
(agree/totally agree)	
a. No immigrants should have voting rights	16.1
b. Immigrants who accept British culture	62.3
c. Those law-abiding for more than 5 years	61.3
d. All immigrants should have voting rights	36.5
2. *Controversial Issues*	
(percentage voting for/against)	
a. Immediately close down nuclear power stations	28.7/15.5
b. Limit speed and private traffic	52.6/11.6
c. Reduction of wages in Scotland to finance	
investments in poorer countries	6.8/59.4
d. Full equality for women	78.4/5.5
e. Use of European army to stop war	54.2/5.8
f. Reduce immigration into Scotland	26.1/22.3
g. Minimum price for Third World goods	21.3/18.7
h. Increased powers for the police	51.0/17.7
i. European integration and currency	24.8/22.9
j. End religious segregation in education	44.2/18.4
k. Death penalty for convicted terrorists	33.2/30.2
l. Arm all police	25.5/30.2
3. *Motorway through your area*	
(weight to saving: much/very much)	
a. Stone Age religious site	21.2
b. Medieval church	22.9
c. An old factory still in use	17.1
d. War memorial	54.5
e. Residence of a famous dead poet	27.7
f. Nesting site for a threatened bird	44.2
g. Housing scheme	41.3
h. Area of natural woodland	59.7

Table 13.3 Findings from comparison 'test': knowledge/political literacy

Knowledge/political literacy	Modern Studies % correct	Non-Modern Studies % correct
A. Scottish Issues		
Overall	68.3	53.8
1a. Local MP	77.6	60.5
1b. Parliamentary constituency	36.7	13.5
1c. MP's political party	85.7	58.0
2. Leader of SNP	41.8	37.0
3. Two services from local council	67.4	58.8
4. City of Scottish Parliament	77.6	78.2
5. Two parties likely to dominate Scottish Parliament	85.7	74.8
B. British Issues		
Overall	44.3	25.6
1. Snowdrop campaign wanted what?	34.7	27.7
2. Her Majesty's Opposition	35.7	21.9
3. Name of Foreign Secretary	46.9	21.9
4. Leader of Liberal Democrats	65.3	27.8
5. Who delivers the Budget?	38.8	28.6
C. European Issues		
Overall	28.0	25.0
1. European Parliament city	38.8	31.1
2. Spot non-member EU	31.6	21.0
3. Who is Helmut Kohl?	15.3	10.1
4. Local MEP	7.1	0.0
5. John Collins' football club	60.2	66.4
D. International Issues		
Overall	50.2	35.8
1. Who lives 1600 Pennsylvania Ave.?	45.9	25.2
2. Secretary-General UN	27.6	2.5
3. President of Iraq	65.3	55.5
4. Who is Nelson Mandela?	55.1	38.7
5. Where will the next Olympics be?	50.2	57.1

Table 13.4 Findings from comparison 'test': attitudes/opinions

Attitudes/opinions	Modern Studies %	Non-Modern Studies %
1. *Voting rights for immigrants*		
(agree/totally agree)		
a. No immigrants should have voting rights	13.1	19.5
b. Immigrants who accept British culture	52.5	52.6
c. Those law-abiding for more than 5 years	59.6	56.8
d. All immigrants should have voting rights	32.3	34.7
2. *Controversial Issues*		
(percentage voting for/against)		
a. Immediately close down nuclear		
power stations	27.3/19.2	31.4/20.3
b. Limit speed and private traffic	53.5/9.1	42.4/15.3
c. Reduction of wages in Scotland to		
finance investments in poorer countries	5.1/55.6	11.9/51.7
d. Full equality for women	69.7/2.0	64.4/10.2
e. Use of European army to stop war	46.5/7.1	54.2/12.7
f. Reduce immigration into Scotland	29.3/19.2	33.9/25.4
g. Minimum price for Third World goods	16.2/22.2	18.6/17.0
h. Increased powers for the police	44.4/18.2	52.5/11.9
i. European integration and currency	16.2/23.2	29.7/22.9
j. End religious segregation in education	39.4/20.2	46.6/14.4
k. Death penalty for convicted terrorists	36.4/26.3	39.0/29.7
l. Arm all police	25.3/40.4	34.8/40.7
3. *Motorway through your area*		
(weight to saving: much/very much)		
a. Stone Age religious site	19.2	29.7
b. Medieval church	21.2	6.3
c. An old factory still in use	26.3	10.1
d. War memorial	58.6	61.9
e. Residence of a famous dead poet	36.4	40.7
f. Nesting site for a threatened bird	47.5	60.2
g. Housing scheme	45.5	56.8

might have expected modern studies students to realize this, that immigrants are British citizens and thus should have the right to vote along with all others. However, there is virtually no difference between the modern studies and non-modern studies groups.

Similarly with the controversial issues section (Table 13.4 section 2); with the proviso vis-à-vis 'positive' explained above, the results suggest that non-modern studies students were 'more positive' in terms of nuclear power, financing investments in poorer countries, minimum prices for goods from developing countries, European integration and ending religious segregation of schools. On the other hand, modern studies students were 'more positive' in terms of transport policy, full equality for women, immigration into Scotland, police powers, reintroduction of the death penalty and arming the police. Third, in terms of the motorway through a local area (See Table 13.4 section 3), modern studies pupils were keener to save a threatened workplace (26.3 per cent to 10.1 per cent) and slightly keener in terms of the overall most popular choice (perhaps showing the growing popularity of the environment lobby with young people) of saving an area of natural woodland (66.7 per cent to 65.3 per cent). For all the other options, non-modern studies pupils were keener to save the proposed feature. Finally, in terms of the outlook towards Europe in 40 years time, the overall result (Table 13.5) was generally negative, perhaps reflecting the lack of learning in the area and the lack of interest by departments.

TENTATIVE CONCLUSIONS

It can be tempting to overgeneralize from these results, especially as the research is fairly large scale. This has to be avoided because of the individual school differences that can skew the results. However, it can perhaps be argued that the following conclusions can be reasonably drawn.

There is a significant difference in terms of political literacy/institutional knowledge between those S3/4s doing modern studies and those not. In this sense, modern studies teachers have been effective in ensuring that one of the main aims of the subject has been well carried out, although there is often a claim made that this knowledge is a function of interest that brought the pupils to modern studies in the first place.

There is not, however, a generalized significant difference in terms of 'positive' attitudes and 'positive' values between those studying modern studies and those not. There are, perhaps, and again tentatively, a number of possible explanations for this. First, the impact of what goes on outside school has an obvious (and indeed usually welcome) effect on learning and modern studies, like most general teaching involving controversial issues, has stressed the objective non-biased approach of the teacher. As has been suggested by Stradling (1984) and more recently by Ashton and Watson (1998), it is possible

Table 13.5 Findings from Modern Studies national/comparison 'test': Europe in 40 years time

	MS National	MS Control	Non-MS Control
		(percentages likely, very unlikely/ unlikely, very unlikely)	
a. peaceful	18.1/52.6	18.2/39.6	17.8/49.2
b. overpopulated	58.1/8.7	52.5/10.1	61.9/6.8
c. some states exploiting others	37.4/13.9	36.4/17.2	37.1/16.9
d. prosperous/wealthy	30.7/28.4	30.3/21.2	37.1/28.0
e. democratic	47.7/12.6	55.6/8.1	42.4/19.5
f. polluted	74.8/4.5	68.7/8.2	80.5/5.9
g. torn by rich/poor conflict	38.7/25.8	40.4/17.2	39.0/20.3
h. torn by ethnic conflict	34.2/21.9	34.3/30.3	34.7/14.4

that this approach can have the effect of reinforcing attitudes/biases picked up outside the school whether from peer or media or family. Teachers may have to reassess how they deal with this, in particular through developing confidence in strategies for dealing with these controversial political issues. Secondly, the generalized lack of rights (and thus responsibilities) given to young people in schools (and indeed in the wider world) may lead to a lack of the very values and democratic ideals that it is hoped to develop. Dobie (1998) outlined the current research in Scotland on pupil councils in schools, and Hannam (1998) further emphasized some of the weaknesses of the overall practice in Britain, although there are plenty of examples in both works and in others, such as Polan (1989) of more positive developments. Further, in the West of Scotland there has been the recent move towards generalized 'curfews' for young people in some areas of socio-economic deprivation. This is not the place to go into the rights and wrongs of this particular Scottish Office (now Scottish Executive) initiative, other than to say that the one group not consulted about the proposal was those young people affected, the vast majority of whom, it is assumed, are not the troublemakers targeted.

Third, there is the case made that history and geography also have the development of positive attitudes as an aim and this is reflected in these results. Finally, as many have suggested (for example, Arnstine, 1995; Puolimatka, 1995; Levin, 1998), democracy teaching to be effective may have to be taught in democratic structures and Scottish schools at present do not lend themselves well to this description. The case for democratic participation by young people, whilst it may lead to unpalatable decisions on occasion (for example, Polan, 1989) is something that teachers and educationalists will have to take more on board.

REFERENCES

Arnstine, D. (1995) *Democracy and the Arts of Schooling*. Albany: State University of New York Press.

Ashton, E. and Watson, B. (1998) Values education: a fresh look at procedural neutrality. *Educational Studies*, **24** (2): 183–93.

Dobie, T. (1998) Pupil Councils in primary and secondary schools. In D. Christie, H. Maitles and J. Halliday (eds) *Values Education for Democracy and Citizenship*. Glasgow: Gordon Cook Foundation/University of Strathclyde.

Hannam, D. (1998) Democratic education and education for democracy through pupil/student participation in decision making in schools. In D. Christie, H. Maitles and J. Halliday (eds) *Values Education for Democracy and Citizenship*. Glasgow: Gordon Cook Foundation/University of Strathclyde.

Harber, C. (1997) International developments and the rise of education for democracy. *Compare*, **27** (2): 179–91.

HMI (1992) *Effective Teaching and Learning in Scottish Secondary Schools: Modern Studies*. Edinburgh: HMSO.

Levin, B. (1998) The educational requirement for democracy. *Curriculum Inquiry*, **28** (1): 57–79.

Maitles, H. (1999) Political education in schools. *International Journal of Inclusive Education*, **3** (2) (April–June): 181–90.

Mercer, G. (1973) *Political Education and Socialisation to Democratic Norms*. Glasgow: University of Strathclyde.

Polan, A. (1989) An experiment in sixth form democratic participation. *Educational Review*, **41** (1): 9–17.

Puolimatka, T. (1995) *Democracy and Education: The Critical Citizen as an Educational Aim*. Helsinki: Suomalainen Tiedeakatemia.

QCA (1998) *Education for Citizenship and the Teaching of Democracy* (Crick Report). London: QCA.

SCCC (1997) *Higher Still Modern Studies*. Edinburgh: Scottish Consultative Committee on the Curriculum.

SQA (1997) *Standard Grade Arrangements in Modern Studies*. Dalkeith: Scottish Qualifications Authority.

Stradling, R. (1977) *The Political Awareness of the School Leaver*. London: Hansard Society.

Stradling, R. (1984) The teaching of controversial issues: an evaluation. *Educational Review*, **36** (2): 121–9.

Chapter 14

Revisioning Citizenship Education: The Irish Experience

John Hammond and Anne Looney

INTRODUCTION

The process of 'revisioning' citizenship education is an international one. The plea to 'do something about citizenship in schools' seems to be almost universal. If it is true that, as Cuban (1990) suggests, when society has as an itch, schools get scratched, in the matter of citizenship, society must be very itchy indeed! The aim of this chapter is to see what 'itched' Irish society, when, in March of 1993 the National Council for Curriculum and Assessment published its discussion paper on Civic, Social and Political Education (CSPE) and to examine the strategies followed to develop provision in this area in post-primary schools in the Republic. As yet no evaluation has taken place as to whether what has evolved offers a soothing balm or a further irritant for society's concerns. This chapter may represent a first reflective step towards such an evaluation.

THE CHANGING CONTEXT

Civics has been on the school timetable in Irish post-primary schools since 1966. The course focused on knowledge of the institutions and structures of the state – it was very much a matter of education about citizenship, rather than education for or through citizenship. In 1989 a new programme for lower secondary education – the Junior Certificate – was introduced, but the new course prepared for social and political studies was never implemented. Civics was then a low-status subject, marginal to the curriculum, the timetable, the allocation of resources and, largely, the hearts and minds of teachers and students. Teachers rarely chose to teach civics. In fact college degrees in sociology and politics were not recognized for the registration of teachers. Civics had a habit of appearing unannounced on teachers' schedules. And on school timetables it exhibited a tendency to transform itself into anything from extra mathematics to drugs education. Understandable, though not excusable, in a largely monolithic and homogeneous society where the tools of the citizen – mores, norms, values, even voting patterns – were passed down from one generation to the next.

That much has changed in Ireland, and continues to change, has been well documented. W. B. Yeats, writing in the earlier part of the twentieth century compared the emergence of the state of Ireland to the birth of a 'terrible beauty'. Yeats's words are just as relevant in the early years of the twenty-first century. The emergence of the 'Celtic Tiger' economy – one of the fastest growing in the world with a 60 per cent growth in GNP in six years – the transformation of the unemployment crisis in the late 1980s into the labour shortage of the late 1990s and the development of Ireland as a hub of international communications and software development has indeed given birth to terrifying, if beautiful tiger cubs!

While the economic boom has many welcome features, it has significant implications for a people who may have created a national identity out of being impoverished, agrarian and generally in the process of leaving the country for far-flung lands – always in steerage, however, never in first class. Rethinking Irishness has become an urgent task. *Irish Times* critic and writer, Finton O'Toole, wrote at the end of 1999:

> At the moment, punch drunk from the effects of continually having pieces of the old Ireland falling on our heads, we're happier re-furnishing our homes than refurbishing our notion of a homeland. But, if only because the one ineradicable aspect of Irishness is a perverse desire to go against the grain, that, too will change. (28 Dec. 1999)

This task of the forging of a new national identity – symbolized most vividly in the current renaissance in all things Irish – is a process more influenced by Europe than by the rest of these islands. Ireland has been spectacularly successful at being European and benefited enormously from funding available to it as a peripheral country. This Europeanization of Irish society has many manifestations. Modern European languages are taken by the vast majority of students in schools. And you are almost as likely to see the flag of the EU as you are the tricolour on a major national building.

The rapid decline of influence of the Roman Catholic Church in Ireland has been remarkable for its pace and scale. The emergence of a secular culture has brought with it particular implications for civic education. For the most part, Ireland does not have a strong civic ethic. 'Being good' has meant, until quite recently, 'being a good Catholic'. With fewer of the latter now around, there is a need to explore a different rationale for ethical behaviour.

TOWARDS CIVIC, SOCIAL AND POLITICAL EDUCATION

All of these changes, together with the disaffection of young people from political and social institutions, a trend characteristic of developed, wealthy, secular societies, informed the preparation by the National Council for Curriculum and Assessment (NCCA) of the 1993 discussion document on Civic, Social and Political Education and the development of a pilot project. The movement towards revisioning citizenship education in the early 1990s was given greater dynamism by political commitment – the Labour Minister for Education placed citizenship (and sex) top of the curriculum agenda.

The discussion paper prepared by the NCCA proposed that, while citizenship education was the business of the whole school, discrete time should be allocated to CSPE – the equivalent of one class period per week. Such was the case with civics, however, and it had been less than successful as a 'subject' at lower secondary level. The discussion paper went one step further than suggesting provision. It proposed that CSPE be included in summative assessment for certification purposes. However, it stressed that the means by which certification could be achieved should reflect the nature and aims of the course. This principle has been fundamental to the development of the assessment of CSPE. The students who sat the CSPE Junior Certificate examination for the first time in the summer of 1999 had already submitted Action Projects which accounted for 60 per cent of their marks. These projects are based – as the title suggests – on participation in some form of civic, social or political action in their school or community. These range from inviting local public representatives to the school for a question and answer session to protesting on environmental issues; from setting up a student council to surveying local buildings for disability access.

A further development was the clear separation of civic education from personal and social education. They were seen as related but as having a different curriculum base. A strong pastoral dimension was seen as a particular feature of Social, Personal and Health Education, for example, and would have been reflected in the priorities of teachers involved in this area. Civic education, as indicated later, attracted teachers with different priorities.

The discussion paper, which drew in particular on the work of James Lynch (1992), proposed the following rationale for CSPE:

Civic, Social and Political Education prepares students for active participatory citizenship in local, national and international life. It should help students to use their minds well in a constantly changing and complex society. It should produce students who can explore, examine and analyse, who are skilled and practised in moral and critical appraisal and capable of making decisions and judgements through a clarified and reflective citizenship, based on human rights and social responsibilities. (NCCA, 1993, p. 11)

The course which was outlined for the first pilot schools was based around a number of key concepts identified as foundational to active participatory citizenship and as engaging for students at the lower secondary stage. Thus, the concept of 'stewardship' was included but 'due process' excluded.

A similar concept-based course is proposed for the curriculum in Northern Ireland. Pilot work is currently under way by the University of Ulster and the Northern Ireland Council for Curriculum, Examinations and Assessment. There, Social, Civic and Political Education aims to empower young people 'for a plural, just and democratic society' (University of Ulster, 1998).

The rationale, the key concepts and the course units (Govt. of Ireland, 1994), which developed in the Republic over time, give a clear vision of what active participatory citizenship means in a changing Ireland, Europe and world. One of its most salient features is that it is a dynamic and evolving vision. We are all too conscious of the results of concepts of Irishness which are immutable and 'owned'. It is interesting that a similar developmental approach is being taken in Northern Ireland.

Perhaps it is because of this sense of citizenship as dynamic and evolving that we are somewhat bemused at the seemingly agonized attempts elsewhere to 'define citizenship' and capture its core values. The approach we have taken may face accusations of being undertheorized, but its does appear that an overtheorization will succeed only in further distancing citizenship from the young citizens who must shape it.

DEVELOPING CSPE IN SCHOOLS

The introduction of CSPE to schools at lower secondary level took place on a phased basis. The syllabus framework for CSPE developed by NCCA was fleshed out through a feasibility study involving seventeen schools in 1992. The main outcome of the study was the drafting of a CSPE course for subsequent piloting.

A pilot project operated from 1993 to 1996 commencing with the participation of 57 schools and concluding with 138 – approximately 18 per cent of all post-primary schools. The purposes of the pilot were to develop the course with a view to its implementation in all schools; to test appropriate modes and techniques of assessment; to test models of in-career development for teachers of CSPE; and the identification and, where necessary, production of resource material for teaching in this area.

Finally, CSPE was introduced on a mandatory basis to all schools during 1996 and 1997 to be assessed as part of the Junior Certificate Examination (the national examination for all students as they approach the end of the compulsory period of education). The fact that a feasibility study and a pilot initiative preceded its introduction is viewed as having had a positive impact. First, the feasibility of pilot studies created a state of readiness among many students, teachers and schools and the education system in general for the advent of the course. Second, they provided opportunities to develop some commitment, confidence and 'expertise' among pilot teachers who later largely comprised the team charged with the dissemination of CSPE in all schools. Third, they resulted in the production of comprehensive resource material that provided both a secure foundation and the space for teachers to get to grips with the philosophical and methodological challenges of teaching the course. Most importantly, they highlighted the key issues and challenges at all levels that need to be engaged with on a continuous basis to sustain CSPE as a dynamic, developing area of the curriculum. Some of these we will return to later.

IMPLEMENTING CSPE

A comprehensive programme of in-career development was put in place to support the implementation of CSPE. Initially support for teachers focused on providing information and opportunities for discussion at regional seminars. Following this, in-service courses offering training in appropriate teaching practice and methodologies were provided to local networks of schools. Finally, and most recently, the emphasis has been on providing in-career development opportunities at school level for the teams of teachers involved in teaching CSPE and for whole staffs. The latter provision is crucial in enabling staffs to focus on the contribution which all teachers and curriculum areas can and do make to education for citizenship.

A range of additional initiatives has been taken to support the implementation of CSPE. The professional association for teachers of CSPE has been regenerated. Modules on CSPE have been provided in pre-service teacher education courses in a number of universities. Subsidized diploma courses have been offered for practising teachers in two universities. A national newspaper has produced a weekly four-page supplement on CSPE topics targeted at students and their teachers. A wide range of resource materials has been produced in co-operation with non-governmental agencies concerned with issues relating to poverty, homelessness, the environment, human rights and the law, among others.

ISSUES AND CHALLENGES

The implementation of CSPE has given rise to a number of issues which can be broadly categorized under three headings: provision for CSPE at school level; teachers and CSPE; and the role of guidelines and resource material.

The preparation of school management for the introduction of CSPE and their active support during implementation was found to be crucial. School management is instrumental in finding appropriate time and time-slots for CSPE on the school timetable, in clarifying among staff and students the relationship between CSPE and related curriculum areas particularly, social, personal and health education, pastoral care and religious education. Management selects teachers of CSPE. Management underscores or undermines the extent to which CSPE and education for citizenship become whole school issues with cross-curricular manifestations. Management can facilitate or impede school–community links and the nature and scale of action projects and political action. The performance of management in providing for CSPE ranged from wholehearted engagement on all these fronts to those schools who failed to make any provision for CSPE in the first two years of its existence largely in the belief that it was an initiative that would simply fizzle out. Such schools found themselves having to provide 'crash courses' in the third year to placate irate parents who wanted their children to participate in the assessment of the new subject.

The second set of issues is associated with teachers and their interest in and commitment to the subject. Teachers from all subject backgrounds and areas of the curriculum teach CSPE. Many teachers of CSPE come from the sciences and the technologies as well as the humanities and languages. Most come to teach it with no formal education in politics, sociology or philosophy. During in-service, teachers have regularly expressed the view that their decision to teach CSPE is reflective of the reason they opted for teaching as a career in the first place – a belief that the business of teaching was about 'making a difference' to the lives of young people as learners, developing human beings and members of society. They come to teach CSPE as citizens and as educators. In this sense, the subject CSPE has a whole-school dimension in being broadly based across the staff of the school.

However, teachers also articulate the challenges and difficulties they have faced teaching CSPE. Frequently, the lack of expertise in areas like politics and sociology leads to insecurity in handling controversial issues or undertaking Action Projects. Teachers have related the challenge they experience in encountering and revisiting their own value systems as a result of heated classroom debate or engagement with students in an Action Project. They draw attention to the difficulty of sustaining high-quality preparation and teaching practice for a subject with a relatively minor time allocation and, usually, little or no planning time. Difficulties have also been experienced in the dissemination of ideas, information and approaches among teachers within schools. This is essential in order to enlarge the team of CSPE teachers available to teach the subject in a school. Consequently, in these early days of CSPE, where a teacher of CSPE changes schools she can leave a considerable vacuum in her wake.

The provision of resource material/guidelines for the teaching of CSPE – the third category of issues – has been successful. Its existence provided instant 'security' for those taking the subject who felt they lacked expertise. It gave them the confidence to make the leap. The guidelines aimed to strike a balance between assisting a teacher in her task while not impeding her potential to develop her approach to and practice in the teaching of CSPE. Provision of exemplar resource material did not, however, prevent the production and publication of commercial textbooks, some of which were singularly inappropriate in the emphasis placed on knowledge and understanding over the action component of the course.

FUTURE DEVELOPMENT

> I learn by going where I have to go. (Theodore Roethke, from Moore, 1977, p. 425)

In many ways, the experience of developing and implementing CSPE concords with Roethke's perception of change and the learning process. The perceived success of this initiative has given rise to consideration as to how education for citizenship should be provided for at the upper secondary level, as yet uncharted territory for citizenship education. Should students experience further enhancement and development of their education as active, participatory citizens? Should the emphasis be placed on more formal, academic study of political or social science? Should we offer optional tasters of a range of congruent disciplines such as those of philosophy, social science, political science and anthropology? This range of possibilities is currently under consideration.

The experience has also highlighted a number of aspects of CSPE where further development and consolidation is required. What comes to mind most readily in this context is how best we can relate the learning experiences of students in CSPE to the broader school and system aim of education for citizenship. In the context of an increasing emphasis on whole-school planning and development in Ireland, consideration of how the overall educational experience of students prepares them for citizenship in democratic society should be prioritized. How well does each school engender the attitudes and values central to democratic life and society – personal well-being and autonomy, respect for others, civic responsibility and democratic participation? What about lessons other than CSPE classes? Do students learn the value of active participation in the CSPE lesson but find that other lessons are characterized by inaction and lack of participation?

Developments in the area of CSPE and a rolling review of the CSPE course will also need to take cognizance of a wide range of developments – educational and political – at national and international levels. The Good Friday Agreement carries with it responsibility for increased understanding, engagement and co-operation between all citizens of these islands – not simply North/South but East/West also. Ireland's commitment to full participation in the European Union requires that we develop our understanding of European politics and of what it means to be a citizen of Europe. Equally, developments in education in areas such as those of multiple intelligences, emotional intelligence and research into learning impacts on the development of an area of the curriculum such as that of CSPE.

But for the present we must content ourselves with having made a start in turning the aspirations of citizenship education into curriculum provision, in bringing to birth a new school subject and watching it take its first hesitant steps. As for its first words ...

> CSPE teaches young people that their opinion is valued, that instead of waiting for others to help it's a matter of doing it for yourself. It teaches you to stand out from the crowd and make a difference. (Anne-Marie Burke (14), CSPE student, Potumna, Co. Galway)

REFERENCES

Cuban, L. (1990) Reforming again, again and again. *Educative Researcher*, **19**(1): 3–13.
Govt. of Ireland (1994) *The Junior Certificate Syllabus for Civic, Social and Political Education*. Dublin: Government Publications.
Lynch, K. J. (1992) *Education for Citizenship in a Multi-Cultural Society*. London: Cassell.
Moore, G. (ed.) (1997) *The Penguin Book of American Verse*. Harmondsworth: Penguin.
NCCA (1993) *Civil, Social and Political Education at Post-Primary Level*. Dublin: NCCA.
University of Ulster (1998) *Social, Civic and Political Education in Northern Ireland*. Ulster: University of Ulster.

Chapter 15

Education for Citizenship and Identity within the Context of Europe

Alistair Ross

INTRODUCTION

New Labour has maintained many of the previous government's policies: in education in particular it emphasized that it was not interested in adjusting the structures of the curriculum (or of educational provision and administration), and was focusing on 'standards'. Nevertheless, there was a scheduled review of the National Curriculum, and the Qualifications and Curriculum Authority had already signalled that this was to include citizenship education. The Crick Report (QCA, 1998) recommended a new foundation subject for citizenship – to be mandatory in secondary schools, and to be recommended in primary schools. There have been parallel moves in the context of the European Union.

There has also been a series of initiatives designed to improve the understanding of European political institutions, calls for European citizenship and initiatives to foster an understanding of democracy amongst young people.

> Our education programmes should encourage all young Europeans to see themselves not only as citizens of their own regions and countries, but also as citizens of Europe and the wider world. All young Europeans should be helped to acquire a willingness and ability to preserve and promote democracy, human rights and fundamental freedoms. (Council of Europe, Recommendation R (83) 4 of the Committee of Ministers Concerning the Promotion of an Awareness of Europe in Secondary Schools, 1983)

> The European dimension in Education should ... strengthen in young people a sense of European identity and make clear to them the value of European civilisation. (Council and the Ministers of Education, 24 May 1988)

> Citizenship of the Union is hereby established. (Article 8, Treaty on European Union, Maastricht, 7 February 1992)

> Education systems should educate for citizenship; and here Europe is not a dimension which replaces others, but one that enhances them ... Education for citizenship should include experiencing the European dimension ... and socialisation in a European context ... because this enables each citizen to play a part on the European stage ... Teachers should develop a European perspective alongside national and regional allegiances; to make use of the shared cultural heritage; to overcome cultural and linguistic obstacles. (Green Paper on the European Dimension in Education, 29 September 1993)

> The objectives of the Socrates programme include: to develop the European dimension in education at all levels so as to strengthen the spirit of European citizenship. (Socrates Guidelines for Applicants, 1996, Erasmus, p. 6)

However, many educators in contemporary Europe approach the concept of European identity with some caution. While there is some enthusiasm for working in the area of European citizenship, this embraces perhaps a rather different conception from those outlined by the various Councils of Ministers and treaties. Any new notion of citizenship or identity based on the new Europe must be distinctly different from the old citizenships of the nation states: less ethnocentric, more diverse, more inclusive, less wedded to nationalistic conceptions. Osler (1994), for example, urges caution and the development of an inclusive rather than an exclusive understanding of identity and citizenship. Similar qualifications are made by Clough, Menter and Tarr (1995) in their analysis of developing citizenship education in Latvia. They suggest inclusivity rather than equality as a core concept, arguing that citizenship needs in plural contexts to be defined in terms of 'both/and' rather than 'either/or'. Hladnik (1995) argues that European citizenship might be used in a confining manner, limited to those with a legal definition of their status, and raises the important point that refugees should also be regarded as citizens, and that our definition needs to be broad, inclusive and to be separated from historical definitions of citizenship by birth, ancestry or naturalization.

The European programmes make much of the ideas of nested identities, and seek to promote citizenship at European level as part of a self-identity that includes national and regional elements. The QCA citizenship education proposals (for England) are perhaps understandably hazy. It is never clear of what one will be educated to be a citizen? England? The United Kingdom? No: pupils must learn 'to participate in society as active citizens of our democracy'. Citizenship education

> promotes their political and economic literacy through learning about our economy and our democratic institutions, with respect for its varying national, religious and ethnic identities. (QCA, 1998, p. 28)

This is a most unusual sentence: note the plurality of democratic institutions, and the singularity of the 'its' – these various identities therefore seemingly refer to 'our economy'. Perhaps *this* is the entity of which we are citizens?

Moves to educate for citizenship in the UK and in Europe thus both seem to have been initiated by some confusion, at the political institution level, about identity. What are the states, or superstates or unions, with which people identify? States themselves are not natural, but are recent social constructions that were forged at the beginning of the modern period: Unions or Communities of States are more obviously constructions. And as a phenomenon of modernism, it is perhaps unsurprising, in an age of postmodernism, that the legitimacy of states comes into question – both the legitimacy of individual states and the legitimacy of states per se, which may be no more than *Imagined Communities* (Anderson, 1983). And these initiatives are being made when there is a very real decline in understanding, sympathy and trust in politicians and political institutions. The recent European parliamentary elections (June 1999) saw remarkably low participation rates – a quarter in the UK, and less than a half in most countries in which voting is not compulsory. Why the decline? The traditional answer of the politicians, perhaps the obvious answer for them, is that we have not had enough political education. Schools have let down the nation (and the European Union) once again: make the schools tell the kids about the virtues of democracy, and all will be well. Politicians are rightly afraid that without popular endorsement at the polls, they lack authority: getting people to believe in the systems that they stand for might restore their legitimacy. But politicians have a much greater personal identity with the state (or the union) than do other people. Their role depends on the political entity: ours does not. Questioning the existence of the nation state, the boundaries, the rules of membership are challenges to the identity and legitimacy of the politicians and the public service, not to most of us. This is a powerful motivating force for the current political emphasis on programmes for citizenship. (Some non-politicians also feel themselves particularly threatened by the erosion of the idea of the nation state. Those who need the authority of a state, who chose to identify strongly with conceptions of 'their race', their genetic stock, are undermined by questions that challenge the legitimacy of this institution: hence the resurgence of extreme right-wing parties across Europe. The political answer to such individuals is that they need more political education: the current rhetoric for citizenship education is, as noted earlier, interlaced with references for education to promote inclusivity, about challenging xenophobia and racism.)

A second set of problems concern the nature of citizenship education itself. Citizenship 'for democracy' is particularly problematic. As Borhaug (1999) has pointed out, it rather depends on what kind of democracy. Traditional representative democracy puts its energies into ensuring the intermittent participation of the population in elections, through political parties that stand for broad principles. The key actor is the informed voter. The classic 1960s study of *The Civic Culture* suggested that the ideal citizen was a careful mix of the active citizen and the passive subject (and suggested that the leading exponent of this tradition was Britain (Almond and Verba, 1965). But there are other kinds of democratic action, and many people over the past two decades have become involved in more specific political activities than simply supporting broad political parties. The growth of 'single issue' politics has challenged traditional politicians, who have found electors deserting mass parties in favour of pressure groups, such as, in the UK, CND, Greenpeace, Greenham Common, Newbury, Drop the Debt and, in Europe, coalitions of Greens. The old political parties have had their activities and compromises challenged by informed political activists. This is an alternative kind of democracy, one that is less concerned with political structures and procedures than with the issues themselves. The key actor becomes the local activist.

But this is not what politicians and public servants want political education to be about. Their concerns are – quite naturally – with buttressing the systems and institutions that brought them into existence and that maintain them. This is not just the identity question, as I argued above, but also about civic duties and obligations – to participate in political processes, to understand the need for compromise, to accept the decision-making processes. If future citizens can be told how fair the existing system is, how the machinery of government works in the interest of the citizen, how interest groups must (of course) be listened to, but balances struck between competing interests – then they will accept the legitimacy of the political processes, and become part of *The Civic Culture* – the good citizen. Parallel arguments hold for supranational institutions such as the European Union: education seems to have been identified as a key factor in the development of a European 'identity', and as an essential way in which to mobilize legitimacy for the Union.

THE CHILDREN'S IDENTITY AND CITIZENSHIP IN EUROPE (CICE) NETWORK

At the European level, educators have already begun to set up various programmes: their motivation, however, is not quite in accord with European politicians. For example, the Children's Identity and Citizenship in Europe Thematic Network Project (85 European Universities, in 25 states) has members who are particularly concerned with promoting 'European citizenship' as a counter to xenophobia, racism and what they see as a potentially problematic overemphasis on 'local' nationalism (Ross, 2000, pp. 171–81). This chapter will look at some of the views of citizenship and identity within Europe held by members of this group.

An identity can often be defined as a negative: having a particular identity is *not* being 'the other'. A poem by Kafavis, 'Waiting for the Barbarians' (1942), gives a good demonstration of this. The word 'barbarian' comes from the ancient Greek *barbarizmo*: a non-Greek speaker – it is supposedly an attempt to indicate the bar-bar sound that the Greeks perceived foreigners to make when they spoke. A barbarian, then, is simply 'not a Greek-speaker', and a Greek 'not a barbarian'. Kafavis begins his poem with a description of a group of townspeople:

> 'What are we waiting for, gathered in the market-place?'
> 'The barbarians will come today.'
> 'Why is there no activity in the senate?
> Why are the senators seated without legislating?'
> 'Because the barbarians will come today:
> What laws can the senators pass now?
> The barbarians, when they come, will make the laws.'

The day goes on: the waiting continues. The level of anxiety rises:

> 'Why has this uneasiness suddenly started, this confusion?
> How grave the faces have become!
> Why are the streets and squares quickly emptying,
> And why is everyone going back home so very concerned?'
> 'Because night has fallen, and the barbarians have not come.
> And some men have arrived from the frontiers
> And they said that there are no barbarians any more.
> And now, what will become of us without barbarians?
> Those people were a kind of solution.'

The historian Linda Colley has analysed the way in which the United Kingdom defined itself in a similar way. In *Britons: Forging the Nation 1707–1837* (1992) she describes how the new union of Scotland and England invented itself as a unified state: united in its differences from continental Europe – founded on Protestantism, mercantilist profits, on Empire – on not being the Other, not being continental Europe. The national identity that was forged in Britain in the eighteenth century was, she argues, precisely that – a forgery – an invented unity based on opposition. Hobsbawm and Ranger, in an earlier book entitled *The Invention of Tradition* (1983), present a series of case studies from around the world showing how national traditions, often presented as symbols of national unity stemming from time immemorial, are often little more than creations of the recent past – practices 'of a ritual or symbolic nature, which seek to inculcate certain values and norms of behaviour by repetition, which automatically imply continuity with the past' (p. 1). The question this chapter seeks to address is this: in the development of a 'European identity', or 'European citizenship', are we likely to be creating a new sense of division, between 'Europeans' and the rest? Will we be forging a new identity based on Europeans and the Other? Will we devise new myths to establish an imagined past unity (for example, in the names of our joint projects, such as *Erasmus*,

Socrates and *Euridice*)? In order to be 'Europeans', do we need to have barbarians? And what will become of us without barbarians? Do we need those people as a kind of solution, in order to give us an identity?

EUROPEAN EDUCATORS' VIEWS

How do members of the CiCe network envisage citizenship in Europe? What do members of the network want to achieve in terms of identity? Examining what this group sees as the future of the European community, how they identify themselves and why they wish to be involved in this project will perhaps indicate some of the directions – and some of the tensions – that might emerge in the education systems of Europe.

Members of the network were recruited over 1996 and 1997. Older European academic networks were canvassed for support – the ICP on European Citizenship, the Youth and History Project. The International Association for Children's Social and Economic Education provided other members. The requirement of DGXXII that applications under this programme include members from every state and associate state in the Community led to searches for potential members in particular states – at various stages, Iceland, Finland, Belgium, Luxembourg and Portugal were all trawled for members to join the proposal. The initial suggestions were to focus on social, economic and political understanding and learning in the European context, and on children up to the age of about 13: the proposal broadened to include students to the age of 18, and came to select a shorter title that highlighted citizenship and identity. From the outset, the intention was to be cross-disciplinary, and to involve social and economic psychologists, sociologists and political scientists, as well as those involved in teacher education, and other professionals involved with children and young people. But the institutions that joined in the initial proposal were not the product of a representative survey of all the member states: they are an eclectic collection of those interested in the area and those with a track record in the area.

What do they want to do, and what do they hope to achieve? This chapter uses two sources of data to address these questions. In January 1999, I requested all individual members to send in data about their interests, so that the Network could publish a catalogue for members to find and identify potential partners. I believed – from the numbers given by institutional co-ordinators – that the Network had almost 200 individuals involved. We have collected 'Essential Information' data from 150 people – we also have a list of 190 names. This information has been analysed to determine the main sectoral interests of our membership. The second data source was assembled in April 1999, from responses to an e-mailed questionnaire to the 143 individual members who have given us e-mail addresses. About 20 of these addresses failed, and it is likely that not all of the others have yet been read. But 54 responses were received, and these have also been analysed.

In the Essential Information form, members were given a list of seven broad themes, and asked to indicate which ones particularly interested them. If they selected more than one theme, they were asked to indicate an order of strength of interest. For the purposes of this analysis, the themes identified as first and second are described as 'main interests', and the others as 'secondary interests'. For the respondents as a whole, the areas nominated are shown in Table 15.1.

Members were also asked to identify the age range which particularly interested them. Members with different age-interests showed some variation in the themes that interested them most. Table 15.2 shows the distribution of members interested in each age range: most members nominated at least two of the age ranges; some offered all six.

Table 15.1 Themes identified as main and secondary interests by CiCe individual members (n=150)

Theme	Number giving as a main interest	Number giving as a secondary interest
Social education	72	34
Identity	41	43
Cultural education	38	45
Civic education	30	41
Economic education	25	25
Citizenship education	24	64
Political education	24	43

Table 15.3 shows the percentages of members in each age group: note that there is substantial overlapping between the age groups. Major interest is shown in bold type, secondary interest in plain type. The distribution suggests that those with experience and interest in younger children are less concerned with citizenship, political and economic learning, and those with older students are less interested in identity.

There are also some geographical variations in these interests (Table 15.4). The responses were grouped into five major regions: the core of Europe (FR, DE, IT, LU, BE, NL, AT), the Scandinavian countries (NO, SE, IS, FI, DK), the eastern countries (EE, CZ, PO, SI, HU), the southern states (ES, PT, MA, GR, CY) and the British Isles (UK, EI).

Table 15.2 Numbers of members interested in each age range

Age range	0–4	3–7	7–9	9–11	11–14	14–18
Members	11	60	70	82	78	62

The countries of Eastern Europe are particularly uninterested in political education, which is probably a term that still bears overtones of Soviet domination pre-1989. They are also less interested in economic education and citizenship. Social education is a very strong interest in the eastern countries. The British Isles also have a less dominant major interest in political education, perhaps the legacy of the previous Conservative government's obsession with equating political education with indoctrination (though this is compensated for by a very large secondary interest). The British Isles have disproportionately large interests in economic education (perhaps another Thatcher legacy), and in citizenship. The core European Union states are also particularly interested in citizenship, civic education and political and economic education. The Scandinavian members are much less interested in these areas: their interests are in cultural education and social education. The southern states seem marginally less interested in identity as an issue, and marginally more interested in social education, but otherwise are close to the European norm.

Examining the findings from the smaller e-mail survey gives more detailed opinions and attitudes. Though the sample is small, it does appear to replicate broadly the gender difference, the states, regions and age-level interests of the larger CiCe membership. Asked to define the concept of 'Europe', most members saw Europe as either an area sharing trading or economic systems, or as an area sharing a common historical heritage (or both). Many others saw it as geographical unit, or as a political unit: very few would define Europe in terms of a shared cultural or religious heritage. Although the number of respondents was not large, there does seem to be some variation between those interested in different age groups, and those from different regions of Europe. Table 15.5 is constructed by weighting responses to take account of rank ordering and of distributing choices, and show the percentage of total scores in each category.

Those concerned with younger children see Europe more as a set of historical connections than as a geographical expression, and those concerned with older children the opposite. The reasons for this do not seem immediately apparent. The British Isles (and to a lesser extent the Scandinavian countries) are less inclined to see Europe as a common trading area; both are more likely to see it as a geographical expression. Those in southern countries are more likely to view Europe as sharing a historical identity.

Table 15.3 Percentage of members in each age range sharing particular themes of interest

Age range	N	Citizenship	Civic	Cultural	Economic	Identity	Political	Social
0–9	5	**0** 40	**0** 20	**20** 60	**0** 0	**80** 0	**20** 20	**80** 20
0–11/14	8	**0** 75	**12** 62	**37** 50	**0** 25	**62** 25	**0** 37	**50** 25
3–11	21	**20** 43	**15** 40	**33** 24	**15** 10	**20** 15	**10** 43	**47** 29
3–14/18	29	**14** 48	**17** 28	**20** 38	**31** 14	**28** 28	**20** 38	**55** 24
7–14/18	17	**18** 41	**24** 35	**35** 35	**6** 12	**30** 24	**18** 24	**82** 0
9–18	12	**25** 25	**8** 16	**33** 16	**8** 25	**16** 33	**16** 33	**58** 16
11–18	29	**28** 41	**28** 17	**24** 31	**28** 24	**20** 34	**24** 24	**45** 31
0–18	20	**10** 55	**25** 30	**35** 30	**20** 20	**20** 45	**5** 40	**45** 35
All	150	**16** 42	**20** 28	**26** 30	**16** 16	**28** 28	**16** 28	**48** 22

Table 15.4 Percentage of members from different regions sharing particular themes of interest

Region	N	Citizenship	Civic	Cultural	Economic	Identity	Political	Social
Core	27	**31** 48	**33** 33	**22** 33	**33** 22	**30** 22	**30** 22	**41** 33
Scand	35	**11** 29	**17** 23	**34** 43	**9** 20	**29** 37	**20** 31	**54** 26
Eastern	32	**9** 31	**13** 25	**34** 31	**6** 9	**44** 25	**6** 13	**72** 9
Southern	27	**22** 59	**22** 33	**26** 15	**11** 19	**15** 41	**22** 26	**59** 22
British Isles	19	**32** 42	**16** 32	**26** 37	**37** 21	**32** 26	**5** 53	**42** 27
All	150	**16** 42	**20** 28	**26** 30	**16** 16	**28** 28	**16** 28	**48** 22

Table 15.5 'Europe can be defined as': weighted scores of responses as a percentage of each category of respondent

Category	N	a geographical expression	a political expression	Religious/ cultural expression	an area sharing a common history	an area sharing trade/ economies	Other
All	**52**	**20**	**14**	**4**	**28**	**31**	**3**
3–14	*18*	9	11	0	40	34	7
9–18	*18*	30	16	10	14	31	0
0–18	*12*	32	10	3	34	15	5
Core	*10*	13	11	8	28	34	6
Scandinavia	*8*	38	23	0	19	21	0
Eastern	*15*	22	17	9	29	36	0
Southern	*13*	10	13	0	44	34	2
British Isles	*7*	29	14	0	29	14	14

What kind of Europe do CiCe members expect to see develop? I proposed a list of fourteen states not yet within the European Union – including some states not within geographical Europe, such as Israel (nevertheless, a regular contestant in the Eurovision Song Contest), Palestine and Morocco. Which of these did they expect to see join the Union within the next ten years? One respondent confidently predicted that all fourteen would join within this period: the other 49 who responded to this question averaged 3.1 countries. Most popular was Malta (68 per cent), though they have no application pending. The two countries on the list that are currently in negotiation were Latvia (38 per cent) and Romania (36 per cent). Both Switzerland (48 per cent) and the Ukraine (44 per cent) scored higher that these; Croatia was suggested by 26 per cent and Chechnya by 20 per cent.

Nine different possible 'European Identities' were proposed, and members asked to select and rank from these the visions that most closely matched their personal view. The list was partly derived from Risse's (1999) analysis of political discourses in Germany, France and the UK since the inter-war period (his five models are starred in Table 15.6 below). The results show that, among CiCe members, the conception of a Europe of shared values was most popular, followed by a Europe as part of the Western community and the nation state model. Risse suggested that the notion of a Europe of shared values dropped from the political discourses of the UK, France and Germany by the early 1960s, leaving only the nation state and the Western community models, but clearly the shared values model survives strongly within the discourse of education.

Table 15.6 Percentages of categories of respondents (weighted scores) on the future of Europe

Europe's future is as a …	All	3 – 14	9 – 18	0 – 18	Core	Scandinavia	Eastern	Southern	British Isles
n	*50*	*17*	*18*	*11*	*10*	*9*	*16*	*12*	*9*
– a group of nation states, operating between governments*	19	8	34	20	22	31	5	24	21
– 'my' nation state operating with the rest of Europe as 'the other'	3	1	3	6	3	13	3	0	0
– a community of shared values, cultural, historic, political*	30	46	16	31	20	17	38	39	29
– a 'third force', an intermediate alternative to capitalism and Communism*	2	0	4	2	1	0	0	0	7
– part of the Western community, based on liberal democracy and a social market economy*	24	34	13	22	38	29	24	12	18
– strong federation of weak states	5	1	11	4	6	0	9	2	3
– single economic community	12	5	13	11	8	6	18	8	18
– a stronghold of Christian values, based on strong social obligations*	0	0	0	0	0	0	0	0	0
– a weak federation of strong states	5	6	5	4	0	4	2	15	4

Again, there are significant variations between members with different interests. The 'community of shared values' is much stronger amongst those interested in younger children, and amongst members from eastern and southern states. The Europe of nation states is particularly unpopular with those interested in younger children and the eastern countries. The core states most closely matched Risse's analysis (which, of course was based partly on French and German debates).

Members were asked to identify the extent to which they wanted to see further European integration. Twenty-four per cent of respondents wanted a totally integrated single European state, and a further 40 per cent wanted a much greater degree of unity than at present. Eighteen per cent wanted some further unity than at present; 12 per cent felt the status quo was about right, and only 6 per cent wanted rather weaker links than at present. These figures were reasonably consistent across all groups, though the Scandinavian respondents wanted rather less integration than anyone else.

These underlying views of the nature of Europe and its future will clearly be of significance in determining the directions in which the CiCe network project travels. Members were asked about their personal reasons for being interested in children and young people's attitudes and views of European identity. Asked to rank various possibilities, the weighted scores are shown as percentages of the total in Table 15.7.

There is a broad consensus around the first four motivations: there is a strong wish to exert some kind of practical effect on future developments, with a sub-theme of an interesting research topic. While the Scandinavians and the British Isles are more strongly research-motivated, the core states and the eastern countries are less so. The southern states are particularly motivated by the wish to develop informed and critical attitudes.

The attitude to research is particularly interesting, because the intention of the Socrates programme in establishing Thematic Network Projects was to emphasize the development of shared university teaching, rather than shared research (other than research that specifically supports teaching). Members were asked to position their motivation in joining CiCe along a five-point scale, ranging from research-only to teaching-only. Only 24 per cent saw themselves as only interested in research; 41 per cent were motivated partly by research, but also by the links that would support their teaching, and 35 per cent by approximately equal teaching and research possibilities. Broadly, those interested in younger children tended to be more teaching-orientated and less research-orientated that those interested in older pupils. There was little regional variation, other than a tendency for rather more British Isles respondents to be research-only (36 per cent).

A question was asked that attempted to find what particular identities CiCe members used themselves: respondents were asked to select one of a pair of possible identities in fourteen different cases. As Giddens has argued recently, 'a

Table 15.7 Percentages of categories of respondents (weighted scores) on why they are interested in children's/young people's attitudes and views on identity in Europe

I am interested in children's/young people's attitudes and views on their identity within Europe because . . .	All	3–14	9–18	0–18	Core	Scandinavia	Eastern	Southern	British Isles
n	*51*	*18*	*18*	*11*	*10*	*9*	*16*	*11*	*9*
– it is an interesting subject to research	20	23	25	12	11	36	13	18	31
– I want to help children prepare for their future role in society	25	34	28	24	26	21	37	18	17
– I want to contribute to building a more integrated Europe	18	20	12	35	31	4	17	15	24
– I want young people to develop informed and critical attitudes to society	33	24	30	24	31	32	28	49	26
– I am required to do this by my employer/by law	2	0	2	4	0	5	3	0	0
– there is a general belief in favour of doing this, and I am contributing	1	0	2	1	0	2	2	1	2

sense of self is sustained largely through the stability of the social positions of individuals in the community. Where tradition lapses and lifestyle choice prevails, the self isn't exempted. Self-identity has to be created and recreated on a much more active basis than before.' Using a statistical method rather similar to that described by Asensio (2000, pp. 167–70), variations from the random can be established to show which identities are being preferred. For the respondents as a whole (n=34), Figure 15.1 shows the variation. The nation state is selected as a reference point for identity more than any other possibility; and equally, Europe is not selected. The larger European region is more popular (Scandinavia and Benelux were suggested as possible such 'larger' regions). This is not to suggest that the respondents were particularly insular or nationalistic: they identified with 'humanity as a whole' more often than not.

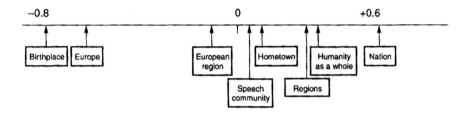

Figure 15.1 Identification with particular identities, greater or less than by chance selection, all respondents

There were considerable variations between members from different regions, too complex to describe fully in this brief space. Most notably, the British were, by far, less likely to identify with their nation (and more likely to identify with Europe or humanity as a whole than the norm). As George Orwell pointed out in 1941, 'England is perhaps the only great country whose intellectuals are ashamed of their own nationality. In left-wing circles it is always felt that there is something slightly disgraceful in being an Englishman and that it is a duty to sneer at every English institution'(p. 95). The Scandinavians were most likely to identify with their nation, with their region and their home town. The identification with Europe showed particular variation, as is shown in Figure 15.2.

What did CiCe members think were the defining characteristics of nationality? As a whole, they came down clearly for a shared culture, a shared language and shared social institutions, but there were some quite marked variations within this. Greek and Cypriot respondents showed a shared religious denomination as being more significant than any other region or nation. One of the options in this category was to describe nations as being artificial inventions: this was included as a reference to Benedict Anderson's analysis *Imagined*

Figure 15.2 Identification with Europe, greater or less than by chance selection, by regional group

Communities (1983), which challenges many assumptions about the cohesiveness of social groups. Only the English respondents gave any weight to this option.

Finally, there were some questions designed to elicit opinions about children's development and education, which will be reported on in this chapter only in brief.

Asked about the factors that were most likely to influence children's development of views about their nation, there was strong agreement that parents were the most significant factor, followed by other family members. There was some disagreement about the respective influences of the media and of schooling in third place. Given the expertise of the CiCe membership, a question asked for the ages at which children begin to define various alternative identities. There was a fairly large measure of agreement between the 40 members who responded: the average ages of the responses were as follows:

Identification as a	family member	2.4 years
	male or female	2.9 years
with	local area	7.0 years
	nation	7.5 years
	local region	8.6 years
	social class	8.8 years
	Europe	11.4 years.

What were the most appropriate ways to develop social, political and economic understanding with young people? There was a clear majority favouring an integrated curriculum approach over those wanting a separate curriculum subject such as civics. More felt that concept-based approaches were more appropriate than issue-based approaches. And opinion was evenly divided about the respective merits of informal and formal exchange programmes.

What emerges from this brief and rather unsophisticated survey of members is a picture that shows in some places clarity, cohesion and a sense of purpose, and in other areas local variations that show significant lack of agreement on the nature of some of the core concepts and issues with which we are engaged. There are significant measures of agreement on the sense of Europe as a shared cultural experience, with common values, and on aspirations to support moves towards further integration. There is agreement on the broad purposes of the work on which we are engaged – to improve young people's critical awareness of Europe and to prepare them for the future. There is a broad consensus on when children develop particular identities, and on the major factors that influence this.

But there are important differences. There are variations in what members consider to be the characteristics of a nation, and wide differences between the various identities that our members prefer. There are differences in emphasis in our various interests – some explicable by the particular age ranges that individual members are concerned with, and others that reflect national and regional experiences and pressures in the recent past.

The discussions and activities that develop during the course of the Thematic Network project will doubtless examine these similarities and differences, and perhaps illuminate them. But it does seem clear that CiCe members are going to approach the issues of identity and citizenship with proper caution: there is no sense of any wish to create a supernationalism that will imitate the nationalisms of the past. Perhaps we will not need the barbarians after all.

REFERENCES

Almond, G. and Verba, S. (1965) *The Civic Culture: Political Attitudes and Democracy in Five Nations*. Boston : Little, Brown & Co.
Asensio, M. (2000) A cross-national way to measure 'Europeanness'. In A. Ross (ed.) *Young Citizens in Europe*. London: CiCe.
Anderson, B. (1983) *Imagined Communities: Reflections on the Origins and Spread of Nationalism*. London: Verso.
Borhaug, K. (1999) Education for Democracy. Paper presented at the CiCe Conference on Children and Young People's Social, Political and Economic Understanding in the European Context. London, May 1999.
Clough, N., Menter, I. and Tarr, J. (1995) Developing citizenship education programmes in Latvia.' in A. Osler, H.-F. Rathenow and H. Starkey (eds) *Teaching for Citizenship in Education*. Stoke-on-Trent: Trentham.
Colley, L. (1992) *Britons: Forging the Nation, 1707–1837*. New Haven, CT: Yale University Press.
Giddens, A. (1999) *The Reith Lectures*. BBC April 1999.
Hobsbawm, E. and Ranger, T. (eds) (1983) *The Invention of Tradition*. Cambridge: Cambridge University Press.
Hosking, G. and Schöpflin, G. (eds) (1997) *Myths and Nationhood*. London: Hurst.
Hladnik, M. (1995) All different – all equal: who defines education for citizenship in a new Europe? In A. Osler, H.-F. Rathenow and H. Starkey (eds) *Teaching for Citizenship in Education*. Stoke-on-Trent: Trentham.
Kafavis, C. (1942; 2nd edn) Ποιηματα (Waiting for the Barbarians). In C. Trypanis (ed.) *The Penguin Book of Greek Verse*. Harmondsworth: Penguin.

Orwell, G. (1941) The lion and the unicorn: socialism and British genius. In S. Orwell and I. Angus (eds) *The Collected Essays, Journalism and Letters of George Orwell. Vol. 2: My Country Right and Left 1940–43*. Harmondsworth: Penguin (1970).

Osler, H. (1994) Education for development: redefining citizenship in a pluralist society. In A. Osler (ed.) *Development Education: Global perspectives in the Curriculum*. London: Cassell.

QCA (1998) *Education for Citizenship and the Teaching of Democracy* (Crick Report). London: QCA.

Risse, T. (1999) *European Identity Project* (http://www.iue.it/Personal/Risse/eirisse.htm). Florence: European University Institute.

Ross, A. (2000) What concepts lie behind 'European Citizenship'? Why are those in European higher education institutions concerned with children's developing ideas of citizenship? In A. Ross (ed.) *Young Citizens in Europe*. London: CiCe.

Chapter 16

Citizenship Education: An International Comparison

David Kerr

INTRODUCTION

In May 1996, as part of its work in monitoring the curriculum in England, the (then) School Curriculum and Assessment Authority (SCAA)[1] commissioned the National Foundation for Educational Research in England and Wales (NFER) to undertake an international review of curriculum and assessment frameworks in sixteen countries[2], to support its evaluation of different methods of curriculum organization.

The aims of the International Review of Curriculum and Assessment Frameworks (IRCAF) Project are:

- to build an accurately researched and ready-to-use resource, comprising a succinct description of the educational aims, structure and organization and the curriculum and assessment framework in each country, collectively referred to as '*INCA*';
- to help QCA analyse the outcomes of international comparisons;
- to provide comparative tables and factual summaries in specific areas of interest;
- to provide detailed information on specific areas to enable QCA to evaluate the National Curriculum and assessment frameworks in England. This is achieved largely through the conduct of thematic studies.

THEMATIC STUDIES

Thematic studies are conducted into specific areas or themes identified by QCA in order to provide:

- richer descriptions of practice in the countries concerned;
- clarification of context; and
- an analysis of fundamental issues, related to the English framework.

They draw on *INCA*, but involve an in-depth thematic study of the literature and/or a seminar, which brings together QCA officers, the project team and invited participants from most of the contributing countries.

The citizenship education thematic study, upon which this chapter is based, was the fourth of the thematic studies[3]. It was designed to enrich *INCA* by examining six key aspects:

- curriculum aims, organization and structure;
- teaching and learning approaches;
- teacher specialization and teacher training;
- use of textbooks and other resources;
- assessment arrangements; and
- current and future developments.

These aspects of citizenship education, for students aged 5 to 16/18, are used to structure this chapter. It is a shortened version of the thematic study. In particular, the sections of the study on the key aspects of teacher specialization and teacher training and use of textbooks and other resources are not included because of length. The thematic study combined material from: the IRCAF Project (from *INCA* and previous thematic studies); specific enquiries about citizenship education addressed to the sixteen countries; discussion at the invitational seminar on citizenship education held by QCA in January 1999; and published sources such as the National Case Study chapters from Phase 1 of the IEA Citizenship Education Project[4] and others. Practice in the sixteen countries studied is outlined where known, although complete information is not available for all of them at this stage. References are to the sixteen countries in the IRCAF Project and cannot be generalized beyond these. The combination of sources was intended to produce deeper insights into policy and practice in this area at individual country level, and to raise fundamental questions about aspects of citizenship education as they emerge from the comparative analysis.

CITIZENSHIP EDUCATION

Citizenship or civics education is construed broadly to encompass the preparation of young people for their roles and responsibilities as citizens and, in particular, the role of education (through schooling, teaching and learning) in that preparatory process. The term 'citizenship education' is used deliberately throughout this chapter as it is the term which describes this area in the curriculum in England. Though there is an attempt to draw a distinction between *citizenship education* and *civics education* later in the chapter, the area of citizenship education is covered by a wide range of terms across the sixteen countries and comprises many subjects. These terms include citizenship, civics, social sciences, social studies, world studies, society, studies of society, life skills and moral education. The area also has links to curriculum subjects and options, including history, geography, economics, law, politics, environmental studies, values education, religious studies, languages and science. The range of terms and subject connections underlines the breadth and complexity of the issues addressed within this area.

Citizenship education is highly topical in many countries at present, at the beginning of the new century, and urgent consideration is given to how better to prepare young people for the challenges and uncertainties of life in a rapidly changing world (Ichilov, 1998). It is no coincidence that the majority of IRCAF project countries are undertaking major reforms of schools and the curriculum which will be in place by 2004. Citizenship education is very much part of this reform process. It is the varied responses of countries to the unprecedented level and pace of global change at the end of the twentieth century which made the thematic study so fascinating and timely. England is no exception to this process. Indeed, the place and purpose of citizenship education in schools was examined in England, as part of the wider ongoing review of the National Curriculum (Kerr, 1999a, b and c; QCA, 1999a and b). It made the thematic study particularly apposite to the English context.

CURRICULUM AIMS, ORGANIZATION AND STRUCTURE

The curriculum aims, organization and structure of citizenship education can only be fully understood by recognizing the important role of context. This fits with the basic philosophy underlying the IRCAF project, namely that context is crucial to an understanding of policy and practice. Context is particularly important in reviewing citizenship education. The complex and contested nature of the concept of citizenship leads to a broad range of interpretations. These interpretations mean that there are many different ways in which citizenship education can be defined and approached. This is underlined in a number of recent comparative studies on citizenship, civics and education for democracy (Torney-Purta *et al.*, 1999; Hahn, 1998; Ichilov, 1998; Kennedy, 1997).

This diversity of approach came though very strongly in the presentations at the invitational seminar. However, participants agreed that though approaches and programmes in citizenship education could be readily transported from one country to another, such approaches and programmes would only succeed if they took due account of the unique historical, cultural and social traditions of the new context. This is an important lesson when citizenship education is being reviewed and renewed. What works in one context cannot simply be transported to another. Careful adaptation rather than wholesale adoption should be the watchword. This applies whether at national, regional, local, school or individual classroom level. A number of the newer democracies among the sixteen IRCAF countries reported difficulties when attempting to introduce ideas and practices from the longer established democratic countries into their schools. This was very evident in Hungary and Korea. It is therefore important to recognize and respect not only the breadth of interpretations of citizenship across the sixteen countries but also different approaches which such interpretations lead countries to take to citizenship education.

Broad contextual factors in citizenship education

A review of *INCA* and other literature sources reveals a number of broad contextual factors which influence the definition of and approaches to citizenship education in the sixteen countries involved in the project. The main contextual factors are:

- historical tradition
- geographical position
- socio-political structure
- economic system
- global trends

There is neither space nor time in this chapter to examine their relative influence and interplay within each country and across countries

Detailed structural factors in citizenship education

The broad contextual factors, in turn, influence the nature of a number of detailed structural factors concerning the organization of the system of government and education in each country. These structural factors are important because they impact not only on the definition and approach to citizenship education but also on the size of the gap between the rhetoric of policy (what is intended) and the practice (what actually happens) in citizenship education. The main structural factors are:

- organization of, and responsibilities for, education;
- educational values and aims; and
- funding and regulatory arrangements.

Organization of, and responsibilities for, education

How education is organized and how responsibilities are held and delegated by governments within education systems is an important structural factor. The sixteen countries in the thematic study can be divided into two groups:

Group A: Those with centralized governments: England, France, Hungary, Italy, Japan, Korea, The Netherlands, New Zealand, Singapore, Spain and Sweden
Group B: Those with federal governments: Australia, Canada, Germany, Switzerland and the USA

There are considerable differences between the two groups in their definition of, and approach to, citizenship education. Countries in Group A have national education systems, and national influence and control can be exercised through a variety of regulatory means. Practice varies in citizenship education from a highly specified, centrally determined curriculum in Singapore, Korea and Japan, to more flexible arrangements with considerable local autonomy in Italy, Hungary and Spain.

In the federal states of Group B, education is the responsibility of the regions and a nationally agreed definition of, and approach to, citizenship education, as such, can only exist provided the regions agree to it both in principle and in practice. Canada, Switzerland and the USA do not appear to have developed centralized guidance, but Australia provides an interesting example of a federal country which is attempting to develop such national (non-statutory) guidance for citizenship education. In Australia, ten national 'common and agreed goals for schooling' have been set out by the Australian Education Council since 1989. Goal 7 'to develop knowledge, skills, attitudes and values which will enable students to participate as active and informed citizens in our democratic Australian society within an international context' and Goal 6 'to develop in students a capacity to exercise judgement in matters of morality, ethics and social justice' make explicit reference to citizenship education.

They offer a structure for co-operation between schools, states, territories and the Commonwealth. A number of states in the USA, among them Kentucky, Maryland and Wisconsin, are also attempting to set standards or expectations for citizenship education through voluntary national standards. These are linked to the establishment of and overarching goals or principles in certain subjects, notably social studies, civics, history and geography.

Educational values and aims

Educational values and aims are an extremely important structural factor. How countries express their values has a marked influence on the definition of, and approach to, citizenship education. The earlier thematic study *Values and Aims in Curriculum and Assessment Frameworks*, conducted by Joanna Le Métais of NFER in 1997, categorized the sixteen countries into three broad groups, according to the degree of detail with which national values are expressed or prescribed in education legislation. It is worth bearing these categories in mind when comparing approaches to citizenship education across the sixteen project countries. The three categories were:

1. *Minimal reference to values in education legislation*
   The countries in this group share a commitment to pluralism and devolved authority. Values are expressed in the Constitution and/or statutes, which provide a framework for the expression of values through devolved educational structures. They include Canada, England, Hungary, The Netherlands and the USA.

2. *National values expressed in general terms*
   In this group of countries, general statements on values are made at national level, but the details are determined by authorities with devolved responsibilities. They include Australia, New Zealand, Italy and Spain.

3. *National values expressed in detail*
   Countries with highly centralized systems tend to express very detailed aims and clear educational and social values. They include Japan, Korea, Singapore and Sweden.

'Values-explicit' and 'values-neutral' citizenship education

The three broad categories correspond with one of the major tensions countries face in approaching citizenship education, namely the extent to which it is possible to identify, agree and articulate the values and dispositions which underpin citizenship. This tension is both philosophical and practical. The response hinges in many countries on the answer to a simple question: is citizenship education 'values-explicit' or 'values-neutral'? Should citizenship education be 'values-explicit' and promote distinct values which are part of a broader nationally accepted system of public values and beliefs? Or should it be 'values-neutral' or 'values-free' and take a neutral stance to values and controversial issues, leaving the decision on values to the individual? The answer determines a great deal about a country's approach to citizenship education.

This tension is part of the broader debate about the balance between the 'public' and 'private' dimensions of citizenship, leading to what the educational philosopher McLaughlin (1992) has termed 'thick' and 'thin' citizenship education. Those who view citizenship as a largely 'public' concern see a major, or 'thick', role for education (through the school and formal curriculum) in the promotion of citizenship and, in particular, for teachers. Those who view citizenship as a largely 'private' affair see a much more limited, or 'thin', role for education (largely through the hidden curriculum). They advocate a much stronger role for the family and community organizations than for teachers. 'Values-explicit' approaches are commonly criticized for the associated dangers of bias and the indoctrination of students, while 'values-neutral' approaches are attacked for their failure to help students to deal adequately with real-life, controversial issues.

Examining the three broad categories it is clear that those countries in the first category take a 'values-neutral' approach to citizenship education (this has certainly been the tradition in England); those in the second category are somewhere between 'values-neutral' and 'values-explicit', depending on the decisions of devolved authorities; while those in the third category are very much 'values-explicit' in approach. The implications of the positions for the linkage between rhetoric of policy and actual practice in citizenship education came through very strongly in the presentations at the invitational seminar. Those countries with a 'values-explicit' approach, such as Singapore and Korea, were much clearer than those from a 'values-neutral' tradition, as to what citizenship education is (aims and goals) and consequently the role of schools, teachers and the curriculum in achieving those goals.

The certainty of such 'values-explicit' approaches is very alluring. Seminar participants were agreed that a clear, publicly accepted definition of citizenship was a tremendous benefit in facilitating effective practice in citizenship education. It enabled everyone involved in citizenship education – schools, teachers, students, parents, community representatives, public figures – to be clear about the aims and goals, to understand their roles and responsibilities in achieving those aims and goals; and provided a strong framework upon which approaches and programmes could be constructed with certainty and purpose. Without such a definition there was a danger that citizenship education became a 'catch-all' for lots of related topics and aspects and that this lack of focus made it a lower status, low priority area in schools. One participant summed up the effect with a quotation from the book of Jeremiah, 'Without a vision the people perish'. A clear vision does not guarantee good practice but it is a vital starting point.

The tripartite categorization is particularly topical given the claims of some commentators that many countries in response to the challenges and uncertainties in the modern world are moving toward a more explicit statement of the values and aims underpinning their education systems. Indeed, this is an interesting development in the current review of the National Curriculum in England. QCA have produced a draft statement of values, aims and purposes of the school curriculum as a potential way of helping schools to develop their own curriculum in a way which reflects the spirit of nationally agreed aims (QCA, 1999b). The challenges and uncertainties are forcing countries to re-examine and adjust many of their underlying cultural traditions, values and assumptions. It helps to explain the considerable debate about the values underpinning citizenship education, particularly in those countries with a tradition of a 'values-neutral' approach.

Funding and regulatory arrangements

Differences in educational funding arrangements and how countries regulate their curriculum and assessment frameworks can also have a powerful impact on citizenship education. These different funding arrangements can influence the emphasis given to citizenship education, particularly in relation to other subjects and areas of the curriculum. This emphasis can be both negative and positive. In a number of countries, the challenge is to maintain the profile and status of citizenship education in the face of a growing national priority on 'basic' aspects of the curriculum. These basic aspects include literacy, numeracy, information and communication technologies (ICT) and science and technology. This challenge is most apparent in Canada, though it is an undercurrent in the discussions about citizenship education in the revised National Curriculum in England. Meanwhile, in other countries the carrot of central funding is being used to promote citizenship education and change practice. For example, in Australia, the federal government has launched the 'Discovering Democracy' initiative with funding for the production of classroom materials and teacher training in a bid to encourage states and schools to get involved.

Common challenges in citizenship education

A review of *INCA* and the literature on citizenship education reveals concern in many countries about how to respond to a period of unprecedented global change. This concern was confirmed by the participants at the invitational seminar. The concern is both immediate – how to respond in the short term through current economic, social and political policies – and more long term – how better to prepare current and future generations for their roles and responsibilities as citizens, parents, consumers, workers and human beings. Seminar participants agreed that there is no simple, 'quick-fix' solution. Though the aims and intended outcomes of citizenship education can be readily drawn up, their successful achievement is a long-term project, often involving more than one generation of students and teachers. The unprecedented global change has thrown up a common set of challenges or issues for countries, which demand a response. They include:

- the rapid movement of people within and across national boundaries;
- a growing recognition of the rights of indigenous peoples and minorities;
- the collapse of political structures and the birth of new ones;
- the changing role of women in society;
- the impact of the global economy and changing patterns of work;
- the effect of a revolution in information and communications technologies;
- an increasing global population; and
- the creation of new forms of community.

The last challenge is of particular relevance in many countries at the moment, with concern about the lack of interest in and involvement of young people in public and political life; what has been termed a 'democratic deficit'.

These challenges touch on complex issues concerning pluralism, multiculturalism, ethnic and cultural heritage and diversity, tolerance, social cohesion, collective and individual rights and responsibilities, social justice, national identity and consciousness, and freedom among others. The education system is a vital part of the response to these challenges. Although countries have similar sets of national aims in dealing with these challenges and issues, including the aim of promoting citizenship and democratic values, they approach those aims in many different ways. This is, in part, because of the influence of the broad contextual and more detailed structural factors highlighted earlier in the chapter.

A continuum of citizenship education

The broad range of approaches to these challenges and issues and the subsequent discussion at the invitational seminar suggests the existence of a continuum of citizenship and citizenship education (see Figure 16.1). Indeed, political philosophers and commentators argue that citizenship is conceptualized and contested along a continuum, which ranges from a *minimal* to a *maximal* interpretation (McLaughlin, 1992). Each end of the continuum displays different characteristics, which affect the definition of, and approach to, citizenship education.

Minimal interpretations are characterized by a narrow definition of citizenship. They seek to promote particular exclusive and elitist interests, such as the granting of citizenship to certain groups in society but not all. Minimal interpretations lead to narrow, formal approaches to citizenship education – what has been termed *civics education*. This is largely content-led and knowledge-based. It is centred on formal education programmes which concentrate on the transmission to students of knowledge of a country's history and geography, of the structure and processes of its system of government and of its constitution. The primary purpose is to inform through the provision and

MINIMAL		MAXIMAL
Thin		Thick
Exclusive	————————	Inclusive
Elitist	————————	Activist
Civics education	————————	Citizenship education
	————————	
Formal		Participative
Content-led	————————	Process-led
Knowledge-based	————————	Values-based
Didactic transmission	————————	Interactive interpretation
Easier to achieve and measure in practice	————————	More difficult to achieve and measure in practice

Figure 16.1 Citizenship education continuum

transmission of information. It lends itself to didactic teaching and learning approaches, with teacher-led, whole-class teaching as the dominant medium. There is little opportunity or encouragement for student interaction and initiative. As the outcomes of minimal approaches are narrow, largely involving the acquisition of knowledge and understanding, it is much easier to measure how successfully the outcomes have been achieved, often through written examinations.

Maximal interpretations are characterized by a broad definition of citizenship. They seek actively to include and involve all groups and interests in society. Maximal interpretations lead to a broad mixture of formal and informal approaches to what has been termed *citizenship education*, as opposed to narrower civics education. This citizenship education includes the content and knowledge components of minimal interpretations, but actively encourages investigation and interpretation of the many different ways in which these components (including the rights and responsibilities of citizens) are determined and carried out. The primary aim is not only to inform, but also to use that information to help students to understand and to enhance their capacity to participate. It is as much about the content as about the process of teaching and learning. It lends itself to a broad mixture of teaching and learning approaches, from the didactic to the interactive, both inside and outside the classroom.

Structured opportunities are created for student interaction through discussion and debate, and encouragement is given to students to use their initiative through project work, other forms of independent learning and participative experiences. As the outcomes of maximal approaches are broad, involving the acquisition of knowledge and understanding, and the development of values and dispositions, and skills and attitudes, it is much more difficult to measure how successfully these outcomes have been achieved.

Although the interpretations are polarized when laid out in this way, nevertheless they provide a useful, if crude, scale for determining where each country broadly stands in its definition and approach to citizenship education. Certainly, seminar participants found the continuum useful in conceptualizing approaches to citizenship education. However, it was pointed out that an equally valid way of conceptualizing approaches is by intended aims or goals. Looked at in this way citizenship education comprises three strands:

- Education *ABOUT* citizenship
- Education *THROUGH* citizenship and
- Education *FOR* citizenship.

- *Education ABOUT citizenship* focuses on providing students with sufficient knowledge and understanding of national history and the structures and processes of government and political life.
- *Education THROUGH citizenship* involves students learning by doing, through active, participative experiences in the school or local community and beyond. This learning reinforces the knowledge component.
- *Education FOR citizenship* encompasses the other two strands and involves equipping students with a set of tools (knowledge and understanding, skills and aptitudes, values and dispositions) which enable them to participate actively and sensibly in the roles and responsibilities they encounter in their adult lives. This strand links citizenship education with the whole education experience of students.

Seminar participants agreed that it was much easier to deliver 'education *ABOUT* citizenship', than the other two strands. However what was taught for one or two hours per week in the classroom was not sufficient to equip students with what was required for their future participation in 'education *FOR* citizenship'. Instead countries needed to set out the values, dispositions, skills and aptitudes underpinning citizenship education and build in experiences (the 'education *THROUGH* citizenship' strand) which complemented the 'education *ABOUT* citizenship' strand. Though this was being attempted in some countries much more needed to be done before the goals of 'education *FOR* citizenship' were achieved.

Whichever way it is conceptualized, in practice, there are two parallel continuua of citizenship education in operation. The first continuum is at the national level within each country. There is constant movement both backward and forward along this national continuum dependent on the interplay of factors. For example, countries in South-East Asia and in Central and Eastern Europe are currently attempting to move from a formal ('education ABOUT') to a more participative ('education THROUGH') approach to citizenship education. This is in line with revised national educational goals which stress the need for more critical thinking and increased initiative and creativity. Meanwhile, in Australia, the new Liberal-National Party federal government has introduced the 'Discovering Democracy' initiative, which is grounded in a more formal 'education ABOUT' approach to Australia's national history and constitution, in contrast to the approach of the previous government. Every country experiences these episodes of introspection and revision of citizenship education. Interestingly, the conduct of the thematic study suggested that these episodes may be becoming more frequent and sustained, with some countries close to a perpetual state of review and revision.

The second continuum is at the comparative level across the sixteen IRCAF project countries. Applying this crude comparative scale places those countries in South-East Asia more toward the minimal, 'education ABOUT' end of the continuum, those in Southern, Central and Eastern Europe somewhere in the middle, and those in Northern Europe and some of the former British colonies such as the USA and New Zealand more toward the maximal 'education FOR' end. However, this scale is indeed very crude and there are exceptions. Australia, interestingly, views itself as somewhere in the middle of the scale but striving for the maximal, while Hungary is attempting to move away from the minimal. Canada probably cannot be placed because of the variation across its provinces.

Approaches to citizenship education

How citizenship is defined in relation to the continuum affects how citizenship education is approached in schools. Tables 16.1 and 16.2 attempt to categorize the terminology, approach and amount of time per week given to citizenship education across the sixteen countries. It must be emphasized that this is an attempt to quantify approaches to citizenship education in the formal curriculum. In most countries, citizenship education is broader than the formal curriculum, involving the hidden curriculum, whole-school and extra-curricular activities, as well as students' everyday experiences of life.

Some countries are attempting to build these activities into the formal curriculum. For example, Japan has special activities, while Singapore has developed a community involvement programme and learning journeys around the key institutions. Other countries have left the choice to schools. In the USA,

Table 16.1 Organization of citizenship education in the primary phase (ages 5 to 11)

Country	Terminology	Approach	Hours per week
England	Education for Citizenship (from September 2000: Citizenship as part of combined PSHE framework)	Non-statutory Cross-curricular	Schools to decide
Australia New South Wales	Human society and its environment (HSIE)	Non-statutory Integrated	Not specified
Canada	Social studies	Non-statutory Integrated	Not specified
France	Civics as part of 'Discovering the World'	Statutory core Separate and integrated	4 hours out of 26
Germany	Sachunternicht	Non-statutory Integrated	Not specified
Hungary	People and society	Statutory core Integrated	4 to 7% of curriculum time
Italy	Social sciences	Statutory core Integrated	Not specified
Japan	Social studies, living experience and moral education	Statutory core Separate and integrated	175×45 minutes per year
Korea	A disciplined life and moral education	Statutory core Separate	Varies dependent on year
The Netherlands	Social structures and life skills	Statutory core Integrated	80 to 100 hours per year
New Zealand	Social studies	Statutory core Integrated	Not specified
Singapore	Civics and moral education	Statutory core Separate and Integrated	3×30 minutes lessons
Spain	Knowledge of the natural, social and cultural environment	Non-statutory Integrated	170 hours per year
Sweden	Social sciences Integrated	Non-core Integrated	885 hours over 9 years of compulsory schooling
Switzerland	Social studies	Non-statutory Integrated	Not specified
USA Kentucky	Social studies	Statutory core Integrated	Time specified per week varies among states

Table 16.2 Organization of citizenship education in the lower and upper secondary phase (ages 11 to 16 or 18)

Country	Terminology	Approach	Hours per week
England	Education for Citizenship (from September 2000: Citizenship)	Statutory Cross-curricular	Schools to decide
Australia New South Wales	Human society and its environment (HSIE)	Non-statutory Integrated	Not specified
Canada	Social studies and also history, law, political sciences and economics	Non-statutory Integrated	Not specified
France	Civics linked to history and geography	Statutory core Separate and integrated	3 to 4 hours out of 26
Germany	Social studies linked to history, geography and economics	Non-statutory Integrated	Not specified
Hungary	People and society with specific social studies, civics and economics courses	Statutory core Integrated and specific	10 to 14% of curriculum time
Italy	Civics linked to history and geography	Statutory core Separate and integrated	4 hours
Japan	Social studies, history, geography and civics and moral education	Statutory core Integrated and specific	175 × 50 minutes per year (Grades 7 and 8) 140 × 50 minutes per year (Grade 9) 140 × 50 minutes per year (Upper secondary)
Korea	Social studies and moral education	Statutory core Integrated and specific	Ranges 170 × 45 minutes to 204 × 45 minutes per year
The Netherlands	Civics and citizenship and social studies	Statutory core Integrated	180 hours over 3 years (age 12 –15) 2 to 4 hours per week (age 16–18)
New Zealand	Social studies	Statutory core Integrated	Not specified
Singapore	Civics and moral education	Statutory core Integrated and specific	2 × 30 minutes lessons
Spain	Civics linked to history, geography and social sciences	Non-statutory Separate and integrated	3 hours per week
Sweden	Social sciences including history, geography and social studies	Non-core Integrated	885 hours over 9 years of compulsory schooling

Table 16.2 *Contd.*

Country	Terminology	Approach	Hours per week
Switzerland	Social studies	Non-statutory Integrated	Not specified
USA *Kentucky*	Social studies including civics and government	Statutory core Separate and integrated	Time specified per week varies among states

there has been an expansion in 'service learning' education based on active partnerships between schools and their local communities. It is a growing area of interest in England through the activities of Community Service Volunteers (CSV) and others. Meanwhile some countries are strengthening the involvement of students in school or class councils. However, it is not easy to obtain reliable information on these broader experiences for all countries.

Table 16.1 examines the curriculum for pupils aged 5 to 11, what is termed in *INCA* as the primary phase. Table 16.2 looks at the curriculum for students aged 11 to 16 or 18, what is termed in *INCA* as the lower and upper secondary phases.

What patterns, if any, are discernible? An examination of both tables enables four points to be made. The first point is that citizenship education and its related issues are addressed in the formal curriculum across the whole age range in every country. The second point to note is the broad range of terms used to describe this area. The third point is the existence of three main curriculum approaches to citizenship education, namely separate, integrated and cross-curricular. In the separate approach, citizenship education or civics is a specific subject or aspect. In the integrated approach, it is part of a broader course, often social sciences or social studies, and linked to other subjects and curricular areas. In the cross-curricular approach, citizenship education is neither a separate subject or topic, nor is it part of an integrated course, but instead it permeates the entire curriculum and is infused into subjects. Some countries adopt a mixed approach to citizenship education, with a broad integrated approach more prevalent in the primary curriculum, giving way to more specialized citizenship education or civics courses in the secondary curriculum. The fourth point is the mixture of statutory and non-statutory approaches to citizenship education. In some countries it is a statutory part of the core National Curriculum, while in others it is non-statutory, with greater freedom left to states, districts, municipalities, schools and teachers. However, the non-statutory nature of provision in some countries means that not all students may encounter citizenship education in their curriculum experience.

The major pattern in the primary curriculum is the organization of citizenship education through an integrated approach of domains or 'brigades' in many countries. It suggests a deliberate emphasis in the intended curriculum, particularly in the early years of this phase, on the integrated learning of the child's understanding of itself with respect to topics and aspects. For example, France links civics with sciences, technology, history and geography under the heading 'Discovering the World'. Hungary has eight curricular areas, one of which is 'People and Society', while Spain uses the term 'Knowledge of the natural, social and cultural environment'. Moral education is also an important component of citizenship education in many countries, particularly those in South-East Asia.

The striking example is that of Korea, which addresses citizenship education through the domain of 'a disciplined life'; an integrated course covering social studies and moral education. Time allocations indicate that moral education features heavily in early education. The same is true for Singapore, where moral education is part of mother tongue teaching, and for Japan. In some countries, the range of the curriculum is extended as the primary phase progresses and there is increased time and focus on citizenship education. In Singapore, for instance, the seven-area curriculum from grade 1 (including civics and moral education) is supplemented by the addition of social studies from grade 4, with subjects increasingly taught through the common medium of English as pupils progress.

Citizenship education in the secondary curriculum is still organized through an integrated approach in most countries, but often as a discrete, explicit component alongside other subjects and aspects. The most common approach is through social studies or social sciences courses, where citizenship or civics is closely linked to the subjects of history and geography. For example, in Hungary, the domain is still entitled 'People and Society' but incorporates specific reference to social studies, civics and economics courses. In Japan, in junior high school (age 12+–15), social studies is divided into three subjects; geography, history and civics to be taught from 2002 alongside a new general studies course: and in high school (age 15+–18), social studies is divided into two subjects; civics, and geography and history, where civics is further subdivided into modern society, ethics and politics and economics. In The Netherlands, citizenship education is part of history and civics at lower secondary (age 12 to 15) and is an integral part of social studies (*maatschappijleer*) courses, while in some Canadian provinces, social studies is linked with history, law, political sciences and economics.

In many countries, the range of subjects that relate to citizenship education is extended as the secondary phase progresses, taking in economics, law, commerce and political sciences. Moral education continues to be an important component in some countries, particularly those in South-East Asia. The other feature of the secondary phase is the increased time given to citizenship education, particularly in the upper years of this phase. This reflects the growing maturity of students and their ability to handle complex, topical issues. It is spurred by the proximity of students to the end of their compulsory or post-compulsory period of education and to their entry into the world as full citizens, with legal, political, economic and social rights and responsibilities.

TEACHING AND LEARNING APPROACHES

Influences on teaching and learning approaches in citizenship education

There are many influences on teaching and learning approaches in citizenship education. The three major influences are culture, content and climate. The interplay between them is very complex and subtle but can have profound consequences.

Culture, in particular is broad and pervasive. It ranges from the cultural traditions and norms in a society, to the particular culture of specific groups (such as teachers, parents and students), of organizations (such as schools, government departments and businesses) and of institutions (such as parliaments, courts and churches). Indeed Carole Hahn found in her comparative study of citizenship education that there are significant differences between countries in terms of their pedagogic traditions and cultural norms. It explains why approaches and programmes of citizenship education cannot readily be transported from one country to another and expect to be successful. In some countries there are also differences between the prevailing civic and classroom cultures. This underlines the profound influence that teacher culture and beliefs have on approaches to citizenship education.

Content covers the various components of citizenship education in the formal and hidden curriculum. For example, in Korea this comprises four aspects: work in curriculum subjects; optional activities based around fifteen cross-curricular themes; cross-curricular activities; and service work. These aspects are identifiable in many countries. Content is vital to effective citizenship education. Research shows that students who take citizenship/civics courses in schools are more knowledgeable about political life (both formal and informal) and therefore more likely to participate in the future. Climate includes the ethos in schools, classrooms and impacts, for example on ability to tackle controversial issues and values with students.

These three main influences impact on policy and practice at three levels. The first level is the general structure and aims of education, including the organization of schooling. The second level is the organization of the curriculum, including content and teaching and learning methodologies. The third level is what students experience in schools and the balance between the formal and hidden curriculum and individual classroom and school ethos.

At the first level, the broad contextual and structural factors outlined earlier in this chapter clearly have a major influence on teaching and learning approaches. They set the official tone and determine the degree of flexibility available to schools and teachers as to how they approach citizenship education. As might be expected among sixteen countries, there are variations in the scope and nature of that influence. For example, teachers in Germany are obliged by law to teach values. Legally speaking, this commitment is just as important as the teaching of knowledge. However, in conformity with the basic law of educational freedom, teachers are free to choose their own methods. In contrast, teachers in Singapore operate within a tightly controlled framework. Civic and moral education are compulsory throughout primary and secondary education, based on a structured syllabus and prescribed textbooks. This learning is reinforced through service programmes (e.g. voluntary work in welfare homes) and by encouraging students to participate in out-of-school club activities. Sweden is interesting in the extent to which the school's responsibility for 'inculcating' values associated with citizenship education is explicitly defined in terms of the development of skills and attitudes, as well as the acquisition of knowledge. The Swedish system also puts great emphasis on the whole school community as a vehicle for learning.

At the second and third levels, the role of the teacher, collectively and individually, is crucial. Actual classroom practice is critical to the successful achievement of the aims of citizenship education, whether those aims are the transmission of formal historical and political knowledge and/or the encouragement of active participation among students. Teachers have to strike the right balance between the content being covered, the chosen teaching methodology and the learning environment that ensues.

The power of teachers in determining the learning environment in schools is noted in a number of the case study chapters from the IEA Citizenship Education Project. The same message was underlined by seminar participants. Teachers are themselves influenced, in their beliefs and actions, by the cultural traditions and norms in a country. This can be both positive and negative. It means that they are generally one or two generations removed from the students they teach. Indeed, they often have more in common with parents than with students. This can lead to a gap in some countries between teachers and students, and also between teachers and the prevailing civic culture. The latter occurs particularly where significant and rapid change in policy is attempted. Research shows that the culture of schools and classrooms is very slow to adapt to change. There was clear evidence of this from the seminar presentations. For example, in Switzerland, teachers in the secondary phase view their primary duty in citizenship education as providing information about national history and politics and describing relevant situations in a didactic and non-controversial way. There is little room or encouragement for other approaches in the classroom.

Countries with a tradition of a formal, knowledge-based approach to this area can also find it difficult to change teacher attitudes and opinions. This is the case in Hungary, where official moves to a more discussion-based approach to citizenship issues in classrooms are being frustrated by the deep-seated belief of teachers that controversial or sensitive issues should be kept out of the classroom. Japan and Korea are encountering similar problems in their official attempts to promote more creativity in schools in what are traditionally conformist and centralist societies. The new teaching and learning approaches which are being encouraged at an official level are viewed as having a Western basis which does not fit with what people feel in their hearts. The power and durability of teacher culture should not be underestimated in attempts to review and renew citizenship education. While it may be true that 'the people will perish without a vision', it is equally true that 'the people will perish if they do not share and support the vision'.

Range of teaching and learning approaches in citizenship education

The IEA Citizenship Education Project national case study chapters highlight the wide range of teaching and learning approaches employed by teachers in covering citizenship education. While a number of countries are still dependent on a passive, didactic, transmission approach as the dominant teaching methodology, there are others who encourage a more interactive, participative approach with room for classroom discussion and debate supported by project and inquiry work, fieldwork, visits and extra-curricular learning. There is evidence in Australian classrooms of structured classroom discussion and debate as the most favoured approach, while in the USA, there are many opportunities for learning through extra-curricular activities and through service learning programmes, national competitions and mock elections. There is an equal range of opportunities available in England through the work of the main citizenship organizations and in the encouragement given to school and class councils.

Some countries have developed specific curriculum programmes which encourage a mixture of approaches to ensure the goals of 'education FOR citizenship' are achieved. They include the Civic, Social and Political Education (CPSE) course in the Republic of Ireland, the Junior Citizenship project in England, the Opening the Schools project in Germany and the 'Discovering Democracy' initiative in Australia among others, but there are far too many to list here. There is an urgent need to map these curriculum projects where they lead to effective practice and to make this practice more widely available both within and across countries. This would also include reference to what is known from effective practice about how students learn best in citizenship education. There was insufficient time in the thematic study to pursue this issue further. However, a number of seminar participants urged the development of a database of projects and resources in order to provide what one participant termed 'effective and inspiring examples from actual practice'.

However, it should be noted that, even in countries with curriculum projects and effective practice, it is accepted that there is still tremendous variety in approach from school to school and classroom to classroom. This means that not all students experience all approaches. Indeed, in most countries, citizenship education teaching still proceeds from the use of the textbook as the predominant teaching resource. Structured teacher exposition of textbook passages and follow-up opportunities for student discussion and questioning is a very common teaching approach.

Some countries are recognizing the need for increased encouragement of active and participatory learning in citizenship education through formal structures and policies. For example, in The Netherlands, there is a move in upper secondary schools to a 'study house' concept, where students are encouraged to move away from traditional teaching methods and organize other forms of working. Elsewhere, there are attempts to achieve greater coherence between what students learn in the formal subject curriculum with what they experience through the hidden curriculum. For example, in Sweden, schools must use democratic working methods with teachers and students deciding in advance the learning goals in each subject. Meanwhile, the province of Ontario in Canada has recently redefined the word 'curriculum' to include all the learning experiences that students have in school.

There are also opportunities in some countries for students to learn about democracy through active participation in school life. In Spain, there are school councils comprising teacher representatives, parents and students that decide, among other things, on curriculum plans, finances and student behaviour. The current reform of the lycée in France aims to give students more say in how their education is conducted, while in England there is growing support for school and/or class councils in every school. However, not all countries have such opportunities. In Australia, school representative councils and youth parliaments are rare. There is a distinct lack of such developments in Hungary, while in others, notably Italy, their existence does not mean they function satisfactorily. It is important to note that such opportunities are often open to only a small percentage of students in a school.

Gap between policy and practice in citizenship education

To a degree, practice often lags behind policy in all areas of education. The issues in citizenship education are the size of the gap, how far it is an accepted part of the education system and what, if anything, is being done to address it where it exists. The gap between policy and practice can exist at many levels, from national policy all the way to policy and practice within an individual school. Indeed, Kennedy (1997) has suggested that the loftier a country's ideals for citizenship education, the less likely it is to have any meaningful practice. As already mentioned, a gap can appear where national policy is attempting to bring a significant shift in teacher attitude and classroom practice in a relatively short period of time. This is the case currently in Hungary, Japan and Korea, with the shift in central policy to encourage more discursive and creative elements in schools. It may well take a generation before new teachers, comfortable with the changed emphasis in practice, begin to close the gap in these countries. Indeed, there is tacit acceptance of this in Korea, where the compulsory retirement age for teachers has been reduced from 65 to 62 in an attempt to increase the number of younger teachers employed in schools.

In other countries, there is a gap which is accepted as part of the system. For example, in Italy, there is a marked contrast for students between the open, participative climate within the hidden curriculum in schools, and the non-participatory climate in the formal curriculum in the classroom. A similar situation exists in Germany, but in reverse. The hidden curriculum in German schools, with its strong emphasis on 'studying for tests' and 'conforming to authority', has a powerful influence on the formal curriculum. Meanwhile, in Canada, it is recognized that actual practice in many provinces is much more conservative and traditional than official policy mandates.

However, these observations should be tempered by a recognition that one of the key points to emerge from the literature in this area is that we have only a limited knowledge and understanding of what actually happens in citizenship education in schools, both in classrooms and elsewhere. Little systematic research has been conducted since the 1970s. Though the research base is growing rapidly with the renewed interest in citizenship education in many countries, it will take some time before research findings and examples of effective practice filter through at international, national, school and classroom level.

ASSESSMENT ARRANGEMENTS

Assessment arrangements for citizenship education

Assessment arrangements for citizenship education show considerable variation across countries, depending on the formal assessment arrangements in operation, attitudes to the purposes of assessment and the particular phase involved. For example, all of the countries with a centralized government and education system have some sort of formal, though not always compulsory, assessment arrangements. Singapore and Italy have compulsory primary school leaving examinations, but these do not involve an assessment of citizenship education. Italy also has a lower secondary school leaving examination at age 14, which includes an oral combined test for civics, history and geography. Indeed, citizenship education is more likely to be part of a formal assessment system in the lower and upper secondary phases because of the way those phases are organized in many countries around formal examination qualifications such as the *baccalauréat* in France and the General Certificate of Secondary Education (GCSE) and General Certificate of Education Advanced (A) levels in England.

Beyond these, the purpose of the assessment affects the structure adopted. Sweden has national tests for students aged 12 and these illustrate that perceptions of purpose may differ. The government sees the role of these tests as supporting teachers and influencing the allocation of funding to pupils who do not pass, while the National Agency for Education (*Skolverket*) stresses diagnosis for the individual pupil and encouraging reflection on teaching by the teacher. There are also concerns in Sweden about tests influencing the curriculum and the use of item banks to provide tests is seen as a solution. Some of the development work on these is being carried out in co-operation with other Scandinavian countries.

Periodic surveys are used to assess the state of citizenship education in several countries, including Hungary, the USA and The Netherlands. The 1998 National Assessment of Educational Progress (NEAP) in the USA looked at civics and government in a representative sample of schools, based on the voluntary national standards for civics and government. The results should be made public at the end of 1999. Other countries favouring this approach include Korea (at ages 10 to 12) and Spain (at age 12). New Zealand has recently set up the National Educational Monitoring Project (NEMP), while the federal government in Australia has announced a baseline survey of student knowledge in civics or citizenship education as part of the 'Discovering Democracy' initiative. Meanwhile, in The Netherlands the National Institute for Educational Measurement (CITO) selects a representative sample of primary schools each year to evaluate pupils' progress in different school subjects, including social structures and life skills. Two-thirds of pupils in The Netherlands also take a voluntary test at the end of the primary schooling, which among other things assesses their knowledge of world studies.

Most of the IRCAF project countries have a mixture of summative and formative assessment arrangements in citizenship education. Continuous student assessment is the responsibility of the individual class teacher in many countries, with formative assessment introduced at a number of natural end points across the school year, often the middle or end of terms. These sometimes coincide with points of transition and exit in the school system, where formative assessment may be part of more formal national procedures. Summative assessment comprises a number of components, including student performance in class tests, the standard of a student's written work and his/her oral contribution in lessons. Indeed, in Sweden, in most grades, schools are free to report on student progress in terms of their creativity, personal conduct and ability to co-operate.

The purposes of assessment are varied. Assessment often helps to inform the teacher and the individual student and may also include some reporting to parents. In Sweden, for example, regular oral and written reports are made to parents, while in Spain, written reports are made to parents every three months. However, assessments may also be increasingly used to monitor the state of citizenship education performance. A number of countries are moving in this direction, through the establishment of national standards for all subjects, with accompanying statements, learning outcomes and testing instruments. This is the case in New Zealand, Sweden and in some Australian and American states. For example, the states of New South Wales and Victoria in Australia are to begin to assess formally civics with history and geography for Year 10 students. Meanwhile in the US state of Kentucky, 57 'Student Academic Expectations' define what students should be able to know and do in five major content areas, including social studies. The social studies expectations stated as learning outcomes, include students demonstrating effectiveness in community service. There are similar developments afoot in Maryland and Wisconsin.

However, it is vital to give careful consideration to the purpose of assessment in citizenship education and its impact on teaching and learning approaches. Seminar participants saw clarity of purpose as the crucial issue concerning assessment arrangements for citizenship education. What was being assessed, how and for what purpose needed careful consideration. Some participants called for an in-depth discussion of the relationship between citizenship education and assessment, and for assessment issues to be a more explicit part of teacher training. They felt that this was long overdue. In some countries, citizenship was only taken seriously as a recognized and valued part of the curriculum when it became an examination subject. This was the case in The Netherlands with the use of end of year written exams at national school level alongside assessment of practical or experiential components (often in project form). There may be a need for more formal, written examinations as part of the assessment of citizenship education in order to raise its status in the curriculum. However, in some countries, the formal assessment system has a negative influence, both direct and indirect, on citizenship education. For example, in Japan, the senior high school entrance exam, which includes social studies, encourages 'teaching to the test'. The same phenomenon is noted in Germany. In Australia, however, the pressure to report on student performance in the Year 12 public examinations is one factor in inhibiting the introduction of citizenship education as a discrete curriculum component.

CURRENT AND FUTURE DEVELOPMENTS

Current position of citizenship education in the school curriculum

In a comparative study of sixteen countries, there are bound to be variations in the position of citizenship education in the school curriculum. However, looking across the countries as a whole, the general position of citizenship education is a healthy one, in that it is a recognized and accepted part of the school curriculum in the majority of IRCAF project countries. The only exceptions are England, and to a lesser extent Australia, where it is yet to establish a firm hold in the curriculum, and Canada, where reforms threaten to weaken severely its curriculum status and position.

Developments in the near future also offer hope. Citizenship education is part of the major reforms of the curriculum currently under way in Spain, France, Hungary, Italy, New Zealand and The Netherlands. It is subject to a change of official emphasis in Japan, Korea and Singapore, as a vehicle for the introduction of more creativity, debate and discussion into the curriculum. The situation is relatively stable in Germany, Switzerland and the USA, with some interesting developments concerning the establishment of standards for citizenship education in a number of US states. Meanwhile, there are promising developments in those countries where citizenship education has yet to take a hold in the curriculum. In England citizenship is to be introduced as a discrete, statutory component in the revised National Curriculum from September 2002 (QCA, 1999c) while in Australia the federal government is attempting to increase the status and take-up of citizenship education across the states and territories. Only in Canada is there cause for concern where citizenship education is being marginalized in many provinces by the national emphasis in education on technology, mathematics and science.

CHALLENGES IN CITIZENSHIP EDUCATION

Many of the current and future challenges facing citizenship education have already been highlighted in the previous sections of this chapter. The main challenges for citizenship education are to:

- achieve a clear definition and approach
- secure its position and status in the curriculum
- address teacher preparedness and teacher training
- increase the range of appropriate teaching and learning approaches
- improve the quality and range of resources
- decide on appropriate assessment arrangements
- develop and disseminate more widely effective practice
- influence the attitudes of young people

What is clear is that many of these challenges are interrelated. As countries reconsider and revise their approach to citizenship education, in order to meet the impact of global change, there is a need to consider citizenship education as a whole package. This means not only examining definition, aims and approach, but also ensuring that the curriculum that is drawn up and the curriculum that students experience support the overall aims and approach. For this to happen, more consideration has to be given to the educative process, to teaching and learning approaches, to support structures and to the needs of teachers and students in terms of training, resources and attitudes. There also has to be much deeper thinking about what is meant by 'effective citizenship education'. It is quick and easy to state as a defining aim of education but difficult, messy and time-consuming to achieve and sustain in practice.

One of the difficulties facing citizenship education is how to keep up with the incredible pace and impact of change in modern societies at all levels and the implications of such change for groups and individuals in society. As Kennedy (1997) reminds us, this is perhaps the major challenge facing citizenship education, namely how to balance global citizenship issues with national developments and with the realities of life in modern society as experienced by young people. There is growing concern in many countries about the attitudes of young people and, in particular, with the signs of their increasing lack of interest and non-participation in public and political life. Effective citizenship education in schools is seen as crucial to addressing this concern. However, there remains considerable debate as to what is meant by the term 'effective' and how it can best be measured.

CONCLUSIONS

The thematic study, upon which this chapter is based, drew the following conclusions, with reference to citizenship education:

- the topical nature of citizenship education and the breadth, depth and complexity of the issues it addresses. The area is under review with planned revisions in most IRCAF countries, as part of the overall reform of the school curriculum;
- the important role of context and culture in understanding aims and approaches to citizenship education. What works in one cultural context cannot simply be adopted and expected to achieve the same ends somewhere else. It requires careful adaptation to suit the new cultural context;
- broad agreement among countries on the common challenges facing citizenship education, even if national responses to those challenges vary;
- a recognition that the explicit statement of shared values underpinning citizenship education can make a difference to policy and practice and may make a difference to outcomes. Those countries with a 'values-explicit' tradition are better able to set out the aims and goals of citizenship

education (policy), how those are to be delivered (practice) and what the end results should be (outcomes) than those countries with a 'values-neutral' tradition. However, it should be noted that clarity of aims does not guarantee successful outcomes;

- a move in many countries away from a narrow, knowledge-based approach to citizenship education, to a broader approach encompassing knowledge and understanding, active experiences and the development of student values, dispositions, skills and aptitudes. However, this transition was proving difficult to manage because of the impact, in particular, of teacher culture and beliefs and the slow adaptation of schools to change;
- the continuing gap between the rhetoric of policy and the reality of practice in many contexts, from a national level to individual schools and classrooms. There is still a long way to go to ensure that effective practice in citizenship education is developed and sustained within and across countries;
- agreement on the centrality of the teacher in citizenship education and on the need for better targeted training for teachers and the development of a broader range of teacher-friendly resources;
- the need for further discussion about assessment arrangements for citizenship education and the importance of clarity of purpose when deciding what arrangements to make. There is a growing debate in some countries about the desirability of terminal, written exams for citizenship education, as part of compulsory, national assessment systems, and their balance with other types of assessment;
- calls for the urgent co-ordination and dissemination of approaches, programmes and initiatives in citizenship education which are developing effective practice. This could be effected through the establishment of a citizenship education database within each country and across countries.

What the thematic study showed, above all, is the commonality of interest, challenge and approach to citizenship education across countries. Once you get beyond the differences in context and in curriculum and assessment frameworks, countries have much more in common concerning citizenship education than they think. Awareness of and in-depth analysis of this commonality is the key to developing more co-ordinated and effective policy and practice in citizenship education. Indeed, active and participatory citizenship requires active and participatory dialogue between all those with an interest in citizenship education – researchers, teachers, policy-makers, curriculum designers, government officials, parents and students. It is to be hoped that this central message will live on beyond the thematic study. It is perhaps fitting to end this chapter with the final contribution to the invitational seminar from the Canadian representative.

> We know enough about how students learn in citizenship education to put in place programmes which are based on the growing research and practice base. We need

to draw out what this research and practice base tells us and then create a partnership with policy makers and curriculum designers.

This spirit of partnership is surely the best way to respond to the current challenges in citizenship education across the world.

NOTES

1. On 1 October 1997, the School Curriculum and Assessment Authority merged with the National Council for Vocational Qualifications to form the Qualifications and Curriculum Authority (QCA).
2. Australia, Canada, England, France, Germany, Hungary, Italy, Japan, Korea, The Netherlands, New Zealand, Singapore, Spain, Sweden, Switzerland and the USA.
3. A full version of the thematic study upon which this chapter is based is available from QCA. For further information contact Karen Senior, Curriculum Review Divison, QCA, 29 Bolton Street, London W1Y.
4. Of the sixteen INCA countries, ten have participated in Phases 1 and 2 of the IEA Citizenship Education Project. Australia, England, Germany, Hungary, Italy, Switzerland and the USA participated in Phase 1 and are also participating in Phase 2. Canada and The Netherlands participated in Phase 1 and Sweden is only participating in Phase 2. The outcome of Phase 1 was a national case study report from each country. These case study reports have been used to supplement *INCA*.

REFERENCES

The main sources and references for the thematic study were:
Material from *INCA*, the Archive of the International Review of Curriculum and Assessment Frameworks Project on sixteen countries;
Le Métais, J. (1997) Values and Aims in Curriculum and Assessment Frameworks (IRCAF Study 1). London: SCAA.
O'Donnell, S., Le Métais, J., Boyd, S. and Tabberer, R. (1998) *INCA: The International Review of Curriculum and Assessment Frameworks Archive* [CD-ROM]. London: Qualification and Curriculum Authority (2nd edn). Also available online at: *http://www.inca.org.uk*
Material from the IEA Citizenship Education Project Phase 1;
Torney-Purta, J., Schwille, J. and Amadeo, J.-A. (eds) (1999) *Civic Education Across Countries: 24 Case studies from the IEA Civic Education Project.* Amsterdam: Eburon Publishers for the International Association for the Evaluation of Educational Achievement (IEA).
Information from official Ministry of Education websites for many *INCA* countries.

Hahn, C. (1998) *Becoming Political: Comparative Perspectives on Citizenship Education.* New York: State University of New York Press.
Ichilov, O. (ed.) (1998) *Citizenship and Citizenship Education in a Changing World.* London: Woburn Press.
Janoski (1998) *Citizenship and Civil Society: A Framework of Rights and Obligations in Liberal, Traditional and Social Democratic Regimes.* Cambridge: Cambridge University Press.

Kennedy, K. (ed.) (1997) *Citizenship Education and the Modern State*. London: Falmer Press.

Kerr, D. (1999a) *Re-examining Citizenship Education: The Case of England*. Slough: NFER.

Kerr, D. (1999b) Re-examining citizenship education in England. In J. Torney-Purta, J. Schwille and J.-A. Amadeo (eds) *Civic Education across Countries: 24 Case Studies from the IEA Civic Education Project*. Amsterdam: Eburon Publishers for the International Association for the Evaluation of Educational Achievement (IEA).

Kerr, D. (1999c) Changing the political culture: the advisory group on education for citizenship and the teaching of democracy in schools. *Oxford Review of Education*, **25** (1-2): 25-35.

McLaughlin, T. H., (1992) Citizenship, diversity and education: a philosophical perspective. *Journal of Moral Education*, **21** (3): 235-46.

Marshall, T. H. (1950) *Citizenship and Social Class*. Cambridge: Cambridge University Press.

QCA (1998) *Education for Citizenship and the Teaching Democracy in Schools: Final Report of the Advisory Group on Citizenship* (Crick Report). London: QCA.

QCA (1999a) *The Review of the National Curriculum in England. The Secretary of State's Proposals*. London: QCA/DfEE.

QCA (1999b). *The Review of the National Curriculum in England. The Consultation Materials*. London: QCA/DfEE.

QCA (1999c) *Citizenship Key Stages 3-4*. London: QCA/DfEE.

Chapter 17

Global Perspectives in Citizenship Education

Roy Gardner

INTRODUCTION

Pupils should be taught about:

i.   the world as a global community, and the political, economic, environmental and social implications of this, and the role of the European Union, the Commonwealth and the United Nations. (QCA, 1998)
ii.   Every child should be educated about development issues so that they can understand the key global considerations which will shape their lives. (DfID, 1997)

The World Trade Organization Ministerial Conference in Seattle in late November 1999 was the scene of huge demonstrations which led to the police having to intervene to restore order. The demonstrators may have had a variety of issues they wished to press upon the delegates and not all of those issues may have been directly related to world trade in terms of trade regulations, tariffs or non-tariff barriers. Some of those issues were related to the impact of trade and its effects on the environment, national development programmes and the exploitation of global resources, both physical and human. The spread of interests exhibited by the demonstrators proves once again the multidimensionality of topics which are often raised and discussed in international fora. The World Trade Organization (WTO) failed to launch a new round of trade negotiations and this indicated the fundamental flaws in the process of establishing global agreements. The complexity of the issues is such that many delegates could not fully grasp the totality of world trade (Mabey, 2000). In particular some delegates from less developed economies were disadvantaged in the discussions because of their lack of prior experience of seeing their way through the intersecting maze of trade patterns, controls and opportunities.

This example of the difficulties of examining the core focus of a major component of global patterns of activity and its spin-off effects is but only one of many that could be cited from the litany of problems that beset the world community. Well-known and well-rehearsed and researched topics include global warming, population growth and control, the inequitable consumption of resources, the gradual exhaustion of finite resources and the inequalities that persist in living standards across the world. This list is not complete but merely illustrative of the wide spread of topics that are available and which attract interest at all levels of education, from the school to the university, and in both national and international debating chambers and agencies. Each of the topics listed is in itself a set of complicated practices and information which react upon each other to provide the dynamism for growth, change and hopefully improvement. Yet again each of the topics listed cannot be treated in isolation with the potential of a solution being found, because each topic interacts with others to produce a diverse, complex and evolving theme which reflects the nature of human life on earth. Such is the beauty of the world in which we live: but we have a major problem to confront these topics and issues and move forward towards a world which will see the elimination of major scourges of poverty, hunger and deprivation and will also see greater equality and equity. Humankind has a clear vision of what sort of world is wanted in the future: what we all have to do is to find ways of working towards the realization of that vision.

This brief foray into global perspectives points not only to the breadth of the topics but also to the interlinkages between them. As educators it is our responsibility to select and mould the topics for our learners and to vary the presentation to match their ages and interests. How can we give to our students at all levels not only the vision of the future that we want – that may already be firmly established in the value systems that are held dear by them – but also ways of contributing to the changes that will be needed to achieve that vision, together with a sense of the opportunities that exist to participate to its realization? Shared human concern, ethical purpose and challenging action lie at the heart of this common vision. Engaging young people in the issues, political awareness and active 'know-how' is the role for citizenship education for global living: putting that role to work is the task.

A GLOBAL DIMENSION: WHAT IS IT? MAKING CONNECTIONS

There are many phrases which are in use to describe approaches to teaching about the issues which face the world. Development Studies, Development Education, Education for Development, World Studies, Global Education and an International Dimension are all in current use. Despite differences between the terms they tend to be used interchangeably and perhaps this does not matter. We all know what we are talking about, don't we? Or do we? Is there a need for a new phrase which would be acceptable to all? Orr (1992, p. 328) points us to 'Reflection is not a detachment, a second thought, but an aesthetic and ethical act of participation in the world, that we might now refer to as "ecological literacy" '. For the purposes of this chapter I propose to adopt 'global literacy' with an emphasis on knowing about the world we live in and the stage of progress it has reached. The emphasis on the global may in itself raise doubts and difficulties over at what ages and under which circumstances learners can begin to associate with others who live in different communities and countries perhaps far from their own. What is needed is to ensure that the learners appreciate why they are asked to look beyond their immediate environment, both social and physical, and to realize that what we do and how we live is not only dependent on other people elsewhere but also has an impact on those same people. It is perhaps the role of this aspect of education to make connections between the self and others, locally and far away.

Globalization as an expression of a trend in world development and change has become commonplace in the last decade of the twentieth century. McGain (1997), however, has reminded us that it is not a new concept. From the time that trade and exchange took place between communities, the individual's perception of the world has changed. Globalization in the past may have taken different forms either through trade, conquest or colonization but it was restricted only in terms of the means of communication available to command a wider coverage than the immediate. As communications have improved so has the sense of the world the individual inherits. Thus today the world for most people is the whole globe where instant contact is the norm for many. Bailly (1998) has suggested: 'Globalization has made us discover another form of citizenship: that of a world that can be viewed through satellite pictures, a world of rapidity and movement, a world united, to address the problems of sustainable development' (p. 199). News items become the text to study current events and lead us to argue for an activist approach to global literacy. At least at Key Stages 4 and 5 this could lead to critical ethnographic studies of community issues.

Globalization in the twenty-first century is marked by wider spatial patterns of participation but it does not yet include everyone on the globe. There are significant areas of the world which are only marginally affected by the trend towards globalization. Indeed, as pointed out by Cairns and Gardner (1997), there are substantial areas which have not been penetrated by modern technology and the last decades of the twentieth century saw the continuance and emergence of local and regional organizations dedicated to the preservation of some degrees of autonomy and local control. However, be that as it may, globalization has led to greater effects on individual lives if only through the greater access to information. The degree of globalization becomes evident through the analysis of the data available and Livingstone (*Independent*, 24

March 1999) has provided a warning example of the impact of globalization through the example of the banana trade. Written at the time of conflict between the USA and the EU on the import of bananas Livingstone noted:

- 80 per cent of the world trade in bananas was controlled by 3 global corporations.
- One-third of the population of St Lucia depend on the banana trade whereas it is 70 per cent in St Vincent.

Livingstone also pointed out that 3 corporations control 83 per cent of the coffee trade, 5 control 77 per cent of cereals and 10 control 94 per cent of agrochemicals. Ian Campbell, Director-General of the Institute of Exports (cited by Livingstone) felt sufficiently strongly about the monopoly of trade to suggest 'It is high time for sanity to prevail. Politicians and bureaucrats need to get round a table and negotiate a way out of this mess before it destroys friendships and important business relationships' (*Independent*, 24 March 1999).

Bailly (1998) identified mobility as the major new factor in the process of globalization. The mobility of people, information, goods and services led Bailly to search for a more flexible concept of citizenship which he thought should be linked to residence and not birth (p. 200). Naturalization in the past has been limited in degree and has been the exception rather than the rule. Bailly thought that the recognition of citizenship based upon residence and not birthplace should become more automatic and would carry with it all the rights and obligations attached to that residence. He went on to reflect upon the way the world has changed from an emphasis on the natural state to the nation state, to supranational communities, to the world system and new regional structures. In answer to his own question of how to build citizenship today and on what scale he proposed the following figure (Figure 17.1).

Regional Communities	Nation States	Supernational Communities	Global Systems
Political and Civic Institutions			
Type of spatial pattern, identity, legitimacy For whom, why, to what purpose			

Figure 17.1 Citizenship for the twenty-first century (on which scale)
Source: Bailly, 1998, p. 201

McGain (1997) thought that, despite the emphasis on economic development and integration, education systems had not changed greatly from the previous systems. The emergence of new theories of learning has led to different approaches to education, especially in the area of programmed learning and the rise of a greater range of media for both face-to-face and especially distance education. However, the continuing stress has been on traditional forms of school-based education. The limited use of radiophonic education and educational television has represented only an introduction to new technologies, especially in low-income situations. The rapid development of communications technology and significantly the rapidly spreading availability of internet contact has offered to education systems opportunities for the rapid overhaul of structures, procedures and provision. Buchert and King (1997) have drawn upon Reich's (1991) focus on knowledge and skills to ensure nations can be globally competitive to emphasize the need for acceptable qualifications. Alexander and Rizivi (1993) have also laid stress on the need for uniform certificates and the standardization of curriculum offerings. The need for qualifications to be transferable across the globe has pointed to the importance of measures of equivalence. These attempts at a measure of agreement on standards has moved a further step towards the globalization of educational awards. Whereas the International Baccalauréate has provided a global standard at the end of secondary education, there has until now been no attempt to secure direct co-operation at university level through external examinations. The announcement (*Guardian*, 15 Feb. 2000) that four UK universities will combine with four American universities to offer degrees and share research and bibliographic resources marks a major step towards the universalization of study for degrees. It can be expected that similar steps will be taken to combine offerings in other parts of the globe.

This chapter so far has sought to show that the move towards globalization is not new and, while economic integration and changes in telecommunications are leading the process and the spread of change, there have been other global trends in the past such as the rise and fall of empires, the humanitarian movement, the present-day movement towards greater democracy and human rights. In education there have been international trends which have seen the transfer of education systems from the north to other parts of the globe. At this time we are witnessing the spread of newer technologies having an impact on the offering and conduct of some aspects of education, especially at the university level. It is to be expected that this impact will continue and grow in speed as the efficiency and complexity of global communication increases.

A GLOBAL LITERACY FOR EDUCATION IN ENGLAND AND WALES

The literature on global education abounds with definitions and intentions and reflects accurately the struggle that has taken place in England and Wales for classes to look beyond the immediate concerns of daily life in school and the community to the world beyond. Gerber and Lidstone (1996, p. 171) have helpfully listed the main texts which have guided teaching about global education:

The Brandt Report: North and South	1980 and 1982
Palme Report: Common Security	1982
Brundtland Report: Our Common Future	1987
European Conference: Stockholm	1992
Earth Summit: Rio	1992
Population Conference: Cairo	1994
Earth Charter	1996

The following major conferences have also contributed greatly:

Land-Ocean Interactions in the Coastal Zone (L01Z)
Land-Use and Global Land Cover Change
Global Change and Terrestrial Ecosystems (GLTE)
Biosphere: Aspects of the Hydrological Cycle
Global Energy and Water Cycle Experiment
Global Change Data Bases (World Data Center, Boulder, USA)

Each of these has provided a plethora of information upon which to draw to formulate inputs into education programmes at all levels.

In addition, there has been ample guidance and justification for including global literacy in school education even before the emergence of the Crick Report (QCA, 1998), and OFSTED (1995) stated that the quality of the education provided should show respect for other people's feelings, values and beliefs (p. 17); and teach pupils to appreciate their own cultural traditions and the diversity and richness of other cultures (p. 19). The Development Education Association (1996–98) went further with:

> Development education in the curriculum is about teaching and learning the knowledge and understanding, skills, attitudes and values that enable young people to become increasingly aware of issues related to development, environment and sustainability and to recognize and evaluate the personal, local, national and global significance of these issues.

Again in 1998, when reporting to the DfEE/QCA on *Education for Sustainable Development in the School Sector*, the Development Education

Association concluded that the key concepts of interdependence (of society, economy and the natural environment) should be infused into pupils' education: i.e., citizenship and stewardship (rights and responsibilities, participation and co-operation); needs and rights of future generations; diversity (cultural, social, economic and biological); uncertainty and precaution in action.

And if more support was needed to justify the inclusion of global literacy in teaching, the views of Gundara (1997) might be used to show that education for development is a process which 'promotes the development, in children and young people, of attitudes and values such as global solidarity, peace, tolerance, social justice and environmental awareness, and which equips them with the knowledge and skills which will empower them to promote these values and bring about change in their own lives and in their communities, both locally and globally.' Thus with steadfast support in official documents from the ministries in the UK and justifications from world bodies the stage has been set not only for citizenship education but also for its international character.

DEVISING A CURRICULUM FOR GLOBAL LITERACY

The movement to infuse global perspectives into the education provided for young people in England and Wales started early in the second half of the twentieth century with the return of volunteers who had worked in low-income countries. These early anecdotal attempts were based on personal recollections of the experiences, both good and bad, that the volunteers wanted to share with their classes. Many of these experiences had been tinged with a desire to shock and to reveal the enormous hardships which many people in other countries faced as well as to encourage the growth of attitudes towards change to alleviate the suffering and the deprivations that people faced. The movement for development education grew through the active involvement of charities and aid agencies as well as of colleges and universities.

Over time the focus was turned onto an analysis of incomes, consumption, inequalities and differentials between countries. Global literacy became a comparative study which illustrated the affluence of the more developed countries as opposed to the poverty of the less developed. The spatial spread of these differentials became the mainspring for the introduction of the concept of North (affluent) and South (exploited). The division was limited to the spatial characteristics of colonialism and the way opened for a full investigation of the legacy of colonialism and its continuing impact on daily life in the latter decades of the twentieth century. Further analysis identified militarization, violence, the abuse of human rights and the role of the multinational corporations among other factors and development education became almost synonymous with the investigation into the causes of world troubles and difficulties.

The content of development education arose not through any systematic planning by government agencies or NGOs but through the interest and passions of those who were concerned about the insular nature of the education being provided by British schools. It was insular in that it was centred upon academic disciplines taken from the nineteenth century and presented as a basis for education for life. It was also insular in that it was inward-looking and paid little attention to the modern-day world outside England and Wales and the changes taking place on the world scene. The introduction of development education began to open up the learning experiences provided. However, its emphasis on the difficulties facing developing countries coupled with a colonial past led perhaps inevitably to a sense of guilt on the part of the teacher and the learners with a heavy stress on the need for both economic and political reform in the nation. For many reasons, this emphasis may have proved too challenging and have led to a sense of anomie and a rejection of the urgent message the material as presented was intended to convey.

Much work has been done to provide a framework for development and global literacy which hopefully will offer a more rigorously thought-through approach to current issues in world development and provide the means to move forward. Oxfam (1997) has provided a very detailed syllabus framework based on values and dispositions; skills and aptitudes; knowledge and understanding. The outline covers the period of compulsory education and is a very valuable basis upon which teachers can plan lessons appropriate for their own pupils. As the section given below shows it provides adequate flexibility (see Table 17.1).

Other writers have sought to define citizenship in multidimensional terms such as Personal, Social, Spatial and Temporal (Cogan and Kubow, 1997) and clearly intended to include a global dimension within any provision for citizenship education. Susan Fountain (1995) went further and identified the key concepts needed for education for development. These were Interdependence; Images and Perceptions; Social Justice; Conflict and Conflict Resolution; and Change the Future. Others have chosen to focus on growth and identify five damaging forms of growth

- Which does not translate into jobs
- Which is not matched by the spread of democracy
- Which snuffs out separate cultural identities
- Where most of the benefits are seized by the rich
- Which despoils the environment (Davies, 1998, p. 5)

Each of these approaches has merit and contributes to the debate about what should be the thrust of global literacy in citizenship education and how these have to be presented. For other subjects, such as history and geography, in the National Curriculum of England and Wales there are schemes of work. For citizenship education there are none and no plans have emerged to develop them. It is to be left to the schools and the teachers to devise their own schemes.

Table 17.1 Global Citizenship: knowledge and understanding

Knowledge and understanding	Pre-KS1 Pre-stages P1–P3	KS1 Stages P1–P3	KS2 Stages P4–P6	KS3 Stages P7–S2	KS4 S3–Standard grade	16–19
Social justice and equity	what is fair/unfair what is right and wrong	awareness of rich and poor	fairness between groups causes and effects of inequality	inequalities within and between societies basic rights and responsibilities	causes of poverty different views on the eradication of poverty role as Global Citizen	understanding of global debates
Diversity	awareness of others in relation to self-awareness of similarities and differences between people	greater awareness of similarities and differences between people	contribution of different cultures, values and beliefs to our lives nature of prejudice and ways to combat it	understanding of issues of diversity	deeper understanding of different cultures and societies	
Globalization and interdependence	sense of immediate and local environment awareness of different places	sense of the wider world links and connections between different places	trade between countries fair trade	awareness of interdependence our political system and others	power relationships North/South world economic and political systems ethical consumerism	complexity of global issues
Sustainable development	living things and their needs how to take care of things sense of the future	our impact on the environment awareness of the past and the future	relationship between people and environment awareness of finite resources our potential to change things	different views of economic and social development, locally and globally understanding the concepts of possible and preferable futures	global imperative of sustainable development lifestyles for a sustainable world	understanding of key issues of Agenda 21
Peace and conflict	our actions have consequences	conflicts past and present in our society and others causes of conflict and conflict resolution – personal level	causes of conflict impact of conflict strategies for tackling conflict and for conflict prevention	causes and effects of conflict, locally and globally relationship between conflict and peace	conditions conducive to peace	complexity of conflict issues and conflict resolution

Source: Oxfam (1997), p. 16

Some schools have made attempts in the past with considerable success. Mill Community School, Bordon, Hampshire, is a case in point (see Crace, *Guardian*, 15 Feb. 2000); and the head, Chris Waller, has stressed the need for a broad school approach towards a holistic curriculum for citizenship education. No doubt many other schools have had similar successes and some were recorded in the Crick Report (QCA, 1998).

THINKING OUR WAY FORWARD FOR CITIZENSHIP EDUCATION WITH GLOBAL LITERACY

Jon Crace (2000) noted that Ken Livingstone on Radio 4 *Question Time* thought citizenship education 'would be the most bunked-off subject on the school timetable', whereas David Blunkett considered it to be a very important introduction into the curriculum. Crace also thought the demands of other subjects, especially those of the literacy and numeracy hours, will lead to citizenship education being squeezed out in the primary school. Should there be a subject called citizenship on the timetable? Some might argue that the word citizenship has pious overtones and it should be avoided entirely.

Citizenship education is to become a cross-curricular theme in the primary phase and a foundation subject in the secondary and with the support of the Government Orders citizenship will have greater presence in the curriculum than previously. Other cross-curriculum themes have had degrees of success, environmental education being one example. This may be because of its more immediate and personal nature with which the learners can easily identify: or potentially because it is associated with evocative issues of animal welfare, forests and global warming. Citizenship education does not immediately offer excitement through voting systems, political parties and rights and obligations even though these are vital to the proper conduct of life in the community. Voluntary work in the community may have little appeal especially for secondary phase students and becoming involved in local issues may not be seen to be worth the effort, given the time that it may take for proposals made to the relevant authorities to be discussed and acted upon. The content and presentation of citizenship education therefore becomes vital for its take-up and success.

What then about global literacy in citizenship education? An honest and realistic review of world issues has dangers of generating rejection through their complexity and through their implied criticism of the North, the UK and the person. What should be the approach to be adopted and what should be the content? Ashok Ohri, (1997) has reminded us of the possibilities of twinning towns and cities in the countries of origin of local minority communities to explaining about their roots. This approach has been adopted by some to good effect. However, some minorities may have less interest in their country of origin than in their adoptive country. There is the need to recognize that the focus of some minorities may now be more local, especially where second-generation minorities form majorities within their own communities. Others have asked how to interpret other cultures and have suggested non-threatening ways such as through art, food and drink. The adoption of a range of aspects of cultures may be of interest but these appear initially to have little to sustain a long-term programme which will attract the attention of students up to 16 years of age.

Both these examples represent piecemeal approaches to teaching about the world. A broad framework is required first to establish a basis on which to work. Such a framework for developing global literacy in the curriculum in the schools was provided by the Central Bureau and the DEA in an insert to the Central Bureau's *News* (Spring 2000).

> The framework identified key concepts of an international dimension as; democracy and citizenship; sustainable development; social justice and a commitment to gender and racial equality; informed perceptions and appropriate images; intercultural understanding and the appreciation of diversity; personal and global interdependence; the resolution of conflict and the promotion of harmony; and human rights. These concepts would provide opportunities for young people and those who work with them to live their lives in a global society; acquire relevant knowledge, understanding and expressions; develop appropriate key skills, aptitude and attitudes; broaden their experience of life by contact with people from a variety of background, countries, faiths and cultures, and by enjoying the cultural diversity that they encounter; address global issues, concerning sustainability, the environment, development and international interdependence; explore their own values and interest as individuals and as members of local, national and global communities and thus to explore and respect the identities and values of others; and increase their self-esteem, confidence and a sense of achievement. (Central Bureau, *News*, 2000)

Perhaps the stage of the development of the global dimension in the curriculum might be to attempt to describe the knowledge, understanding and skills that students might develop throughout their school careers. Table 17.2 is a tentative suggestion.

CONCLUSION

Frameworks and statements of levels are all useful ways of seeking to define and refine the concept of a portion of the education offered to young people in school. Such instruments need further analysis and refinement before teachers can begin the exacting task of translating codes and perceptions into learning situations and experiences. This is an even more exacting task when the goal of the intended education is not solely the inculcation of data, strategies and processes related to specific subjects areas but also related to a wider agenda of personal development. This may lead to a commitment to promote equity not

Table 17.2 Knowledge, understanding and skills in global literacy

Level	Knowledge, understanding and skills
Level 1	Knowledge of the location of countries and continents on the globe. Realization that each country including the UK is made up of groups each with its own customs, beliefs and values. Respect for other cultures.
Level 2	Knowledge of the variety of economic and social conditions in and between countries. Avoidance of the exotic, unusual and touristic views of cultures. Knowledge of lives of young people in different location in one or more countries. Concept of growth and stagnation.
Level 3	Knowledge of origins of the UK and past and present relationships between more developed and less developed countries. An understanding of the effect of past events on today and possibly future developments and change.
Level 4	An acceptance that change is a continuous process and it will be a continued fact of life. An understanding that the rate of change varies between groups and countries, and an understanding of the reasons for these differences.
Level 5	Knowledge of different interpretations of the term development and the factors which help or hinder development. Alternative routes to development. North–South and underdevelopment. Knowledge of local developments and their advantages and disadvantages.
Level 6	The pattern of trade of the UK and changes in patterns over time. Analysis of the concept of interdependence. Role of international trade agreements. Source of aid and the need for aid.
Level 7	Knowledge of the international agencies and their role in international development. Assessment of success and failure of international organizations. Non-governmental organizations.
Level 8	Patterns of consumption of the world's resources and the need for sustainable development. The possibilities for action to support sustainable development. The misuse of resources and the political and economic costs.

Source: Based on Gardner, 1990, pp. 184–5

only locally and nationally but also internationally. The promotion of ideas of citizenship which go beyond the instrumentalities of civics carries with it the responsibility of the development of values which have currency spatially and temporally. To do this, teachers and pupils must have a conception of what a good citizen is and here Davies *et al.* (1999) provide a pointer with a focus on social concerns of the welfare of others, moral and ethical behaviour and the tolerance of diversity; and on a knowledge of government, current events, the world community and the ability to question ideas (p. 45).

Others may wish to go further in specifying the particular attributes of good citizens who are globally literate and who are committed to supporting and encouraging growth and change. The role of citizenship education would thus make a broad contribution to the promotion not only of local and national commitment but also to local and national communities as part of the world community to which we all belong.

Time will tell how citizenship education, its global focus and impact will evolve but perhaps this chapter might conclude with a plea for care by those who will have the responsibility for providing international and global perspectives to maturing minds. The statements given above on global literacy are depersonalized as curriculum statements often are. It is the interpretation of those statements into the focus of planning and lesson development which will be vital in encouraging or discouraging interest in the classrooms. Our energies must be directed to planning which takes account of young people as they engage with all their learning experiences. For example, the ways in which young people experience their history and culture; power relationships and personally useful knowledge and socially useful knowledge should shape future directions in integrating global literacy into the National Curriculum. Citizenship may remain the focus but the wider context of the whole curriculum is paramount.

Is there not an opportunity now to think deeply about the character of the international dimension provided? Certainly inequality, disaster, poverty, tragedy are with us throughout the world, at home and abroad, and these cannot be forgotten or played down. But is there not also the opportunity to balance the tragedy with other aspects of life – the developments that have taken place, increased longevity, better food production, the preservation of cultures and cultural patterns which add to the richness of our perception of the global community. News broadcasts stress the tragic: good news is not newsworthy. In schools and colleges is there a need to focus solely on the tragic? I hope not. David Hicks (DEA/IoE,1997) made a similar point:

> Global education for the twenty-first century – is about educating in a spirit of hope and optimism which fully recognizes the rights and responsibilities of both present and future generations. We can no longer make sense of everyday life unless we set [the school curriculum] in the context of living in a global society.

REFERENCES

Alexander, D. and Rizivi, F. (1993) Education, markets and the contradictions of Asia–Australia relations. *Australian Universities Review*, **36** (2): 16–20.
Bailly, A. (1998) Education for new forms of citizenship through history and geography. *Prospects*, **106** (XXV111).
Buchert, L. and King, K. (eds) (1997) *Learning from Experience: Policy and Practice in Aid to Higher Education.* The Hague: Center for Studies on Education in Developing Nations. CESO Paperback No. 24.

Cairns, J. and Gardner, R. (1997) The Hermeneutics of Rimology: a counterpoint to globalisation. Unpublished Conference Paper.

Central Bureau for International Education and Training (2000) *News* (Spring). London: British Council.

Cogan, J. J. and Kubow, P. R. (1997) *The Citizenship Education Policy Study Project Final Report*. Minneapolis: University of Minnesota.

Crace, J. (2000) The new citizens. *Guardian*, 15 February 2000.

Davies, I., Gregory, I. and Riley, S. (1999) *Good Citizenship in Educational Provision*. London: Falmer.

Davies, L. (1998) *Global Goals and Own Goals in Education*. Birmingham: TIDE.

Development Education Association (1996–98) *Global Perspectives in the National Curriculum*. London: DEA.

Development Education Association (1998) *Education for Sustainable Development in the Schools Sector*. London: DEA.

DfEE (1999) *Citizenship Orders*. London: DfID.

DfID (1997) *Eliminating World Poverty: A Challenge for the Twenty-first Century*. London: DfID.

Fountain, S. (1995) *Education for Development*. UNICEF: Hodder and Stoughton.

Gardner, R. (1990) (ed.) *An International Dimension in the National Curriculum: An Imperative for 1992 and Beyond*. London: Institute of Education.

Gerber, R. and Lidstone, J. (1996) *Developments and Directions in Geographical Information*. Clevedon: Channel View.

Gundara, J. (1997) Global and Intercultural Dimensions in Teacher Education. In DEA/IofE *Global Perspectives in Initial Teacher Education: Training Teachers for Tomorrow*. London: DEA/IofE.

Hicks, D. (1997) *Global Perspectives in Initial Teacher Education*. London: DEA/IoE. Quoted in *Learning for Global Society*. London: DEA

Livingstone, J. (1999) Quoted in *Global Issues*, No. 2. Belfast: One World Centre.

Mabey, N. (2000) Learning from Seattle in WTO Seattle Ministerial Conference III. In *Connections* (Feb.–Apr.) London: UNED/UK.

McGain, N. F. (1997) Impact of globalisation on national education systems. *Prospects*, **101** (XXVII).

OFSTED (1995) *Frameworks for the Inspection of Schools*. London: OFSTED.

Ohri, A. (1997) *World in Our Neighbourhood*. London: DEA.

Orr, D. W. (1992) *Ecological Literacy: Education and the Transition to a Postmodern World*. Albany, NY: State University of NY Press.

Oxfam (1997) *A Curriculum for Global Citizenship*. Oxford: Oxfam.

QCA (1998) *Education for Citizenship and the Teaching of Democracy in Schools*. (Crick Report). London: QCA.

Reich, R. B. (1991) *The Work of Nations*. New York: Vintage.

Index

Printed in the United Kingdom
by Lightning Source UK Ltd.
125432UK00001B/205-210/A